Springer Series on Social Work

Albert R. Roberts, D.S.W., Series Editor

Graduate School of Social Work, Rutgers, The State University of New Jersey

Advisory Board: Gloria Bonilla-Santiago, Ph.D., Sheldon R. Gelman, Ph.D., Gilbert J. Greene, Ph.D., Jesse Harris, D.S.W., Michael J. Smith, D.S.W., Barbara Berkman, Ph.D., and Elaine P. Congress, D.S.W.

Margaret Gibelman, DSW, is Professor and Director of the Doctoral Program at the Wurzweiler School of Social Work, Yeshiva University, in New York. She teaches in the areas of social welfare policy, management, and child welfare. She has also taught at Rutgers University and The Catholic University of America.

Dr. Gibelman has worked in the human services as a clinician, supervisor, educator, and manager. In the latter category, she has served as Executive Director of the National Association of School Psychologists and the Lupus Foundation of America. She was also Associate Executive Director of the Council on Social Work Education, the accrediting body for social work education programs in the United States. She is a frequently contributor to scholarly journals on nonprofit management, privatization, professional education, women's issues, and service delivery systems.

Harold W. Demone Jr., PhD, is currently a Visiting Scholar at Florence Heller School for Advanced Studies in Social Welfare, Brandeis University and an Emeritus Professor II in Social Work and Sociology and former dean of the School of Social Work at Rutgers University. His publications on the human services exceed 120 in number.

With a professional career spanning more than 40 years, about equally divided between the practice and academic arenas, Dr. Demone has had frequent opportunities to both practice and observe many of the facets of privatization, even long before it was known as such. Dr. Gibelman and Dr. Demone have teamed on several articles on the subject of privatization and co-edited *Services for Sale: Purchasing Health and Human Services* (Rutgers University Press, 1989).

The Privatization of Human Services

Case Studies in the Purchase of Services

Volume 2

Margaret Gibelman, DSW
Harold W. Demone, Jr., PhD
Editors

 Springer Publishing Company

Springer Publishing Company, Inc.
536 Broadway
New York, NY 10012–3955

Cover design by Margaret Dunin
Acquisitions Editor: Bill Tucker
Production Editor: Pamela Lankas

98 99 00 01 02 / 5 4 3 2 1

The Library of Congress has catalogued Volume I as follows:

Library of Congress Cataloging-in-Publication Data

The privatization of human services : policy and practice issues /
Margaret Gibelman, Harold W. Demone, Jr., editors.
     p.   cm.—(Springer series on social work : 28)
    Includes index.
    ISBN 0-8261-9870-8
    1. Human services—Contracting out—United States.
2. Social work administration—United States.
3. Privatization—United States. I. Gibelman, Margaret.
II. Demone, Harold W. III. Series.
HV95.P737   1997
361.973—dc21   97-28506
                                                                                  CIP

Library of Congress Cataloging-in-Publication Data

The privatization of human services : cases studies in the purchase
of services
Margaret Gibelman, Harold W. Demone, Jr., editors.
Margaret Gibelman, Harold W. Demone, Jr., editors.
     p.   cm.—(Springer series on social work : 29)
    Includes index.
    ISBN 0-8261-9871-6
    1. Gibelman, Margaret. II. Demone, Harold W. III. Series.
HV95.P737   1997
361.973—dc21   97-28506
                                                                                  CIP

Printed in the United States of America

This book is dedicated to
William John Curran, LL.B., S.M. Hygiene, L.L.D. (HON.)
(1925–1996)

Professor Curran was the Frances Glossner Lee Emeritus Professor of Legal Medicine on the faculties of Medicine and Public Health, Harvard University. Until his death he continued as the Director of the Harvard–World Health Organization International Collaborating Center on Health Legislation, which he helped establish in 1986.

Bill was also a close family friend, a colleague in several undertakings, a collaborator, personal attorney, and Cape Cod neighbor.

His outstanding chapter in this book, which reviewed the several legal issues raised in the case histories, is illustrative of his long-standing scholarly work as the "father of health law." It was also his final professional writing, prepared during that brief interval of remission under chemotherapy.

We will miss him very much.

Harold W. Demone, Jr.

Contents

Foreword

Simplistic assumptions and excessive expectations: These are the invariable precursors of cynicism. Both are dangerous—potentially even fatal—to the health of democracy. The only cure, the only preventive, is a combination of solid data, realistic analysis, and a positive commitment to accountability.

That the "privatization" of functions previously performed by government can often lead to more successful outcomes at lower cost is undoubtedly true. To suppose that privatization is appropriate to most government services most of the time would be a simplistic assumption. Its inappropriate indulgence, nonetheless, is already having and could increasingly have damaging side effects. The great merit of this timely book, therefore, is that it uses the direct examination of concrete situations as a means of uncovering the potential for a creative balance among competing considerations, choices, and trade-offs.

An earlier volume produced by the same editors combined a survey of selected service areas—mental health, mental retardation, and alcohol and drug treatment—with an overview of such overarching requirements as the demand for accountability. This second volume employs a series of case studies for the purpose of bringing into focus a broad array of practical, ethical, legal, and interorganizational issues. The editors of both volumes are uniquely well qualified for the task. One, Margaret E. Gibelman, now the Director of the Doctoral Program at the Wurzweiler School of Social Work, Yeshiva University, served as Associate Executive Director of the Council on Social Work Education. The other, Harold W. Demone, Jr., a former Professor of Social Work and Sociology and Dean of the School of Social Work at Rutgers University, is now a Lecturer in Heath Policy and Management at the Harvard School of Public Health. Their wealth of experience both in the academy and in the field has been brought to bear here in a way that takes solid data and sound analysis by informed observers and transmutes them into a whole more intelligible than the sum of its parts.

The first case study following Dr. Gibelman's Introduction is by Michael Dukakis, for 12 years the governor of Massachusetts at a time of rapid acceleration in the privatization of services. His opening paragraphs make plain the need for this book by pointing to the differences between contracting for social services and contracting for the kinds of things—roads, weapons, and transportation, for example—that governments have always procured from somebody else. It's not too hard to make sure that a highway is well constructed, that a fighter plane meets its specifications, or that a shipment has been delivered. By contrast, the results called for by a contract for social services are hard to measure. Not only is it difficult to tell whether or not taxpayers are getting their money's worth but it's also difficult to pin down exactly what they thought they were buying. Beyond that, there are usually many fewer qualified bidders for a social services contract than there are qualified bidders for a highway contract, and the weaker the competition the more difficult it is either to reduce costs or to improve quality.

In an insightful examination of the influence of privatization on politics and the press, Harold Demone points out that in 1971 Massachusetts was spending only $25 million on the purchase of human services. By 1985–1986 the Commonwealth had negotiated some 4,700 contracts with more than 1,200 provider organizations for a total of $614 million. Much of the impetus for this phenomenal increase stemmed, not surprisingly, from zeal to "diminish the size of government." The protagonists of this aim are thus prone to use as measures of success the elimination of x government agencies through reliance on contracts with y private organizations and the layoff of z government employees. But these are misleading measures. The same services are still being performed by the same or similar kinds of people. Government agencies, moreover, are still assigning the services to be performed and prescribing the standards of performance. And at the end of the day the same taxpayers are still paying the bill. The real tests are whether quality has been improved, economies have been achieved, and accountability has been maintained. The great value of this book thus lies in the remarkable extent to which it sheds light on factors influencing quality, efficiency, and cost. As the cases also demonstrate, privatization makes it all the more important to monitor and—better yet—to evaluate performance.

A second less political but even more influential contributor to the growth of privatization was the wave of deinstitutionalization that occurred from the 1960s into the 1980s. In an illuminating case, Barbara Bailey Etta's study of St. Ann's Infant and Maternity Home in Washington, DC, conveys a vivid sense of the tremendous pressure generated in those years to diminish the population of public institutions and to close as many of them as possible. This and other cases also drive home the proposition that there is no substitute for resources. Arbitrary cuts in spending, delays in contract payments, and budgetary uncertainties undermine the efficiency and quality of contracted services. They demonstrate as well the fundamental distinction between cost and cost-effectiveness while also underscoring the need for services integration, community-based models, and the indispensability of alert public oversight.

Having spent many years overseeing human services programs, I can assure the reader who stays the course that she or he will come away with a firm grasp of the key questions that need to be addressed, a keen appreciation of how hard it is to get the answers, and outrage toward the distorting influences of politics as usual. It is devoutly to be hoped that many such readers will be moved to think harder and act more vigorously. That will be the definitive demonstration of the value of this book.

ELLIOT L. RICHARDSON, LLB, AB
Former Secretary of Health,
Education, and Welfare,
and U.S. Attorney General

Contributors

Barbara Bailey Etta, DSW
Director of Field Instruction and
    Assistant Professor
National Catholic School of Social
    Services
Catholic University of America
Washington, DC 20064

Lois Camberg, PhD
Health Research Scientist
Health Services Research and
    Development Program at the
    Brockton/West Roxbury VA
    Medical Center
Instructor in Medicine
Harvard Medical School
Needham, MA 02192

Andrea Canter, PhD
School Psychologist
Minneapolis Public Schools
Minneapolis, MN 55409

**William J. Curran, JD, LLM, SM,
    Hygiene, LLD (Hon.) (Deceased)**
Former Director
Harvard–World Health
    Organization International
    Collaborating Center on
    Health Legislation

Frances Glessner Lee Emeritus
    Professor of Legal Medicine
Schools of Medicine and Public
    Health
Harvard University
c/o Doris M. Curran
169 Clinton Avenue
Falmouth, MA 02540

Harriet Davidson, PhD
Research Associate
Harvard University
School of Public Health
Cambridge, MA 02138

Margaret B. Davidson, MA
Research Assistant
Harvard University
School of Public Health
Cambridge, MA 02138

Robert A. Dorwart, MD, MPH
Professor of Psychiatry
Harvard Medical School and
    Harvard School of Public
    Health
Harvard University
Cambridge, MA 02138

Michael Dukakis, JD
Distinguished Professor
Department of Political Science
Northeastern University
Boston, MA 02115

Ruth Fishbein, MA, MSW
Project Director
Quality Improvement
  Collaborative for Health and
  Addictions Research, Inc.
Boston, MA 02116

Elaine Hickey, MSN, RN
Nurse Researcher
Health Services Research and
  Development Field Program
Bedford MA VA Medical Center
Co-Investigator
Veterans Ambulatory Assessment
  Project
Natick, MA 01760

Philip W. Johnston, MA
Executive Director
Citizens Programs, Inc.
Boston, MA

James R. Kelly, MA
Former Director of Extended
  Care Services
Veterans Health Administration
Boston, MA

Donald C. Kern, MD, MPH
Assistant Professor
Boston University School of
  Medicine and School of Public
  Health
Boston, MA 02118

Steven Kraft, MSW, JD
Assistant Professor
University of North Dakota
Department of Social Work
Grand Forks, ND 85203

Dennis McCarty, PhD
Research Professor
Brandeis University
Florence Heller School for
  Advanced Studies in Social
  Welfare
Waltham, MA 02254-9110

1

Introduction

Margaret Gibelman

One of the major themes in the latter part of the 20th century is that of "privatization." This broadly encompassing term basically refers to the divesting of government responsibility for the funding and provision of products or services—mostly services, as government has not played a major role in the direct manufacture of products. An intermediary step in privatization widely used in the human services is that of purchase of services (POS), in which the government retains a primary role in service funding but delegates, through contracting, service delivery responsbility to the private sector (Gibelman & Demone, 1989; Gibelman, 1995).

Purchase of services is consistent with and an example of privatization: the shift of functions and responsibilities from government to the private sector. POS, however, is both an important building block toward privatizing and a free-standing, frequently used technology that may be driven more by pragmatism than by ideology.

Traditionally, state and local governments have elected to meet part of their responsibilities through financing the provision of care and services by nongovernmental organizations. The general satisfaction with these arrangements is evident in their continued and expanded use. Although the practice of contracting is far from new, its expanding scope and boundaries calls forth an array of practical, ethical, legal, and interorganizational issues that demand exploration.

PURCHASE OF SERVICE FRAMEWORK

As a political symbol, privatization constitutes the polar extreme of the welfare state (Leat, 1986). The reality, at least in the human services field, is a modified form of privatization in which government delegates service provision responsibility but maintains some or all fiscal responsibility. Purchase of services falls within this latter category and encompasses the concept of public-private partnerships. Government, at the federal, state, and local levels, purchases services from for-profit organizations, proprietary groups, other governmental units, and not-for-profit organizations.

Purchase of services thus concerns both the act of transmitting public funds to private service-providing sources and that of making decisions about how services are to be delivered. It is an organized procedure by which an entity of government enters into a formal agreement with another entity for goods or services. In the case of purchase of human services, the focus is on those services provided to individuals, groups, or communities to prevent, ameliorate, or resolve environmental, physical, or psychosocial problems (Demone & Gibelman, 1989).

The original intent of POS was to provide an alternative means of delivering services that would better achieve public purposes in the public interest (Gibelman & Demone, 1989). As the concept and practice have evolved, however, POS has become a means to further the goal of reducing the size and scope of government. As defined in the Reagan and Bush administrations, privatization meant divesting government of as many functions as possible. These include not only operations but also planning, administering, monitoring, and sometimes even licensing the services. Public services ranging from air traffic control to management of prisons were considered fair game for contracting out. President Clinton (1993) is continuing in this same tradition, with the goal of "reinventing government" to make it leaner and more effective.

The ultimate goal is to have the private sector assume responsibility for both service delivery and service funding and to encourage the application of market criteria to control costs and ensure quality. Nevertheless, within the human services, attainment of this goal would suggest the total dismantling of the welfare enterprise, an occurrence more likely to occur in rhetoric and degree than in fact or totality.

Government contracting of human services has traditionally been smaller in scale than contracting for other government services, such as defense, and has, until recent years, been primarily confined to relationships with the not-for-profit sector. Privatization of the human services marks an about-face of social policy development since the Great Depression, which increased the roles and responsibilities of the public system (Gibelman & Demone, 1983).

The absolute and relative extent of POS depends not only on the perceived wisdom of contracting out but also on the dollars available within the federal budget in a particular service or functional area. Purchased services may be provided to targeted groups of people, such as AIDS education oriented to teenagers in public schools, or to special populations, such as runaway youth or children who have been abused. In some cases the type of service or the number of people to whom services may be rendered within a group may be limited by statute, regulations, or agreement, or it may be open-ended. As budgets tighten, open-ended arrangements are less frequently found, a fact highlighted in several of the case studies in this volume.

The growth of contracting has its parallel in the national growth of not-for-profit organizations. In 1950 the number registered with the federal Internal Revenue Service (IRS) was about 50,000. Fifteen years later the number exceeded 300,000. In 10 more years (the mid-1970s) the number was above 700,000 (Hall, 1995). By 1992 the IRS was reporting the existence of more than 1 million tax-exempt organizations (General Accounting Office, 1995).

But organizations come and go. Bielefeld (1994), in a panel study in Minneapolis/St. Paul, found that 20% of not-for-profits ceased operation between 1980 and 1988. As Gibelman notes in chapter 7 of this volume, reliance on POS contracts may actually accelerate the demise of some organizations.

Purchase of services can take several forms, depending on the desired buyer–seller relationship and the nature of the services to be purchased. One method is to purchase the service(s) for particular individuals or classes of individuals who have identified problems or needs and are deemed eligible to receive services. Contractual arrangements may be long- or short-term. The provider may offer services based on selective screening or serve all who are referred by the contracting agency who fall within the established criteria; this will depend on the specifications of the contract. These types of purchasing arrangements are typical within the human services. The contract period may be for 6 months to several years. Contracts may, however, be terminated if the provider fails to live up to the agreement or if public funds dry up.

Purchase of services constitutes only one of several options for planning and delivering services. Savas (1982) identified nine alternative mechanisms, some of which have gained wide attention and favor in recent years: (1) service rendered by a single government agency, (2) agreements between governments, (3) purchase by contract, (4) franchises, (5) grants, (6) vouchers, (7) free market, (8) voluntary services, and (9) self-service.

Boundaries

The boundaries of POS arrangements are continually expanding within the broader context of the desire to privatize as many government functions as possible. Within the human services, several areas that were exclusively within the province of government are now being reexamined to identify alternative delivery methods, including social security (Kenworthy & Dewar, 1990). To date, POS has been applied to group homes, day care, child protective services, substance abuse services, foster care, mental health services, and residential care, among others. Very few areas remain untouched by contracting. A notable exception is protective services (adult or child), for which the service includes a legal determination process and cannot be delegated by government to another provider.

The extent to which POS dominates a particular human services field is subject to a wide range of influences, including political and philosophical forces and social values and preferences. Purchase of services, as one means to actualize privatization (albeit still using public funds), is reflective of and integrally related to changing conceptions of the roles and functions of government and the private sector of this society.

The increased use of POS must thus be understood within the context of prevailing priorities, values, and preferences affecting social welfare policies and programs. The use of not-for-profit and for-profit human services providers as an alternative to public service delivery is political expedient and a realistic and effective way to circumvent negative public sentiment about government's size and role. Its use is likely to continue unabated, despite some real or alleged problems that have surfaced in contracting experience.

Advantages and Disadvantages of POS

In recent years there has been a growing literature about experiences with the purchase of human services and issues arising from its use. The growing body of experience with POS has led to various claims and counterclaims concerning the weaknesses and strengths of this form of service delivery. The arguments in favor of and against POS can be summarized as follows:

Advantages
    Cost-effectiveness
    Administrative efficiency
    Ease of altering or terminating programs
    Circumvention of civil service regulations
    Promotion of citizen participation
    Enhancement of quality of services
    Increased professionalism
    Flexible use of personnel
    Program flexibility
    Promotion of innovation
    Promotion of competition
    Addressing the mistrust of government
Disadvantages
    Difficulty in ensuring standards
    Loss of public control and accountability
    Increased cost
    Poorer services
    Loss of protection for the poor and neediest ("creaming")
    Loss of autonomy for private agencies
    Difficulty in monitoring
    Subjection of private agencies to public policy shifts
    Unreliability of contractors (Demone & Gibelman, 1989, 1997).

What is an advantage to some organizations or individuals may be seen as a disadvantage by others. As the case studies in this volume suggest, the perceived advantages and disadvantages are crystallized in contract implementation.

IMPLEMENTING POS: EXAMPLES FROM THE FIELD

American culture has long supported the concept and practice of individual or group purchase of needed goods and services; this is a fundamental tenet of the free enterprise system (Mills, 1985). The application of this value to human services has had a less certain history, in part because of the paternalism that has characterized support of public health, welfare, and social services. Nevertheless, the growing body of experience with POS in the human services is suggestive of the range, advantages, and pitfalls of this kinds of arrangement.

Given the enormous industry that has evolved to implement POS (rate-setting systems, contract administration, negotiating and compliance-monitoring procedures, etc.), how POS works to achieve its intended public purposes is a subject of utmost importance. The high expectations surrounding POS, despite a growing list of documented problems, also suggests the need for a comprehensive exploration of the implementation and outcome of these arrangements. An emphasis on outcomes also helps to focus on the people ultimately intended to benefit by improved methods of service delivery: the consumers of services.

This volume thus focuses on POS in implementation and examines, through case studies, a number of human service areas in which services are now being purchased. These services share in common their goal of preventing, ameliorating, or resolving health, mental health, social, or environmental problems that afflict individuals, families, groups, and communities.

The case studies provide an in-depth look at POS experiences. These examples of POS contracting for human services are selected to show the range and breadth of such arrangements and their impact on clients, agencies, and government and the interrelationship between the public and private sectors. The nine case studies of purchased services are explored in relation to the rationale, implementation experience, trends, lessons, and future prospects associated with this method of service delivery. The majority of chapters focus on POS at the state or local level, the traditional locus of most direct human service delivery programs within the province of government.

The case studies are authored by individuals who have expertise in their particular area of POS and have engaged in substantial research of a qualitative or quantitative nature. Several have written recent or earlier dissertations on the subject (Gibelman, Etta); others have conducted independent or organizationally sponsored research (Davidson et al.; Canter, Fishbein & McCarty). Still others have personal experience in contracting from the perspective of government and/or private providers (e.g., Dukakis, Johnston, Gibelman, Demone, Kraft). Substantive areas of purchase practice include child welfare, substance abuse, school mental health services, veterans' services, and homemaker/home health aide services.

Several of the cases focus on contracting experiences in the commonwealth of Massachusetts. Although not planned, it is also not accidental that Massachusetts is overrepresented, given this state's long history with contracting and the extent of its use.

When libertarian William Weld first ran for governor in 1989, as a Republican, to succeed the retiring governor, Michael Dukakis, contracting for services became politicized with its conversion to privatization. It was a major Weld platform. (Elsewhere in this volume, former Massachusetts governor Dukakis discuses the public administration principles he used to determine when his administration chose to contract or not to contract.) But candidate Weld was not the first to see the political possibilities in the concept of privatization. It has its advocates in other states, at the national level, and internationally as well.

In his second term, Governor Weld became a more subdued advocate, for just as privatization has potentially positive political implications it has a similar potential for negative side effects. By 1994, language adjustment was in favor. The state's transportation secretary was describing his department's efforts as "competitive contracting." The secretary of administration and finance acknowledged that privatization had become a "polarizing term . . . a misnomer for some of their initiatives" (Polner,1994, p.17). Massachusetts, with a Republican governor and both branches of the legislature controlled by the Democrats, provided a natural breeding ground for controversy especially given the earlier Democratic support (see chapter 2, by former governor Dukakis).

Two of the chapters provide personal reflections on POS from the vantage point of those responsible for decision making. Michael Dukakis, as governor of the Commonwealth of Massachusetts, presided over an unprecedented expansion of contracted services during the 1980s. He sees this expansion within the context of fundamental changes in social welfare policy, including deinstitutionalization and the need for rapidly developing community services for the mentally ill and developmentally disabled.

Mr. Dukakis illustrates the explosion in contracting in Massachusetts with the case of the State Division of Youth Services. His observations make it clear that planning and capacity building are essential first steps in a POS system. Mr. Dukakis believes that the experience over the past decades has provided important lessons about what works and what doesn't work in POS. We agree. Among the lessons he cites are the following:

- The larger the number of qualified bidders, suppliers, and contractors, the better.
- Contracting for social services is more difficult than purchasing concrete services such as road construction.
- Management systems must be revamped.

- Potential cost savings are frequently exaggerated.
- Privatization increases the possibility of corruption.
- Some services should not be purchased but publicly provided. These include adult corrections and services for the severely and chronically mentally ill.

Johnston also speaks from personal experience about the evolution of social services contracting in Massachusetts. Johnston served as secretary of human services in the Dukakis administration. Bridging the public-private sectors in multiple roles as administrator, policymaker, and legislator at both the state and federal level has provided Mr. Johnston with a unique vantage point. Successes and failures are noted but with some satisfaction of a task well done. He notes several danger signs, however, in light of changing economic and political circumstances:

1. The reimbursement of private direct-care workers has remained stagnant for several years. The minimums were established in 1986. These are the core providers in many settings.
2. A new focus for POS is surfacing—faster and cheaper is better.
3. Leaner and meaner is the behavior.

Johnston's creative solution is to organize the board members of the voluntary associations into a statewide federation to lobby for more responsible behavior on the part of the state. These people are among the more influential and verbal members of our society. They will be heard.

Formalization

Johnston, Etta and Kraft, and Gibelman provide historical perspectives on the evolution of contracting. These authors share in common their observations about the growing formalization of public–private relationships. In the early days of contracting, arrangements were "loose," and available providers in the community were approached for their existing expertise. Contract requirements were general in nature, typically specifying only the time period, dollar amount, general population to be served, and type of service. Reporting requirements also were minimal. This situation was to change with relative speed; the reasons, however, are unclear. As more and more voluntary providers became interested in contract funds, it is likely that the pool of agency applicants increased to such an extent that a more formal bidding process was required. In addition, bureaucracies tend to clone themselves, and once the immediate start-up needs were met, public agency staff ensured their own jobs and future by creating contracting procedures and systems that took the place of the service-rendering role for which they had previously been responsible.

Another common theme, noted by Johnston and by Kraft and Gibelman, among others, relates to problems with prompt payments. Cash flow was affected by consistently late payments, a situation that continues into the late 1990s, as Gibelman portrays in the case example of the District of Columbia. In that case the cash-strapped District handled, in part, its own cash flow emergency by simply halting payment to contractors.

The majority of authors perceive contracting to be a mixed bag. They agree, further, that the continuation of these arrangements is a given and that fiscal dependency has largely replaced earlier motivations for the public-private relationship. Contract funds have come to represent the greatest source of revenues for many private agencies. The programs they support have developed constituencies of their own, and there is pressure from internal agencies, boards, communities, and clients to preserve them.

The dollar amount of contracting within the human services arena began as relatively small and grew exponentially. For example, Johnston notes that in Massachusetts, during the period 1984–1991, contracting increased from about $400 million per year to $1 billion per year. Demone, also in this volume, cites 1996 figures that estimate the total Massachusetts contracting at $5 billion or, using this higher estimate, approximately 30% of the state's operating budget. Purchasing services from not-for-profits alone has grown into a $15-billion-a-year industry annually (Smith & Lipsky, 1993). If the Massachusetts experience were to be generalized, the national figure would approximate $150 billion, not $15 billion. Although it is clear that estimates vary considerably, the scope of contracting remains significant.

One of the rationales for contracting is the perceived lower costs of service provision. Contracting, as it has evolved, has had its impact on keeping costs down. Human services are labor-intensive, and the highest costs typically involve personnel expenses. By suppressing wages (placing a lid on reimbursable salaries), as noted by Johnston, the public funding agencies have been able to control costs. But at the same time, this choice of tactics has had an impact on the competitive position of nonprofits in attracting the most highly qualified professionals.

In 1990 estimated employment within the independent sector was 14.4

million, or 10.4% of the total labor force. Excluding volunteer time, the 1990 independent sector work force constituted 6.3% of the total U.S. labor force (Hodgkinson & Weitzman, 1992). However, the recent expansion of the for-profit sector and the growing number of human services employment within it suggest that the voluntary sector may be loosing out in the competitive struggle to recruit and retain the best-qualified work force. An analysis of the composition of the membership of the National Association of Social Workers indicated that the greatest growth between 1988 and 1995 occurred in the proportion of social workers employed under for-profit auspices. Salaries also tended to be higher for those employed by for-profits or public agencies (Gibelman & Schervish, 1997).

Another perceived advantage of POS is the flexibility it affords. Private providers have long been seen as having greater ability than the public sector to mount new programs quickly. The chapter by Davisdon, Hickey, Camberg, Davidson, Kern, and Kelly explores the implementation of a Homemaker and Home Health Aide (H/HHA) program in Veteran Affairs (VA). When the need was perceived to provide noninstitutional health-related services to eligible veterans, the Veterans Health Administration determined that the program should use a POS mechanism to deliver these services on a national basis.

The use of POS in this example provided both opportunities and challenges. In the first 20 months of operation over 3,000 patients received services through 119 VA medical centers. Purchase of services allowed VA the flexibility of providing needed services at each facility without developing its own expertise and staff or building or expanding permanent structures. The challenges of providing quality services to a geographically dispersed patient population require monitoring of access, costs, and patient outcomes on a nationwide basis.

Here, the results were positive. The program's evaluation demonstrated a high degree of satisfaction among patients and families with the community-based services and VA facility administrators as well. Program costs were controlled. This case study is instructive in that it shows purchasing care can be used with success in a federal program.

The Contracting Business

Contracting for service has become big business with big stakes. Often, voluntary and for-profit providers are pitted against each other in competition for contract funds. Sophistication in marketing one's agency has become essential to succeed in this competitive environment.

Dukakis notes that there is money to be made in contracts and cautions that care must be taken to ensure that the system is not exploited. He urges attention to ethical standards for the contracting process.

The "big business" side for government is the amount of dollars (and discretion) they have to offer. For potential and actual contracted service providers, the stakes are high. As Kraft and Gibelman observe, the cumulative impact of contracting can be an alteration of the client population served, technology used, and services offered. Even when boards of directors and management are aware of the costs of contracting to their mission and purpose, the enticement of dollars may neutralize these concerns. Practicality often rules.

Quality and Quality Control

A long-standing question in contracting for services concerns the relative cost and quality of these services compared to those provided directly by public agencies. Canter examines the quality dimensions of school psychological services that are contracted out. Traditionally provided by school district employees, school psychological services increasingly face significant modification, reduction, or elimination in favor of purchased services from the larger professional community. Purchased services may allow a district to expand its current resources or may appear to offer a cheap alternative to salaried employees. Little empirical data exist comparing purchased and employee services in school settings in relation to cost or quality.

Canter's chapter provides an overview of service models, standards, and practical issues regarding purchased school psychological services, followed by several case studies illustrating positive and negative outcomes of contractual arrangements and comments regarding future directions. Unlike child welfare or substance abuse services, school psychological services may be purchased from an individual contractor as well as from another organization.

Canter concludes that the continuing quest to solve financial problems favors the use of a contract model, despite indications that such arrangements have had negative consequences. Those psychological services purchased tend to be narrow in scope, forfeiting a more comprehensive approach to service provision. Cost savings may be largely illusive because the services purchased are frequently less encompassing than those provided directly by school-based psychologists. In this example the decreased dollars spent by contracting likely mean decreased services.

The growth in contracting has been accompanied by, as noted above, increased formalization and accountability demands. Accountability has evolved to more than fiscal reporting and process adherence. The demand is more and more for documenting the outcome of services, and there is movement toward reimbursement systems based on outcome measures. This portends of things to come.

Fishbein and McCarty, in their chapter on quality improvement for contracted substance abuse services, suggest that monitoring and accountability processes can be contracted out in much the same way that services are purchased. State and local agencies that use POS contracts usually develop quality assurance mechanisms to document that services are delivered as required and meet minimal expectations for quality. As service systems become more complex, however, inspectors may have a large workload and may be relatively unfamiliar with specialized services. In such cases the inspection is often cursory and offers little sense of the value of the services.

The Massachusetts Bureau of Substance Abuse Services, in collaboration with alcohol and drug abuse treatment and prevention services, has replaced much of its quality assurance process with a contract that supports the development of continuous improvement systems in programs that contract to provide addiction treatment and prevention services. The development and implementation of the Quality Improvement Collaborative (QIC) is reviewed in the chapter by Fishbein and McCarty. Principles for continuous improvement systems are outlined and delineate the philosophical base for the initiative. QIC's structure and process are described, and the technical assistance provided to treatment programs is illustrated. Finally, the program's influences on system development during the first years of operation are reviewed.

Emerging Issues and Cautionary Notes

As more and more experience is gained with POS, issues of planning, performance, role delegation and delineation, interorganizational relationships, service monitoring, and evaluation and accountability, among others, have surfaced. The case studies in this book suggest the range of issues that have affected POS arrangements from their earliest inception (see, e.g., the chapter by Etta) to the present.

As the case studies illustrate, contracting for services is not without its problems. As with any mechanism for the delivery of services, experience may deviate from intent. Thus, attention is also focused on the some of the negative experiences and issues related to contracting, including role conflict and boundaries, corruption, and accountability.

By the mid-1980s, POS had come under considerable attack and scrutiny, and human services contracting has not been immune. Such criticisms range from inadequate accounting procedures to ineffective services. The *New York Times* and the *Washington Post*, two of the major national newspapers, contain consistent and numerous articles about allegations, investigations, and outright scandals concerning contracted services. Although a majority of these reports have concerned the defense industry (by virtue of the sheer volume of defense contracting), contracting problems related to the human services have also surfaced in the media. Demone's chapter "Privatization, Politics, and the Press," highlights the role of both politics and the press in human services contracting. This case history follows several private human services providers in Massachusetts for a 33-month period after a series of front-page stories in the *Boston Herald* alleged a variety of contract misdeeds. One of these agencies is examined in some depth. The conclusions include the following:

- Negative allegations were not well founded.
- The allegations were not symptomatic of extensive transgressions.
- The role of the press was deleterious.
- The elected officials protected themselves at the sacrifice of important services.
- The senior bureaucrats and the private agency executives and their staffs behaved responsibly.
- The likely individual losers are those public and private officials subject to continual political and press attack.

Demone notes three major failings of government: the structural layers that inhibit effective action, the multiple protections of employees embodied in the combination of civil service and organized labor, and the constant political meddling in the operations of the agencies. In this latter regard, Demone echoes a common theme in these case studies: some of the structural organizational failings of the public sector are being transferred into the daily operations of contracted agencies, with likely negative results.

Unlike Demone, who found many of the allegations in the press to be unfounded, Gibelman highlights the responsible role the press can play in publicizing legitimate contracting problems. The case study offered by Gibelman in this volume offers some insight into the types of problems that can emerge in contracting, as revealed through press accounts. The transgressions were almost exclusively focused on the government of the District of Columbia, a relatively easy target in light of the District's history of mismanagement, if not outright corruption. The press clearly sided with the not-for-profit contracted providers who were left in the lurch by delays in payments and contract renewals.

These examples indicate the range of implementation problems that occur with federal, state, and local POS arrangements, with fault attributed to the government agency, to provider agencies, to both, and/or to the relationship between the two. Although problems are far more likely to receive media attention than successes are, their occurrence does raise questions about monitoring and accountability. Criticisms have, not surprisingly, led to some proposals to reform the contracting system. In general, such proposals aim to control discretion, tighten public monitoring, encourage competitive bidding, and ensure that conflict of interest situations are avoided. But as noted above, even these oversight functions are now actual or potential targets for contracting out.

Forecasting

Contracting out for the delivery of services is far from a static phenomenon and may at times be viewed within a continuum of a preferred solution or a new type of accountability and administrative problem. Unlike contracting for concrete services (computer services) or products (construction of housing units), the use of purchase arrangements for human services is more complex, and the methods of monitoring, evaluating, and performance standards are more elusive.

Experiences with purchasing human services have shown mixed results. This finding, however, is neither surprising nor unexpected. The implementation of many, if not most, American social policies has been marred by too high expectations, insufficient funding, short time frames, and vague and often competing goals.

Criticisms about POS range from the very general (perpetuation of inadequate service delivery or insufficient steps toward privatization because POS is based on public funding) to the more specific—lack of standards, lack of long-term planning, inadequate staffing of contracted programs, poor communication and relationships between government and contracted agencies, inadequate rate setting and/or payment procedures, and so forth.

Despite the general and specific criticisms of POS, it is noteworthy that there remains substantial unanimity about continuing this form of public–private partnership in the delivery of human services. The goal has been to bring about incremental change in the contracting system rather than to discard it. There may, however, be a lack of real alternatives in a time when public provision is political unacceptable and total privatization (including funding responsibility) is unrealistic within the human services. On a more optimistic note, POS may satisfy the disparate requirements of a wide segment of the American political and general publics.

Cautionary notes are, however, in order. The reliance on government funds has led to substantial changes in the nature of not-for-profit agencies, including primary service focus, types of programs offered, operating mode, and management style. These impacts are clearly seen in the case studies offered herein by Gibelman, Kraft and Gibelman, Dukakis, and Johnston. The desire to initiate, expand, or supplement existing or new programs may lead voluntary agencies to enter financially dependent relationships with government with little consideration of the long-term impact.

The issue of financial dependence is long-standing. The chapter by Etta traces the reliance of one sectarian child care institution on POS contracts over the span of 100-plus years. Contracting has become its major means of organizational survival. The forces, factors, and methods developed and utilized to maintain the viability of this agency, when other child welfare agencies were not able to adapt, are discussed. Variables are identified that are instructive and generalizable to other organizations during periods of crises. Finally, a prognosis regarding POS contracting for this agency is presented.

Financial dependence on the part of the voluntary sector may be hazardous to the longer-term viability of these agencies. One of the key advantages to purchasing services, from the point of view of government, is that contracts can be terminated. The general status of the economy and the consensus among Democrats and Republicans alike that the budget deficit must be reduced suggest that no area of government spending, direct or through contract, is sacrosanct. And as Gibelman points out in relation to the District of Columbia, government cash shortfalls may lead to unilateral decisions to curtail contracts or delay payment to contractors.

Gibelman's chapter explores the recent history of the purchase of social

services in the District of Columbia within the context of the city's growing fiscal crisis and changes in prevailing views about the merits of social
welfare programs. One stimulus to enlarge the scope of contracting in
the District was to meet court-ordered mandates to revamp the child welfare system. However, political decisions about how to address the city's
serious fiscal woes placed many voluntary agencies in an untenable position. This case highlights the sometimes precarious nature of contractual
relationships. Extrapolating from the experiences of the District of
Columbia, contracted services may be highly vulnerable to the budget ax
as municipalities across the country seek to reduce expenditures.

Long-Term Impact

Two concluding chapters are devoted to reviewing and analyzing issues
of planning, performance, role delegation and delineation, and interorganizational relationships, as reflected in the individual and collective
experiences explored in the case studies. Faced with decreases in federal
dollars, it is not unusual for state and local governments to respond first
by curtailing contracts. Scarce resources, as noted by Johnston, can also
lead funding agencies to freeze reimbursement rates.

Professor William J. Curran, the draftsman of the 1966 mental
health/retardation legislation cited in the chapter by Demone, has provided a chapter in this book that looks freshly at the legal issues arising
with the growth of privatization.

It should be clear that POS contracts are a tool—a legal tool—for achieving public governmental objectives. Comprehensive privatization plans
in the human services area are best achieved by legislation that lays down
guidelines for carrying out the programs.

All parties to POS contracts in this field should be aware of general
policies and requirements for public contracting, as detailed in this chapter. The role of public agencies is proactive in seeking appropriate contractors and in promoting high-quality services. Public agencies are also
legally bound to provide and enforce monitoring and evaluation of the
services delivered under these arrangements. Liability suits against local
community contractors and against supervising public authorities can
raise serious questions about duties under these contracts.

A final chapter, by Demone, explores the implications of the use of contracting in the human services in regard to redefining the role of government, the impact on voluntary and proprietary agencies, quality of

service, and furthering the public interest. Experience suggests that POS arrangements are likely to be an increasingly used tool to provide human services, particularly in light of political and social pressures to diminish the size and role of government. Even if government maintains fiscal responsibility, the appearance of divestiture is made possible through the contract method. And despite a checkered history, the weight of evidence is in favor of continued and widespread use of POS.

Audiences

Potential users of this volume include public policymakers, public and private human service managers, and social service practitioners. Procurement agents, contract and grant managers, and financial officers at the federal, state, and local levels will also find the book relevant and useful. Educators who seek to prepare students for the realities of current practice will find the case studies adaptable for classroom use.

The volume can stand alone or in combination with its companion volume as a text in master's- and doctoral-level public policy and social administration courses in the fields of social work, political science, and public administration. Finally, interested citizens concerned with how their tax dollars are being spent or how the human services work to promote or inhibit high-quality service delivery may find this volume instructive.

REFERENCES

Bielefeld, W. (1994). What affects nonprofit survival? *Nonprofit Management and Leadership, 5*(1), 19–36.

Clinton, W. (1993). *A vision of change for American.* Washington, DC: U.S. Government Printing Office.

Demone, H. W., Jr., & Gibelman, M. (1989). In search of a theoretical base for the purchase of services. In H. W. Demone, Jr., & M. Gibelman (Eds.), *Services for sale: Purchasing health and human services* (pp. 5–16). New Brunswick, NJ: Rutgers University Press.

General Accounting Office. (1995). *Tax exempt organizations* (GAO/GGD-95-84RO). Washington, DC: Author.

Gibelman, M. (1995). Purchasing social services. In R. L. Edwards, (Ed.-in-Chief). *Encyclopedia of social work* (19th ed., pp. 1998–2007). Washington, DC: NASW Press.

Gibelman, M., & Demone, H. W., Jr. (1983). Purchase of service: Forging public–private partnerships in the human services. *Urban and Social Change Review, 16*, 21–26.

Gibelman, M., & Demone, H. W., Jr. (eds.). (1989). The evolving contract state. In H. W. Demone, Jr., & M. Gibelman (Eds.), *Services for sale: Purchasing health and human services* (pp. 17–57). New Brunswick, NJ: Rutgers University Press.

Gibelman, M., & Demone, H. W., Jr. (1997). Private solutions to public human service problems: Purchasing services to meet social need. In S. Hakim, G. W. Bowman, & P. Seidenstat, (Eds.), *Privatizing government Services*. New York: Praeger.

Gibelman, M., & Schervish, P. (1997). *Who we are: A second look*. Washington, DC: NASW Press.

Hall, P. D. (1995). Theories and institutions. *Nonprofit and Voluntary Sector Quarterly, 24*, 5–13.

Hodgkinson, V. A., & Weitzman, M. S. (1992). *Dimensions of the independent sector: A statistical profile*. Washington, DC: Independent Sector.

Kenworthy, T., & Dewar, H. (1990, January 20). House Republicans push anew for privatization of social security. *Washington Post*, p. A4.

Leat, D. (1986). Privatization and voluntarization. *Quarterly Journal of Social Affairs, 2*, 285–320.

Mills, J. E. (1985). Moving toward a tripartite marketplace in the human services. In *The social welfare forum, 1982–83*. (Pp. 108–116). Washington, DC: National Conference on Social Welfare.

Palmer, T. C., Jr. (1994, March 15). Sloganeers try to stay one word ahead of critics. *The Boston Globe*, p. 17.

Savas, E. S. (1982). *Privatizing the public sector: How to shrink government*. Chatham, NJ: Chatham House.

Smith, S. R., & Lipsky, M. (1993). *Nonprofits for hire: The welfare state in the age of contracting*. Cambridge, MA: Harvard University Press.

2

Personal Reflections on Purchase of Service: A View from a State Capitol

Michael Dukakis

There is nothing new about the government contracting for goods and services. We've been doing it since the beginning of the Republic.

Contracting for services is not simply an issue that faces the public sector. Whether to "make or buy" a service or product has always been an important question for private businesses as well. Does General Motors, for example, manufacture all the components of its cars within the GM organization? Or does it contract with independent parts and component suppliers? Who cleans the corporate offices at the end of the day? Who does the landscaping around the company buildings? If the company president has to fly on a business trip, do you buy him or her a corporate jet or does he or she fly commercially?

Very few governments in this country have ever run their own public works construction operations on anything but relatively minor jobs. Although the federal government operated federal arsenals and shipyards for decades prior to World War II, most of those facilities have been closed, and for at least the past half century almost all of the manufacturing of military arms and equipment has been done under contract with private companies—occasionally with less than satisfactory results.

It is a rare state or local government that has in-house architects or engineers to do the sophisticated design and engineering work required on major public works projects, and many state and local governments have for years contracted with private contractors for waste disposal and snow removal.

Some governments try to handle major bond issues in-house, but the majority hire private firms at very attractive fees to underwrite and sell their bonds and provide the legal opinions that the financial world requires before they will buy them.

Nor is there anything new about governments contracting for the purchase of social services. Years ago, many communities paid a local doctor to provide medical care for the indigent. Since the passage of Medicaid by Congress in 1965, health care for the poor has operated almost entirely on a contracted basis with thousands and thousands of health care providers. Furthermore, most state social service departments have for years used foster care as a means to provide security and a stable home environment for abused and neglected children—a service that they routinely "purchase" from hundreds of foster families that provide such care for a set fee.

What is different today is the explosion in social services that has taken place since the 1960s and the dramatic expansion in the amount and variety of contracting, often in areas that are both difficult and complex and pose enormous challenges to those providing the services. I was one of the governors who arrived on the scene in 1975 at the time when purchase of services (POS) was beginning to take off. After an involuntary sabbatical from 1978 to 1982, I returned to the governor's office and presided over an unprecedented expansion of contracted services during the 1980s.

In part, this expansion was fueled by fundamental changes in policy— the closing of large institutions for the mentally ill and retarded, for example—that demanded a whole range of community services for those leaving the institutions. A new and expanded focus on services for children with learning disabilities was accompanied by extensive contracting for their education with a host of private or nonprofit schools, which either had been or were then established to provide specialized learning for these youngsters.

In Massachusetts one of the most dramatic examples of this fundamental change in policy took place in the State Division of Youth Services in the early 1970s under Commissioner Jerome Miller. Miller, who arrived in Massachusetts from a teaching job at Ohio State University with some interesting but not particularly detailed views about the handling of delinquent juveniles, rapidly came to the conclusion that the traditional "reform school" system was hopelessly beyond repair. In one of the most dramatic revolutions in social policy in the history of this country—and with the support of a number of us in the Massachusetts legislature who had come to the same conclusion—Miller closed the reform schools, sent home a lot of the children in them, and then proceeded to try to develop a community-based system from the ground up where none had ever existed. I was the governor who inherited the early results of the Miller revolution, and I spent my first 4 years trying to bring some stability and community support to a wildly exciting but often chaotic experiment in deinstitutionalization.

In short, we have had a lot of experience with what many today call privatization. What too many, including the advocates *and* opponents of POS have failed to do, however, is to look at our experience over the past decades for the lessons it teaches us about what works and what doesn't work in the POS business. Fortunately or unfortunately, that is not a luxury that elected chief executives have. Before we leap into the privatization stew, we had better know what we are doing. Otherwise, we will be retired to private life 2 or 4 years hence.

What follows is an effort by at least one retired elected chief executive to draw some lessons from my own experience on the front lines of the POS battleground.

1. *The larger the number of qualified bidders, suppliers, and contractors, the better.* One of the reasons competitive bidding on highway jobs works reasonably well in this country is that there are a lot of contractors, and we know how to estimate construction costs. That does not mean that we don't have problems on construction jobs with private contractors. Some of them turn out to be incompetent or irresponsible. There is ample room for collusion between contractors and inspectors. Contractors on public works jobs are often pressured to make campaign contributions to elected officials or candidates. (More on this later.)

But the fact that there are so many of them makes it possible to have a genuinely competitive bidding process that can produce quality work. And if a contractor happens to screw up, you can throw him off the job and look to the performance bond, which he must post as a contractor for winning the bid, to pay for the completion of the work.

The same is true of contract cleaning. Early in my second term as governor I became increasingly dissatisfied with the conditions of the Greater Boston metropolitan transit system. We finally decided to go to contract cleaning. Not only did we get cleaner stations, we also saved a lot of money. Why? Because there are dozens of cleaning companies that will bid and bid aggressively for the work; and if they don't do the work well—something that is easily verified by a simple visual inspection—there are 20 other companies waiting in the wings to do the job.

2. *Contracting for social services is a (helluva) lot tougher than bidding road*

jobs and cleaning contracts. Trying to contract for social services is a whole different kettle of fish. Social services are much harder to define and quantify. There are not 20 or 30 social service organizations standing around with ample financial resources and a long history of successful operations waiting to bid on these contracts.

Furthermore, the contracting process itself is far more difficult. How do you describe the services you want? Can you quantify them in a way that gives you accurate cost estimates? How do you know you are getting a fair price and value for your money? Are the organizations capable of providing the service? And what do you do if, God forbid, one of the agency's clients runs or escapes and commits a heinous crime while out on the street?

Moreover, once you have shut down your state operations and opted for a system based largely on contracted services, you have effectively lost your capacity to deliver the service if your contractors fail or collapse. I had that precise experience in my first term as governor when one of our major providers of services to delinquent youth went bankrupt on a Friday afternoon (it *always* happens on a Friday afternoon, usually *late* Friday afternoon). The provider had responsibility for literally hundreds of youngsters, for whom it had agreed to provide services in a variety of settings.

Talk about panic attacks. We went nuts trying to find the kids, find alternative services and organizations that could provide for them, and do so before one of them went out and did something crazy or worse. We certainly couldn't put them temporarily back in reform schools. The reform schools were gone. Nor were there any state-run group homes or other alternatives.

What we were forced to do was to plead with a handful of existing nonprofit providers to take these children at a time when they had their hands full trying to do what we had already contracted with them to do. Needless to say, we were in no position to drive a hard bargain with them. In fact, we had to beg them to take these kids—and fast.

3. *If you decide you are going to rely wholly or substantially on contracted services, you had better have an entirely different management system in place before you do so.* One of the things that made Jerry Miller's tenure as commissioner of youth services such a stormy one was that he had inherited a system that depended almost entirely on institutional care run by the state. Each institution had its own superintendent and its own budget and line items. A large percentage of the staff of the institutions had been doing the same job for a long time, and the agency was loaded with political patronage.

Suddenly, policy decisions were being made that would virtually eliminate the institutional system and rely almost exclusively on nonprofit organizations to provide services, either in the community or through a series of group homes and facilities, none of which existed at the time Miller made the decision to deinstitutionalize.

That situation was—and is—not unique to Miller. It is not simply the fact that organizations and private agencies, often with little or no experience in the particular field, must be persuaded to get into the contracting business. State government itself must create an entirely new management system that has nothing to do with running the institutions but everything to do with managing a complex and decentralized network of mostly nonprofit providers in a way that accurately defines the service we want; prices them accurately; engages in extensive, ongoing monitoring of the provider's performance; and is ready and willing to take action if their performance fails to meet acceptable standards.

The transition from an institution-based system to one that contracts and monitors is not only difficult; it requires people with skills that are very different from those required of the people who staff and run institutions. These new skills include the capacity to manage a decentralized network of regional offices that can work directly with local providers; design and draft appropriate contracts; develop "should cost" models that attempt to put a reasonable price on the services being requested; undertake case management, as well as procedures and staff for auditing and evaluating performance; and have a clear sense of how and under what circumstances a provider must be dumped, especially when the public agency has lost its own ability to deliver such services.

Miller had to create his own management system out of whole cloth, and he himself had never managed anything larger than a small program for emotionally troubled youngsters of service personnel when he was an officer in the air force. Moreover, there was no handy-dandy guidebook to tell him how. As a result, many providers didn't get paid for months. The commonwealth's own budget and management system were not equipped to help him develop the kind of management system he needed. Designed as it was for a largely institutional system, it was instead a constant burden on him and his staff as they developed their new approach to the care and custody of delinquent youths.

In fact, it is not an exaggeration to say that the budget and personnel procedures in the state Office of Administration and Finance were as big a problem for Miller as the fact that he had nothing even approaching the kind of management system required for the POS operation within his own department.

The results were predictable. A revolutionary approach to the care and treatment of delinquent youth almost came to grief because of management and administrative failures. It took several years and a lot of starts and stops before we had such a management system in place.

4. *Politicians should not exaggerate the potential savings from a POS system. Good services purchased from the private or nonprofit sector cost money.* Back in the 1960s and 1970s, when many of us were talking about deinstitutionalization and POS, we assumed almost automatically that contracted services would be cheaper and better. If such services are properly conceived and run, both goals can be achieved.

But it is a terrible mistake to exaggerate the financial savings from contracting, or what these days is more commonly called privatization, especially of social services. Dealing with violent young people, for example, requires small, well-staffed settings with security *and* services. Making progress with difficult kids won't happen on the cheap.

My successor as governor, Bill Weld, learned that the hard way in 1993. I had been forced to make budget cuts in virtually all social service programs as a result of revenue shortfalls during the recession that hit Massachusetts and the Northeast in the late 1980s. Some of these cuts fell on the Department of Youth Services. Unfortunately, Weld failed to move to restore those cuts as the state's fiscal situation improved in 1992 and 1993. Suddenly, we were confronted with a revolving-door situation in which young people arrested for violent crimes were being released to the community under the worst possible circumstances because of a lack of beds in our network of small, secure facilities. In fact, eight residents of one of those facilities in western Massachusetts escaped together, provoking outrage from a lot of citizens and embarrassment for the administration.

Those cuts have now been restored. But they are a reminder that POS by itself is not a magic cure. Resources are required, particularly for those who are either severely disturbed emotionally or likely to engage in violent conduct.

The new Speaker of the House of Representatives, Newt Gingrich, is apparently learning that same lesson. Even if orphanages made sense for youngsters (an early Gringrich proposal to "solve" the problem of teenage pregnancy, among others) from dysfunctional and abusive families—and they don't—good care in a well staffed group residence will easily cost five or six times more than it will in a stable, well-trained foster family.

5. *Privatization increases the possibility of corruption. Tough standards of integrity must be established and enforced.* Putting the arm on public works

contractors for gifts, bribes, or campaign contributions is as old as American politics itself. In fact, I cut my political eyeteeth in the Massachusetts legislature over scandals in the hiring of architects and engineers for the state building projects. I had been elected to the state legislature for the first time in 1962, and I was aware even then that the best architects in Massachusetts—and we had some of the best in the world—wouldn't touch a state job with a 10-foot pole. The reason, it turned out, was not hard to find. State architectural and engineering contracts were being parceled out routinely to architects and engineers willing to buy tables for the fund-raising dinners of incumbent governors and their opponents. And those architects and engineers were thoroughly bipartisan. They gave to both sides.

I and one of my colleagues in the legislature proceeded to blow the whistle on this racket, which had been going on for years. We finally forced the incumbent administration and the legislature to buy the notion of a Designer Selection Board (DSB) that would get the process out in the open. We hoped to get politics out of it and top-notch architects and engineers into it. By and large, the DSB has been a success, but the fact that we had to create it in the first place is an early warning sign for the advocates of privatization.

If there is money to be made in state contracts—and there is—and if the criteria for awarding those contracts are often largely qualitative, particularly in social services—and they are—the opportunities for abuse can multiply exponentially. For that reason, POS and privatization advocates must pay a lot of attention to ethical standards that have to be set as part of the contracting process.

Should providers and their principals be barred from contributing to political campaigns? If not, should they be required to list their organizational or professional affiliations as part of their contribution? In Massachusetts it is a criminal offense for a state employee to solicit or receive a campaign contribution from anyone. But that doesn't prevent the governor's fund-raisers from going after state contractors, and many of them do so with a vengeance.

There is a related problem that arises all the time, particularly in social service contracting. As institutions are closed and services shifted to non-profit, community-based providers, state employees are often encouraged to join the community-based network. That, however, creates potential conflict of interest problems. In my state no employee can have an interest or participate in any matter that was the subject of his or her general responsibilities for at least a year after he or she leaves the state payroll.

In cases where the matter was part of their specific responsibility, they are barred from participation for life.

Furthermore, even if a state employee did not have responsibility for a particular program, hiring on with a non-governmental provider gives that employee and his or her new employer access to the contracting process that others don't have. In short, purchasing social services under contract involves the same potential revolving-door problem that the Pentagon and its retiring generals have been wrestling with for years.

This problem is not just theoretical by any means. There were numerous occasions during my 12 years as governor when we had to confront a real or potential conflict of interest as state employees left state service for better-paying jobs in the POS system. Fortunately, my state has an ethics commission authorized to provide departing state employees with advisory opinions that tell them what they can and can't do.

But the ethics commission doesn't make up its rules as it goes along. It needs guidance, either under existing or amended conflict of interest laws or a code of conduct that is designed specifically to deal with potential POS conflict problems. Massachusetts has one of the toughest conflict laws in the country. It was approved, however, in 1962, long before the explosion in the POS business. We and every other state should be taking a long look at existing codes and laws to ensure the highest standards of integrity in the POS environment.

Promulgating standards is only the beginning. Governors and mayors must be equipped to investigate and report violations of them. Ethics commissions and attorneys-general can do some of the job. I found, however, that I needed internal investigative capacity to track down rumors and allegations of wrongdoing *before* we referred them to the ethics commission or the attorney-general. For that reason, I created a special investigations unit (SIU) in the office of my secretary of public safety, staffed by a small, experienced, and savvy group of state police officers whose responsibility it was to investigate these matters. My secretary of human services had his own investigating unit to pursue this kind of problem even before it got to my office and the SIU.

6. *There are some services that no governor in his right mind ought to privatize.* It ought to be obvious by now that I support contracting for social services as long as governors and mayors and those who work for us understand what is involved, are ready to manage a first-rate POS system, and are alert to the dangers that POS brings with it.

There are some services that governments provide, however, that I would never contract out to private or nonprofit organizations. One of them is adult corrections.

This may come as a surprise to some advocates of privatization and to some of the companies that are providing correctional services under contract to state governments. But the security problems associated with turning the care and custody of violent adult offenders over to the private sector are very serious and potentially disastrous. And the correctional business is tough, about as tough as any job our citizens expect their state governments to do.

What do you do if prisoners riot? What happens if your contractor turns out to be a dud? Talk about the dangers of being overly dependent on a handful of contractors! It was bad enough when we faced the problem on the juvenile front. I would never put myself in the position of having to scramble for someone to run my adult maximum security institution under any circumstances.

Halfway houses and transitional facilities are something else. In those cases we would occasionally contract with a private or nonprofit agency for a limited number of inmates who were within a few months of parole date, and even that can be a tricky proposition if one of the residents of the facility breaks the rules and decides to run.

But turning over all or even some maximum- and medium-security correctional facilities to the private sector is a risk that I, for one, would never entertain. Appointing a top-notch corrections commissioner who has the management and people skills to run a first rate adult correctional system and giving him or her the resources to do the job is the way to go. Privatization is not.

I feel just as strongly about the care and treatment of the severely and chronically mentally ill. Don't get me wrong. I was a strong advocate of deinstitutionalizing our mental health system in the 1960s and 1970s and closing or eliminating unnecessary beds and facilities as modern medicine and community-based services combined to make it possible for thousands of previously hospitalized patients to live and work and prosper in the community.

But the notion that the private sector can and will provide continuing care for severely and chronically mentally ill people is, in my judgment, a pipedream. And the consequences of such a policy, as anyone can plainly see from walking down the main street of any city in America, are cruel and barbaric.

General hospital psychiatric units and private psychiatric hospitals can provide good care for a relatively short time to acutely mentally ill people. Dramatic advances in psychopharmacology are making it possible for millions of Americans to live good and healthy lives despite recurrent bouts of depression and related illnesses. New advances in the treatment of disorders like schizophrenia have transformed the lives of thousands of previously "hopeless" patients. And genetic research will undoubtedly produce even more dramatic breakthroughs in the years ahead. In fact, I don't rule out the possibility that short stays in the hospital, followed by supportive therapy and continuing medication, may eventually be the answer to virtually all of the diseases of the mind with which the human species has been afflicted.

In the meantime, however, there are thousands of our fellow citizens who suffer from chronic and severe mental illness and who deserve better than being bounced around from short-term hospitalization to a homeless shelter and back again. For them, extended hospitalization in a first-rate state facility may be required, and they are entitled to it. State governments can and should be able to provide that kind of care at the same time that we are building and expanding community services. Community services can be provided largely by contracting, but long-term hospitalization is something the public sector should do—and do well.

3

Personal Reflections on the Purchase of Human Services in Massachusetts

Philip W. Johnston

THE EVOLUTION OF PURCHASE OF SERVICES IN MASSACHUSETTS

During my career I have been an active participant in the development of human services contracting in Massachusetts. My early days in the field coincided with the first recognition by state policymakers that rapid reforms in human services programs could happen only by a radical restructuring of the entire state apparatus. True, subsequent to that period—the late 1960s and early 1970s—the state had contracted with a relatively small number of nonprofit agencies, mostly in child welfare programs. Generally, these were old, well-endowed, highly professionalized agencies like the New England Home for Little Wanderers, the Italian Home for Children, Catholic Charities, and the Nazareth Home. Many were affiliated with churches and supported by both state contracts and wealthy board members with a special interest in helping abused and neglected children.

At the time, I was a very young CEO of a fledgling nonprofit children's agency established to honor the memory of Robert F. Kennedy. Our agency began contracting with the Department of Public Welfare in 1969 with a $250,000 contract to operate a short-term intensive residential diagnostic center for young (ages 6–12) children recently separated from their biological families. Of course, the $250,000 was not paid in a lump sum monthly or annually, which would have allowed for some planning. Instead, our arrangement—similar to that of all other agencies at the time—

involved payments from the state based strictly on the number of children actually residing in the program, multiplied by the number of days the child stayed. And because the daily rate was hardly generous, we were under constant pressure to keep the program filled to the maximum.

I am using the term *contract* very loosely. The "contract" consisted of a few paragraphs outlining a general understanding between the two agencies, signed by the state director and me. The stories of managerial chaos in those days are legion. I served as executive director of the nonprofit for about 5 years, or 60 months. During those 60 months we never received an accurate payment from the state. For a new, undercapitalized nonprofit agency, with no endowment fund to dip into when the state payments were delayed or inaccurate, cash flow became a matter of desperation. My agency survived by means of a line of credit it obtained with a Boston bank, arranged by a state legislator who served on our board. Many other young, energetic nonprofits were not so fortunate—they simply disappeared.

Later, when I served in the state legislature, I watched the network of new nonprofits grow and stabilize, in large part because of better management on the rate side. Whereas the first chief of rate setting for residential child care programs previously was a meat retailer, the state agencies gradually tightened up the process and began to hire people with some knowledge of contracting to supervise the nonprofits. Moreover, when I paused for breath in the mid-1970s and looked back on the previous 5 years, I realized that my agency had participated in one of the rare true revolutions in social policy.

Jerry Miller, Joe Leavey, John McManus, and a few other creative state managers had figured out that contracting with private agencies led to the policy shifts they wanted to achieve. Civil service, collective bargaining agreements with public employee unions, and political interference by the legislature explained in part the reasons the old system resisted change. I think the principal reason for that resistance was the simplest and most obvious: size. It's just very difficult to bring about change within any large organization, whether it's the automobile industry or a state-run social services agency. The new community-based agencies ran *small* programs with limited staff and clients. That made all the difference. Over the years, I've observed that the best human services programs are those with clear missions and a willingness to remain small. As a general rule, human beings do not thrive in large institutional settings; this is even more likely to be true for people with serious emotional or physical problems.

What was spawned by the explosion of state contracting with hundreds of small community-based agencies in Massachusetts was truly remarkable. The antiquated institutions warehousing the retarded, the mentally ill, and juvenile offenders were emptied. The state handled the development of some alternative programs better than others. For example, by the late 1970s, the Department of Youth Services, which deals with juvenile delinquency, had been transferred from a national disgrace to a national model. To replace abusive and uncaring state institutions, Jerry Miller and his successors worked closely with nonprofit agencies and developed a continuum of care remarkable for its flexibility and its capacity to address the individual problems and needs of each youth. A major study by the National Council on Crime and Delinquency in 1990 showed that the Massachusetts juvenile justice approach resulted in the lowest recidivism rates and the lowest per capita costs in the country.

RESULTS: A MIXED PICTURE

The contracting changes created real energy and creativity among citizens concerned with the problem of juvenile crime across the state. But again, it's important to remember that juvenile justice is a system that is highly focused, with relatively small numbers of people needing care. A youth enters the network of programs within the Department of Youth Services only through a court commitment. The number of youths in custody at any time usually hovers around 2,000, and the department spends about $60 million per year. Compare these numbers to the Department of Social Services, with 72,000 families served and a budget in the 1990s of about $500 million; or the Department of Mental Health, with 80,000 clients and a budget of $514 million.

The sad reality is that contracting did not lead to the reforms we hoped for in other areas. In most cases the problems or failures had less to do with the nonprofit world and more to do with a fundamental lack of resources. In mental retardation, for example, it was through the intervention of a federal court that we were able to obtain the money to provide high-quality community-based settings for thousands of disabled citizens. In mental health, Massachusetts made the same mistake as did many other states: we deinstitutionalized before we had alternatives in the community. In 1986, Governor Dukakis and I (during my tenure as his secretary of human services) fought for and won passage of a $360 million mental health reform package that, among other things, provided for a quadrupling of housing units for the mentally ill, most of which would have been operated by nonprofits. We were barely under way when the bottom dropped out of the Massachusetts economy, and our project was stopped in its tracks.

Despite this mixed record of successes and failures, I continue to believe that private contracting in human services often makes a great deal of sense. Although critics frequently charge that such contracting is riddled with fraud and waste, my experience was quite the contrary. During my tenure as secretary of human services (1984–1991), contracting with private agencies increased from about $400 million per year to about $1 billion. When we consider that the $1 billion went to 1,200 nonprofits, one might worry that financial abuses would be common. In fact, however, I can count on one hand the number of nonprofits caught stealing public funds. Even the number of agencies shut down because of fiscal mismanagement, in which actual corruption was not at issue, has been quite small over the years. I think several factors help to explain this relatively clean record in the state's human services contracting.

First, most nonprofits have strong boards with serious interest in programs. They tend to be looking over the shoulders of managers and thus act as effective deterrents to inappropriate behavior.

Second, in our administration we instituted tight fiscal requirements for agencies wanting to do business with the state. These include rigorous prequalification standards for new contractors, in which the entire financial history and current status of the agency are reviewed. The agencies appreciate this process because, once qualified, the rest of the process is streamlined and they can avoid the kind of paperwork that previously had been so burdensome.

Third, we initiated an early warning system that detects agencies experiencing financial difficulties. For example, a program's failure to pay withholding taxes would prompt the Department of Revenue to provide that information to state human services managers to allow for early intervention in the problem. This protects not only the public dollars invested in the program but also the clients, who could be displaced if the agency were to collapse.

Fourth, regular audits by the private agencies' auditors, the state auditor, and the state contracting agency further diminishes the chance for corruption or mismanagement. Indeed, many private agency executives believe auditors are now tripping over each other in human services. I agree. The private agency's own audit should suffice in most instances, with sporadic checks by state auditors.

CURRENT PERSPECTIVES

In the 1990s, as the contracting network has matured, unanticipated downsides have become more apparent. To a large degree they involve the fight for scarce resources in a conservative era in which the elected officials who allocate the dollars are not especially sympathetic to the needs of poor and disabled citizens. Moreover, human services providers increasingly are seen by politicians as representing an "industry" or a "special interest." Today we find ourselves at an important crossroads in human services; the stakes are enormous, not only for providers but also for the people they try to serve. I see three major overarching dilemmas that will need to be resolved if the current arrangement between the state and the nonprofit providers is to survive.

Salary Discrepancies

First is the dilemma of finding the public and private dollars to upgrade the salaries of direct-care workers. Currently, the disparity in salaries between private nonprofit employees and state workers performing essentially the same tasks is dramatic. For example, the average salary of a direct-care worker in private nonprofits serving the mentally retarded in 1994 was $16,224; a comparable position in state government pays about $7,000 more per year. In 1986, I established a floor of $15,500 for direct-care workers in private programs serving the mentally retarded. That floor has not been changed in nearly a decade, although inflation has lowered the purchasing power of $15,500 by about one third. As public employee unions routinely reach collective bargaining agreements with state contracting agencies, state workers' salaries generally have kept pace with inflation and often exceeded it. Private agency workers' salaries have not.

During the past few years a Republican administration in Massachusetts has closed most of what remained of the state facilities for the mentally and physically disabled and has transferred thousands of clients to private nonprofits without increasing their rates. As a consequence of this policy, the private sector is struggling to cope with the most profoundly disabled citizens in the state—who tend to be the most expensive to care for as well—with no additional resources. This leads to an endless cycle of low salaries, high staff turnover, inadequate training and supervision, and far weaker private programs.

The strategic question of how to persuade a reluctant legislature to provide sufficient funds to increase direct-care salaries is crucial. Discussions between the Service Employees International Union and a number of executive directors of nonprofit organizations are an indication of how desperate the private agencies feel about the salary issue. For years the nonprofit managers and boards were frightened by the specter of unionization. The fact that some now see that affiliating with a union that is popular with legislators as their only route to survival is startling.

At the same time, the workplace itself is undergoing dramatic change. Client empowerment means that disabled citizens themselves, rather than state agencies, often decide which provider will serve them. This fundamentally alters the employer-employee relationship; issues regarding salaries and benefits, work rules, and the like become even more complex as a result. Clearly, however, increasing salaries to a livable level must be achieved if private providers are to survive and offer the range and quality of services expected of them. Underpaid and undervalued workers care for the neediest people in our society. Today many of these workers are eligible for food stamps, fuel assistance, and Medicaid. Yet we make great demands on direct-care workers: college degrees, paramedical training, long hours, and incredible physical stamina. They are great assets to every citizen; we must address their problems if we are to retain them in the human services field.

Static Reimbursement Rates

The second dilemma also is linked to the problem of resource scarcity. State managers now make program decisions based on an understanding by all parties that there will be no significant rate increases in the foreseeable future. The reasons for this are twofold: first, state revenues are relatively flat, and second, neither governors not legislators want to increase taxes to pay for upgrading social services programs. This has led recently to a move on the part of state human services managers to introduce what we know as managed care in the health arena into social services and mental health. Indeed, it is quite likely that most human services programs in Massachusetts will be provided within a capitated rate structure within the next few years. As a result, I think we'll begin to see the same corporate behavior in social services that we have seen in health care: mergers of large agencies and a rapid move away from residential care into cheaper services like family counseling and day programs.

Thus, the broad continuance of care that has worked quite well in

Massachusetts for the past 20 years may soon be extinct. My own feeling is that this is probably quite a dangerous development. In many other states, providing fiscal incentives to move clients out of residential care back into their own communities might be a positive change because most states still have an overreliance on residential services. In Massachusetts, however, both its juvenile justice and foster care programs were deinstitutionalized years ago, leaving only the most disturbed clients in residential care. One must worry about a new system that will provide for 24-hour care on an extremely limited basis. What will this mean for emotionally disturbed children and their families?

Alarm bells should go off whenever we find services retreating from a full panoply of treatment choices. Such retreat or narrowing is spawned by ideologies on the one hand and budget cutters on the other. Each camp is usually surprised to discover its new bedfellows. In this case the ideologies are human services advocates who consider it immoral to place anyone in a congregate setting. In joining forces with budget cutters who do not want to pay for such services, a powerful political engine is roaring down the track and will be difficult to stop.

Psychologist Abram Chipman put it this way in a column in the *Boston Globe*:

> Non-state-run facilities are increasingly under the control of "managed care,"
> with its emphasis on doing what is quickest and cheapest for the sake of the
> bottom line. To get to know hard-to-reach, distrustful patients and keep
> them "under wraps" long enough to feel safe "unwrapping" them eventu-
> ally, requires much effort and time and high-level professional investment,
> all of which cost money. Paying for such things, never all that profitable, has
> become politically unpopular. And so here we are; as a caretaking society,
> "leaner"—and, in ways both direct and indirect, meaner. Sometimes change
> is not progress.

Diminished Advocacy

The third dilemma looming before us goes to the heart of the mission of a nonprofit human services agency. It can best be posed by asking this question: Does an agency compromise its ability to advocate freely on behalf of the poor and disabled once it accepts funds from the government? Regrettably, my observation is that too often it does. Political assaults against women and children on welfare are commonplace today, yet few voices from the nonprofit world are heard protesting state policies. The reason is quite simple: providers are now dependent on the administration in power in the state at any given time. They are unable or unwilling to risk the possibility that they might lose existing or future contracts if they are critical of a governor's human services policies. In a real sense this dilemma has taken the soul and passion from the providers' mission. They now must act as any other business would in their dealings with the government—carefully. It is a great tragedy for the poor and the disabled because they have lost many articulate voices that should be speaking on their behalf.

One way to resolve this dilemma is for providers to organize their boards of directors as a statewide political force advocating improved human services. The board members are an untapped source of great political strength. They tend to be prominent and respected throughout their communities, often with strong connections to business and academe. These board members could play a pivotal advocacy role if they acted *together*. Obviously, it is awkward for the CEO who is negotiating daily with state agency heads who are part of a gubernatorial administration to be in an adversarial position with those state managers. Moreover, the CEO is considered by many to be self-interested because he or she is on the payroll of a private agency. But board members have far more credibility with the legislature, the press, and the public and should be raising their voices on key human services policy concerns. To be effective, of course, the CEOs and agency staff must keep board members involved and informed.

OUTCOMES

Finally, I want to talk about *outcomes*. A myth persists in the social services field that we cannot measure success or failure in our programs. I've always believed that this myth is related to the traditional 50-minute therapy hour with a psychiatrist—it's hard to quantify any real progress in that kind of setting. Yet many of the problems that afflict people who require human services are very specific: high school dropout rates, teen pregnancies, unemployment; substance abuse, and sexually transmitted diseases. State contracting agencies should enter into performance-based contracts with providers to push more services that can have the most substantial impact on individual life. It may be helpful to an acting-out adolescent to live in a group home setting with support and love from peers and staff. But if the program does not address the youth's remedial education needs, for example, he or she will fail when s/he returns to the community.

During the Dukakis administration we had great success in our Employment and Training Choices Program (ET) when we used performance-based contracts with agencies responsible for finding jobs for welfare recipients. The contract between the state and the provider stated that the provider would be paid a fair price if a job was obtained; otherwise, the provider received nothing. Despite initial grousing, this worked very well—at least until the economy soured and the jobs dried up.

During my last 2 or 3 years as secretary I began to implement the following contracting mechanism in many of our state agencies. In contracting with providers we made it clear that we expected specific outcomes: lower pregnancy rates; lower out-of-home placements; lower recidivism rates; lower dropout rates, higher employment rates, and so forth.

In the battle for resources, which is certain to last many more years both within Massachusetts and nationally, it is important to demonstrate positive results. Those who oppose public financing of social services programs maintain that the poor and the disabled are hurt by such efforts, that they merely become dependent on the services. The beauty of a diversified, decentralized, community-based network of programs is that this model allows us to experiment and to create innovations that work more effectively. But measuring the success or failure of each initiative must be a central element in the model in order to prove to the skeptics that we are achieving a major goal of human services—to help poor, disabled and underprivileged citizens to become *independent* members of society. We know that we cannot always reach that goal, but we must never stop trying.

4

Quality Improvement for Publicly Funded Substance Abuse Treatment Services

Ruth Fishbein and Dennis McCarty

Skepticism about the use of purchase of service contracts to provide publicly funded mental health and substance abuse treatment services challenges service providers and the contracting state agencies to document outcomes and demonstrate effectiveness. Increasingly, states require evidence of effectiveness and link contract evaluation and continuation to outcome measures.

This chapter reports on the efforts of one state agency, the Massachusetts Bureau of Substance Abuse Services (BSAS), in collaboration with alcohol and drug abuse treatment and prevention services, to replace much of its quality assurance process with a contract that supports the development of continuous improvement systems in programs that contract to provide addiction treatment and prevention services. The philosophical base for the initiative, and development and implementation of the Quality Improvement Collaborative (QIC) is reviewed, and principles for continuous improvement systems are outlined. QIC's structure and process are described, and the technical assistance provided to treatment programs is illustrated. Finally, the program's influences on system development during its first years of operation are reviewed. QIC has facilitated a transition from mechanistic quality assurance procedures to comprehensive continuous improvement systems and supports alcohol and drug abuse service providers in the continuing development of health care services.

PRECEDENTS IN CONTRACTING FOR QUALITY IMPROVEMENT SERVICES

Examples from Tennessee, Maine, and Georgia illustrate some of the strategies being tested to engender more confidence in the value of purchased services. Specifics vary from state to state but common threads are apparent: increased attention to consumers and an emphasis on measurable products. These elements are essential features of quality improvement strategies.

Tennessee piloted the use of outcome funding for substance abuse prevention and early-intervention services (Rensselaerville Institute, 1994). Nonprofit community-based agencies specified customers, products, and performance targets for services working with adolescents, young adults, and school systems. In Maine the state authority for alcohol and drug abuse treatment services collaborated with treatment providers to establish performance expectations for detoxification and residential and outpatient substance abuse treatment services and initiated performance-based contracts (Commons, McGuire, & Riordan, in press). Agencies that fail to meet the performance goals may have funding reduced during the following contract period. Georgia's legislature mandated a reorganization of mental health, mental retardation, and substance abuse services and emphasized the development and delivery of services that promoted consumer choice and empowerment (Georgia Department of Human Resources, 1994). Georgia's primary measure of effectiveness has been consumer satisfaction.

The Massachusetts BSAS also began an ambitious quality improvement initiative. To implement a statewide program of quality improvement for almost 200 detoxification, residential, outpatient, methadone, and prevention services in the commonwealth, the BSAS issued a request for proposals, selected a community-based agency to develop and implement a technical assistance program, and initiated a contract for the systems development service. The service, its goals, and its effects are described below. A brief overview of the Massachusetts publicly funded system for treatment and prevention of alcohol and drug abuse describes the context for the quality improvement program.

SUBSTANCE ABUSE TREATMENT AND PREVENTION SERVICES IN MASSACHUSETTS

Creation of a Division of Alcoholism in the Massachusetts Department of Public Health in 1950 marked the beginning of the commonwealth's efforts to address the social and health consequences of alcoholism and drug abuse. An independent Office of the Commissioner of Alcoholism was created by the state legislature in 1956 to coordinate work in state agencies that dealt with the consequences of alcoholism and alcohol abuse. The two alcoholism authorities were combined within the Department of Public Health in 1959.

Because funds were limited in the early years, efforts to build a statewide system of publicly funded alcoholism treatment services emphasized the use of contracts to develop outpatient programs in community-based hospitals. By 1959, 15 hospitals were funded to provide outpatient alcoholism clinics for residents of the commonwealth (Caramello, 1959). In 1971, Massachusetts was among the first states in the nation to decriminalize public intoxication and promote the development of a comprehensive system of addiction treatment services (U.S. Department of Health Education and Welfare, 1972). Services were purchased through contracts, and the total annual budget expanded from less than $1 million prior to 1970 to more than $2 million in 1973, when federal formula grants were awarded for the first time. State and federal funds were used to contract with community-based organizations and develop a continuum of treatment services to address the needs of men and women seeking sobriety. The evolution of the treatment system continued, and in 1982 the state legislature added the state authority for the treatment of drug abuse (the Division of Drug Rehabilitation) to the Department of Public Health. The two authorities (Alcoholism and Drug Rehabilitation) were administratively merged in 1986 to form the BSAS within the Department of Public Health.

Today (state fiscal year 1996) the Massachusetts prevention and treatment system for alcohol and drug dependence and abuse includes 3 shelters for homeless men and women actively using alcohol and other drugs, 20 detoxification centers (medically managed but not affiliated with acute care hospitals), 60 residential programs for long-term (approximately 6 months) rehabilitation, 10 shelters for alcohol- and/or drug-dependent women with their children, 80 outpatient clinics, 12 methadone clinics, 10 outreach services for out-of-treatment injection drug users, programs for AIDS education and HIV risk reduction, and 10 prevention centers.

State and federal appropriations allocated to substance abuse treatment and prevention exceed $80 million. About 95 of the budget for substance abuse services in Massachusetts is used for more than 400 purchase-of-service contracts with 150 different community-based organizations. During state fiscal year 1995, programs with state contracts reported more than 105,000 admissions (mean age = 34 years, 28% women, 37% African American and Hispanic, 73% unemployed, 80% abusing alcohol, 65% using one or more illicit drugs, 42% using cocaine, 29% using heroin, and 18% reporting injection drug use).

The expansion of the service system from a handful of contracts for outpatient services in the late 1950s to more than 400 contracts for a variety of services required not only a sophisticated service system but also a well-developed bureaucracy for quality assurance. State agencies that purchase services must report to the legislature and oversight authorities that state appropriations are spent appropriately and that state residents receive quality services. Typically, state employees conduct quality assurance inspections and reviews to document the quality of contracted services.

Unfortunately, the continued expansion of the commonwealth's comprehensive and sometimes complex set of addiction treatment and prevention services taxed the ability of the licensing unit to adequately monitor multiple levels of care and assess the quality of service. Hiring limitations made it difficult to add employees to assist with the inspections, and salary freezes inhibited competitive job offers for the most qualified men and women. As a result, the licensing and quality assurance staff included individuals with little or no experience in clinical settings. Thus, in addition to an excessive workload, many of the inspectors lacked the experience to identify and assess clinical practices that were either noteworthy or unacceptable. Inspections were primarily mechanical reviews of documents, not assessments of provider strengths and weaknesses.

A solution began to form from discussions about the application of total quality management technology to the delivery of public health services, including substance abuse treatment and prevention. The state agency staff, however, did not have the expertise either to develop or to evaluate clinical protocols for continuous improvement of treatment services. It was apparent that a contract for systems development and continued oversight was necessary. In addition, because it was necessary for treatment programs to engage in retraining staff and reshaping their views of service delivery, it was essential to involve treatment programs and their staffs in the process of developing and evaluating the process.

A complete reorientation of the quality assurance process emerged. The focus changed from a mechanical inspection of forms and records to an interactive transaction that emphasized the use of peer review to encourage and direct the development of mechanisms to continuously monitor treatment processes. In Massachusetts the quality assurance process has become a systems development initiative in which treatment programs assume responsibility for improving their own services. The early conceptualization was formalized, and a request for proposals was issued to select a community-based organization that would coordinate the development and implementation of the revised approach to quality improvement and assurance.

THE QUALITY IMPROVEMENT COLLABORATIVE

The Bureau of Substance Abuse Services (BSAS) evaluated five responses to the request for proposals and in November 1992 awarded a contract to Health and Addictions Research, Inc. The Quality Improvement Collaborative: A Substance Abuse Program Peer Initiative (QIC) began in April 1993 to implement a peer review system for continuous improvement of the substance abuse treatment system and assumed responsibility for quality assurance monitoring of treatment providers.

Because QIC addresses federal requirements for peer review of addiction treatment services and state requirements to provide quality assurance, there are potential conflicts in roles. Monitoring and regulatory responsibilities may conflict with continuous quality improvement efforts. The potential conflict means that QIC staff must maintain a balance between the needs of the project's two primary customers: the state (payer/regulator) and the program providers (users of the QIC services). Generally, however, both parties have similar goals: enhanced services for women and men seeking treatment for alcohol and drug dependency. Thus, QIC is able to maintain autonomy and work to achieve both its quality improvement and monitoring objectives.

The Quality Improvement Collaborative adapts traditional quality management concepts and tools to a large systems framework to effect improvement across a broad continuum of care. Four key concepts were adapted and integrated to support systems development: leadership, customer involvement, scientific thinking, and transfer of knowledge.

Critical Role of Leadership

Plesk (1993) observed that "without strong effective leadership . . . improvement efforts may not happen or, if they do happen, may quickly dissipate because of neglect and lack of integration with other activities in the organization" (p.71). In a traditional hierarchical organization, leadership is clearly identified by the formal organizational structure. In a large system there is no single leadership structure. Instead, a process must be developed to identify and recruit leaders: QIC used the state provider organization and the state regulatory authority to nominate individuals to serve on a steering committee and form a "quality council." Members are recognized leaders in their field who can effectively represent the project, contribute to its development, and champion it with peers and colleagues.

Customer Involvement

Customer involvement at all levels is critical to the success of a continuous improvement project. This model assures customer involvement. Membership on the steering committee and its subcommittees (i.e., interagency teams) includes both service providers and payers. The steering committee assumes responsibility for project development and implementation. Regular meetings are conducted with the larger constituent group, that is, the professional trade organizations within the state and state agency staff. Baseline data–gathering tools (site visits, management information system (MIS) review, reports) are designed by the customers. Site visits include broad customer participation; site visit report drafts are reviewed and edited by the customers. Peer surveyors participate in all site visits. Finally, client focus groups are conducted on all site visits when feasible.

Scientific Thinking and Transfer of Knowledge

The project introduces the notion that improvement must be based on data. The site visits are a key data-collection tool. Individual program and system-wide data are aggregated and analyzed to provide information on current practice, system strengths, and areas for improvement. These data are used to identify system training and technical assistance needs.

The Quality Improvement Collaborative uses every opportunity to teach the principles and techniques of continuous improvement to program staff. This is accomplished through peer surveyor training, demonstrations during site visits, technical assistance initiatives, consultation, and training. The collaborative intends to see the system integrate these concepts and techniques and take on primary responsibility for quality improvement and peer review functions.

GOALS

According to its mission statement, QIC strives to

> Maximize the effectiveness and efficiency of the substance abuse treatment system by working with treatment providers to develop and implement continuous quality improvement systems within individual programs and across the treatment system. The results of this effort will be enhanced quality of services along the continuum of care.

The Quality Improvement Collaborative provides the substance abuse treatment system with an opportunity to change the way it does business to meet the demands of the future.

During Phase I (April 1993–September 1995), QIC had two project goals. First, the introduction and integration of continuous improvement systems in the substance abuse services in Massachusetts would lead to (a) measurable organizational change and improvement; (b) continuous improvement training at all levels of the organization and across organizations; (c) a self-directed cadre of continuous improvement experts within the system—peers, external consultants, and QIC staff; and (d) customer involvement at all levels and in all phases of project activities, including clients, staff, third-party payers, the community, and regulators. The second goal was to demonstrate the potential for using system development strategies to facilitate the integration of continuous improvement in a health care treatment system.

To achieve these goals, QIC completed a cycle of site visits for baseline data collection to all funded treatment programs. Site visit data were analyzed and aggregated to create summary reports for each service category and to inform policy and programmatic decision making. The site visit process was continuously monitored and revised to assure that the visit met customer needs and expectations. System training needs were assessed, and a training plan was developed.

Phase II of QIC's development began in September 1995. A technical assistance/training structure that supports the project goal of knowledge transfer is used to encourage more self-directed provider improvement activities. Bimonthly training sessions support continuing quality management education. Interagency quality improvement/system design teams were established to address important service system issues and provide training on quality management tools and techniques. Peers are used more frequently as system consultants. A cadre of consultants with specialized expertise (e.g., in board development, fiscal management, primary prevention) is available to provide technical assistance and training.

There are eight goals for Phase II:

1. Expand system capacity to respond to changing health care needs and priorities.
2. Establish provider performance and practice standards for each treatment/service modality.
3. Operationalize outcome measures for each treatment/service modality.
4. Measure program improvements in treatment and prevention service programs that improve client health status.
5. Expand collaborative initiatives with key stakeholders and communities.
6. Transfer primary responsibility for site visit/peer review and related activities to the peer reviewers.
7. Use data to confirm that site visit/peer review activities are a cost-efficient and effective mechanism for significant program improvement and development.
8. Continue to model the integration of continuous improvement in a health care service system.

QIC STRUCTURE

Funding for QIC for fiscal year 1996 in the amount of $410,000 supports five staff members (project director, three project coordinators, and an assistant project coordinator) plus stipends for peer reviewers, mileage reimbursement for in-state travel, and administrative costs. The QIC staff provide support to peer surveyors to conduct site visits at treatment programs and to review clinical operations. The peers contribute to the development of site visit protocols, participate in the site visits, and review reports from the visits. The steering committee provides program direction and gives customers input into QIC's operations. Finally, an advisory committee of national and local experts in the areas of health care and non-health care quality management is available for technical assistance and to lend broader perspectives.

Peer Surveyors

A central feature of total quality management is participation by those involved in the very processes being reviewed. Provider staff serve as peer surveyors on each site visit. Volunteers are selected from within the modality being evaluated but come from a geographical region other than the target site, to avoid any suggestion of conflict of interest or competition. A peer surveyor training module is designed for each service category. The module includes discussion of the project mission, orientation to the principles of total quality management, review of the site visit process and key program processes, and definition of the peer surveyor role. Peer surveyor training provides an opportunity to clarify the relationship of the QIC with the BASA (the funding agency), further define the project's quality management focus, and address provider questions and concerns. It is also an opportunity for customer input into the planning process.

Peer surveyor training is open to management-level staff from treatment programs within the treatment category. Peer training is held at regular intervals to maximize opportunities for participation and ensure adequate numbers and varied expertise. As peers become more experienced with the site visit process, they take an increasingly active role, allowing teams to divide up responsibilities for more efficient use of time. Peer surveyors are reimbursed for their travel expenses, and their agencies are paid a stipend in exchange for allowing staff to participate in this process.

A primary QIC goal is knowledge transfer, that is, that through formal training and site visit experience providers will take over the peer review process and use the QIC in a consulting role. Peer surveyors were active participants in Phase I, lending their expertise and experience to the development of key program processes. The role and expectation of the peer surveyor should increase during Phase II. Training opportunities for peers, in addition to their surveyor orientation, is offered bimonthly. Peers are expected to assume greater responsibility on site visits.

Steering Committee

The steering committee, the project's "quality council," is a small work group that plays a central role in overall project design and implementation; it charts the course of QIC. It advises the project staff on issues and strategies and contributes to the development of site visit, training, and technical assistance activities. Membership includes project customers (i.e., payers and service providers), an ethnically and culturally diverse group of providers, and represents the range of service modalities and geographical regions in the state. Two members represent the BSAS. Members are recruited on the basis of recommendations from peers in the provider groups and BSAS staff. Steering committee member recruitment is an ongoing activity. Orientation for new members, including both written material and an orientation meeting, is provided periodically as the membership changes.

The steering committee meets monthly. Initial meetings established the project mission, defined the committee structure and member roles, and stimulated (a) survey tool development; (b) site visit design, including key process identification; (c) peer reviewer recruitment and training; (d) report design; and (e) identification of potential stumbling blocks to the quality improvement process. Meetings continue to focus on mission/vision development, strategic planning, project development and implementation, and technical assistance/training initiatives. Committee members are vocal in their support for project activities. They communicate this commitment to their peers and contribute to the positive reception received on site visits.

The project's focus on quality management, applied to the steering committee, has made this an effective leadership group. Task groups are convened to address emerging improvement issues. The steering committee's subcommittees are quality improvement teams, or cross-functional work teams, organized to study a particular process and effect process improvement. Members are selected on the basis of their familiarity with the steps of the process to be studied.

Advisory Committee

Experts in the field of substance abuse and quality management were recruited to participate on an advisory committee, formed in September 1993. The committee now includes representatives from national health care accrediting organizations, managed care organizations, health care consulting firms, industrial quality management, substance abuse research groups (academic and private), treatment providers, the BSAS, and project staff. This group provides a broad perspective on national trends in health care, quality, and substance abuse services for the development and management of the QIC. They help establish the vision of continuous quality improvement in the Massachusetts substance abuse service system. This committee is a very powerful resource in planning the future of the QIC.

SITE VISITS

Each treatment program was visited by QIC to begin the development of continuous improvement activities. The steering committee established the structure and process of the peer site visits and identified peer surveyor training needs. Site visit teams include a QIC staff member and a peer surveyor; the visit is completed in 1 working day. Using provider input as an essential resource, the site visit team collects baseline information on a program's operation and lays the groundwork for continuous improvement activities.

The use of a quality management tool—flow charting—facilitates the dialogue between QIC site visitors and program staff about key program processes. Flow-charting key processes clarifies the actual operation of essential program components (e.g., admission, treatment, discharge), revealing strengths as well as redundancies, inefficiencies, bottlenecks, or other opportunities for improvement. Technical assistance and training needs are identified, and, in consultation with program staff, recommendations are made for program improvements. The collaborative also identifies resources for the necessary technical assistance and training through peers or independent consultants.

Site visits are on a continuous repeating cycle that allows for the evaluation of change over time. Initial baseline-data gathering was completed in Phase I. Phase II site visits are more focused and address the critical areas identified during the initial visit (e.g., board development, financial management).

Presite Visit Activities

Project staff coordinate site visit schedules and arrange for peer surveyors. The project coordinator contacts the program, introduces himself or herself and the project, and asks the program personnel if they would be willing to participate. Site visit participation is theoretically voluntary, however, QIC's relationship with the BSAS provides a strong incentive to participate. Although one program initially declined participation, the group became a willing and active participant after QIC provided additional information and reassurances.

Approximately 1 week before the site visit, programs receive a briefing package that includes (a) confirmation of the site visit date, (b) the names of the peer and QIC staff surveyors, (c) the visit agenda, (d) sample flow charts, and (e) sample site visit tools (e.g., record review forms, facility review forms, and a data request form). Submission of any pertinent materials before the site visit (e.g., data sheets, methadone program client manuals) is encouraged.

Project staff and the peer surveyors review provider profile materials, including client demographic information, contract and utilization reports, and any information provided by the program. The BSAS licensing file may also be reviewed prior to the site visit. Both the licensing office and regional managers are advised of the site visit schedule and are encouraged to share any information or ideas about programs with the project staff.

On-Site Activities

Site visit schedules are tailored to specific program needs (i.e., time frames, duration, agenda items, etc.). Visits include an overview of QIC, an explanation of its relationship to the BSAS and its regulatory responsibilities to the state, and the purpose and design of the site visit. Programs are advised that QIC is obligated to report to the BSAS any serious licensing or contract compliance issues identified during the site visit. The BSAS has agreed, however, and programs are advised that should such a situation arise, the BSAS notification will include documentation of a technical assistance/improvement plan that the QIC develops with the program to correct the deficiency. The agenda, which identifies the key processes to be surveyed and time frames for site visit activities, is reviewed. Programs are assured that nothing will be in the written site visit report that was not discussed during the visit and that they will have the opportunity to review and edit the report before distribution to the BSAS.

The QIC staff and peer surveyors facilitate a discussion of the steps involved in each of the key processes identified in the agenda. Programs are encouraged to have those staff members most closely involved with the process participate in the discussion. For example, staff with responsibility for some aspect of admissions participate in the analysis of the admissions process. Inclusive staff participation captures a range of perspectives and enriches the understanding of key processes. Generally, between 3 and 10 staff members take part in site visit activities.

If program staff are willing, focus groups are arranged to encourage the direct participation of clients. Participants are oriented to the project and site visit process and asked to comment on the strengths of the program and areas for program-specific or system-wide improvement. Focus groups have proved valuable for obtaining client feedback on treatment and the treatment system.

Site visits conclude with an exit conference. This is often an opportunity for broad-ranging discussions about program strengths, opportunities for improvement, and agency-specific and system-wide technical assistance needs. The site visits have also resulted in a valuable exchange of information and ideas among peer reviewers and program staff that can contribute to significant program improvement. A few examples follow:

- Sharing client tracking and billing procedures among methadone programs.
- Helping to ensure a comprehensive documentation/billing system.
- Sharing vendor information for purchase of methadone and lab services, resulting in program cost savings.
- Sharing detoxification clients' clinical record forms.
- Sharing information on economical access to computer resources.
- Sharing waiting list management systems in residential programs.
- Sharing client registration and intake systems to reduce the frequency of "no-shows" in outpatient programs.

Site Visit Reports

Site visit activities and observations are documented in a written report that is reviewed by the program before it is finalized. The report flowcharts key processes and assesses process effectiveness and efficiency, the results of which provide useful information for program development and improvement. Reports indicate strengths and areas for improvement, technical assistance and training needs, and compliance with regulatory requirements. The first round of reports provide baseline information to be compared with information from future visits, providing a measure of program improvement.

Aggregate data from these reports help describe the specific treatment modality, including system-wide strengths, opportunities for improvement, compliance with regulatory requirements, and system-wide technical assistance and training needs. This information is used by both the QIC and the BSAS to evaluate project activities and by the BSAS and treatment providers for policy development.

Finally, questionnaires are sent to project participants to evaluate the success of peer site visits and assess the perceived value of site visit reports. Participation in the evaluation is voluntary and anonymous; confidentiality is assured. Evaluation data are used to refine and improve project activities.

TECHNICAL ASSISTANCE

The Quality Improvement Collaborative is developing a technical assistance and training component to facilitate integration of continuous improvement within agencies and across the treatment system. Requests for technical assistance often involve concerns shared by multiple treatment programs. During Phase I, QIC developed special assistance projects with detoxification centers, methadone services, and outpatient clinics. Detoxification centers identified a need for improved clinical record-keeping systems and formed the Client Record Quality Improvement Team (CRQIT) to develop and implement a model clinical record. The need for client treatment outcome measures in outpatient programs led an interagency quality improvement team to draft protocols for assessing outcomes among outpatient clients. The collaborative is also collaborating with methadone programs.

Requests for technical assistance may be agency-specific. Program-specific requests include assistance with a clinical services billing system, simplification of admission processes for detoxification, record modifications to comply with regulatory documentation requirements, and assistance in improving the range and quality of clinical services. The QIC staff provide consultation at no expense and may, if appropriate, refer programs to peers or independent consultants.

The collaborative also promotes staff and management training. Because total quality management (TQM) approaches influence QIC's orientation, much of the training is designed to familiarize programs with the principles of TQM. An executive leadership workshop on quality management introduced TQM concepts and demonstrated their application to the substance abuse treatment system. It also highlighted the key role executive leadership plays in facilitating the organizational transformation to TQM.

Such skill development sessions continue. A 4 half-day, hands-on TQM training workshop (4 half-days) included 11 agencies. Each program selected a key process for improvement and established a quality improvement team. Team members learned basic TQM concepts and techniques in the context of an actual improvement project in their own organization. The half-day workshops were supplemented by face-to-face and telephone consultation with QIC staff. After the formal workshops were finished, QIC worked with the participants to continue their continuous quality improvement efforts and complete their improvement projects.

RESULTS

During Phase I (April 1993–September 1995), QIC completed 160 site visits: 19 detoxification centers, 17 methadone programs, 56 residential programs, and 68 outpatient clinics. The perceived effectiveness of the peer site visits and site visit reports were assessed by sending a peer site visit evaluation questionnaire and a report evaluation questionnaire to each visited program. Site visit evaluations assess surveyor skills/knowledge, responsiveness, and effectiveness; usefulness of information imparted; and organization of site visit. The report evaluation questionnaire assesses accuracy, usefulness and organization of draft reports.

Participation in the evaluation is voluntary, and confidentiality is maintained. The evaluation forms are anonymously returned to the attention of the executive director of Health and Addictions Research, Inc. Responses were obtained from 68 of 92 site visit evaluations and 51 of 92 site visit report evaluations. The mean response for all questions fell between "above average" and "excellent." Questionnaires also provided an opportunity for the customers (i.e., programs) to make comments and suggestions and to inform the project of changes made as a result of the site visit. Areas for QIC improvement identified included peer surveyor skill/knowledge, length of site visit process, length of reports, and report turnaround time. These criticisms led to changes in QIC protocols: enhanced peer training, briefer Phase II site visits, data-based site visit reports, and improved report turnaround time. A secondary measure of project effectiveness is increased requests for technical assistance. The collaborative is working with 18 individual agencies and 4 inter-agency teams from four treatment modalities.

Report timeliness has been the major problem. Currently, the BASA does not see a report until the program has reviewed and edited the draft.

This produces extensive delays and diminishes the value of the information to the BSAS. The QIC has made this issue a major initiative in Phase II, to be addressed by report format redesign and improved systems to ensure timely report generation by QIC and turnaround by providers.

Measurable system changes have been produced by QIC. Detoxification centers developed and implemented a model clinical record, and methadone services are moving toward standardized evaluations of client progress in treatment and designated phases of treatment. Generally, the treatment system is engaged in collaborative efforts to address significant programmatic and clinical issues. Interagency teams are now focused on the critical areas of outcome measurement and practice standards and are assisting programs to be more viable in managed care environments.

Site visits have also led to significant program changes. Agencies report that improvements have been made in (a) HIV education and assessment programs, (b) client orientation and admission policies and procedures, (c) treatment programming, (d) medical services and health care case management, (e) clinical record management, (f) physical facilities, and (g) billing and fee collection. Several programs have also begun to use quality management tools and techniques, particularly quality improvement teams, to guide internal change initiatives.

LESSONS

The Quality Inprovement Collaborative is an effective resource for facilitating the transition to continuous improvement in the Massachusetts substance abuse treatment system. Quality management concepts and techniques were introduced to the treatment programs, their staff, and the BSAS. A cooperative, peer-centered approach builds communication and trust among the system members, reduces the anxiety often associated with program reviews, and permits open dialogue about improvement opportunities. The first 2.5 years of the QIC program provided lessons in the value of customer involvement, communication, use of data, leadership, involvement of stakeholders, and the feasibility of using a contractor to facilitate implementation of quality improvement processes.

Customer focus is essential to the success of this initiative; QIC involved the state agency, the providers, and program clients. The BSAS participated in all aspects of project design and development. The BSAS director and deputy director are members of the advisory committee. BSAS staff are members of the steering committee. The BSAS staffs play a role on interagency teams, representing both payer and regulatory interests. While maintaining its status as "separate from" the BSAS, QIC has successfully managed to include the BSAS as an integral player.

Treatment providers are also included in all facets of QIC. Provider representatives on the steering committee designed the site visit processes and established categorical provider task groups. Management staff from treatment programs participate as peer surveyors on site visits. Evaluation surveys permit anonymous feedback on the quality of the site visits and stimulate QIC's own continuous improvement effort. Finally, training initiatives are based on assessment of customer needs. Site visits also include client focus groups to ensure sensitivity to the needs of service users.

Communication is critical. The newsletter, meetings with key groups, and presentations have proved to be extremely important to the customers. These are vehicles that reduce customer anxieties and teach important quality management concepts.

Reliable, objective data are valued. Programs recognize the need for data including the need to respond to purchaser demands for accountability and better manage limited resources. Program management acknowledges the value of data-based program planning, program development, and decision making. All QIC efforts rely on data and teach the use of data.

Leadership plays a critical role in supporting the change process. The collaborative relies on the support of leaders in the state agency and treatment programs. The steering committee serves as a de facto "quality council" and assumes leadership responsibility for collaborative activities.

The collaborative works with key stakeholders. From the start, QIC established and maintained relationships with key project stakeholders (e.g., Medicaid, Medicaid's managed care organization, and the Department of Mental Health). The support of these stakeholders is important. For instance, the outpatient providers are on the verge of establishing a formal collaborative arrangement with Medicaid's managed care entity (MHMA) to develop and collect data on treatment outcome measures. Collaboration with the Department of Mental Health on management and treatment of the dually diagnosed client is beginning to emerge.

Perhaps the most important lesson is that a purchase-of-service contract can be used to stimulate system change and modify approaches to quality assurance, and TQM technology can facilitate large system change. Interagency teams are an effective method of maximizing resources and reducing redundancy of effort.

The peer model is proving to be an effective tool for program improvement and for knowledge transfer. Peers are becoming quality experts in their own agencies and in the system. Potential conflicts of interest between the BSAS and QIC can be effectively managed so as not to interfere with the goals of the project. The parameters of regulatory responsibilities and requirements to report serious deficiencies to the BSAS are clearly established. When problems are identified, QIC works with programs to develop improvement plans that correct identified problems; reporting to the BSAS includes a description of the problem, steps planned to correct the problem, and a review of the technical assistance QIC will provide to support changes and improvements. Extraordinary interventions are not required in most situations. But even when the state agency must be informed, the solution is still peer- and provider-generated.

The Quality Improvement Collaborative has transformed a traditional regulatory process and mechanical review into a dynamic systems-change process. The quality assurance need is better addressed, and services for the men and women seeking services for alcoholism and drug abuse are improving.

Health care service systems and funding structures are changing rapidly. Payers are demanding seamless service systems and organizational capacity to provide the broadest continuum of health care. Mergers and acquisitions are common within the substance abuse service system and across the health care system. Payers expect documented service outcomes using measures of client satisfaction and improved client health status. Payers demand demonstrated cost efficiency and implement utilization management systems. Competition for increasingly limited resources is fierce. The architecture of entitlement programs may change dramatically in the immediate future. Financial resources for health care, particularly for the indigent population, will continue to decline. The demand for accountability will continue to increase. The demand for measurable benefit for dollars spent will increase. The capacity to demonstrate significant positive treatment/service outcomes will determine who remains in the "game." The Quality Improvement Collaborative provides the substance abuse service system with a vehicle to respond effectively to current and future demands.

REFERENCES

Caramello, A.V.(Ed.). (1959). *Commonhealth,* 7 (November/December), 1–16.

Commons, M., McGuire, T. G. & Riordan, M. H. (in press). Performance-based contracting for substance abuse treatment services in Maine. *Health Services Research.*

Georgia Department of Human Resources. (1994). *Common ground: A strategic vision for substance abuse services in Georgia.* Atlanta, GA: Substance Abuse Services Section, Division of Mental Health, Mental Retardation, and Substance Abuse.

Plesk, P. (1993). Tutorial: Quality improvement project models. *Quality Management in Health Care, 1*(3), 69–81.

The Rensselaerville Institute. (1994). *Applying a results mind set to substance abuse programs.* Rensselaerville, NY: Author.

U.S. Department of Health, Education and Welfare. (1972). *First special report to the U.S. congress on alcohol and health* (DHEW Pub. No. HSM 73-9031). Rockville, MD: National Institute on Alcohol Abuse and Alcoholism.

5

Privatization, Politics, and the Press

Harold W. Demone, Jr.

The case study that follows illustrates a near-universal finding in regard to public contracting with the private sector. The late Speaker of the House of Representatives, Tip O'Neal, described all politics as local. A corollary is suggested. All public human service contracting is political at some time. This is not to imply that politics dominates all or even the majority of contracts but that all public human service contracts, given the appropriate circumstances, are open to political considerations. Further the definition of what is of political interest is determined by the politician(s) in authority, not by the public bureaucracy or by the provider. Thus, those entering into contractual relations must factor potential politics, for good or bad, into their behavior. The role of the media as collateral, significant, and symbiotic actors in the contracting must also be appreciated.

The public body in this case history is the Commonwealth of Massachusetts. The public agency under discussion is principally the Department of Mental Retardation (DMR). The private vendors are several in number. Documentation comes largely from three sources: the print media, personal interviews, and personal observations, some of the latter as a participant-observer. To complement and place in context these observations, brief references will be made to other jurisdictions and subject areas.

HISTORICAL PRECEDENTS

Public contracting for human services in Massachusetts has an honorable history beginning prior to World War II. For example, the State Health

Department has long contracted for services to children and the chronically ill. The thoracic surgeons who operated at the public tuberculous sanatoria were often affiliated with medical schools and teaching hospitals. The surgeons were hired as consultants.

When alcoholism was added to the department's portfolio in the early 1950s, the new clinical operation was based exclusively on contracting with hospitals, mostly voluntary, acute care, general hospitals, but including some municipally operated general hospitals and one specialized hospital, the Washingtonian. Thus, the state alcoholism authority did not directly provide any specialized alcoholism services although other Massachusetts state agencies with overlapping responsibilities did directly serve alcoholics. Noteworthy among the latter would be programs in mental health, corrections, probation, parole, tuberculosis, and chronic disease, the last two also under the Department of Public Health. The chapter by Fishbein and McCarty in this volume examines some of the current issues in contract management for substance abuse services, now an annual $80 million venture.

The Massachusetts state retardation agency, made free-standing from mental health in 1987, also has contracting precedents. Its preschool nursery program, first operationalized in the 1950s, was largely a contractual operation consistent with the Department of Mental Health's post–World War II partnership with mental health outpatient clinics.

The locally based public child guidance movement with public employees can trace its Massachusetts history back more than 80 years. Notwithstanding these very modest community-based efforts, the public mental health and retardation system was dominated by the large public institutions operated across the state. The state commissioner of mental health, who sat on top of this single decentralized operation, had limited authority for most of that history. The state hospitals and state schools absorbed most of the department's employees and budget. The superintendents were often very powerful, sometimes in conjunction with local legislators and mayors. Political patronage was common.

During the mid-1960s the evolving community mental health movement, new legal protections for the mentally ill, and the advent of psychotropic drugs collectively stimulated the substantial shift to community-based services. Nationally, from a crest of 559,000 patients in 1955, the daily census of state psychiatric hospitals is now less than 100,000 (Butterfield, 1996).

The revised Massachusetts state mental health and retardation enabling legislation in 1966 for the first time explicitly sanctioned contracting as a program delivery tool. Contracting began to accelerate. Retardation programs followed, using the models developed by the mental health senior partner (retardation had long been the stepchild in this alliance) and eventually separated. (In some states retardation programs had a larger budget than mental health and more contracts and community-based activities.) Now a handful of downsized expensive mental hospitals and state schools, many of questionable quality, still remain.

Costs of Care

With finite resources, the appropriate distribution of the limited budget is a matter of considerable debate. The Dever State School, under court order for several years, costs the Commonwealth of Massachusetts approximately $160,000 per client per year ("Healey Case," 1995). The average expenditure for care in a four-client, community-based residence is approximately 53% of the average cost of care in an institutional setting (Krauss & Seltzer, 1995). Comparative 1994 figures from New Jersey show an annual average cost for the retarded in state-operated institutions exceeding $120,000. In New York, for 1995 the state calculated annual costs for patients in mental hospitals at about $88,000 per year. State prisons cost about $44,000 a year (Nordheimer, 1995). For each of the several populations being served by these existing institutions there are superior alternative, smaller-scale programs.

Annual Expenditures and Number of Vendors

According to the *Boston Herald*, in 1971 Massachusetts was spending $25 million on the purchase of human services. By fiscal year 1985–86 more than 1,200 provider organizations had negotiated more than 4,700 contracts with the commonwealth for $614 million, an amount about equal to the state's Medicaid expenditures for the same year (McGovern, 1989). By early 1993 the contract expenditures stood at $1.2 billion (Armstrong, 1993a).

In fiscal 1994 the Executive Office of Human Services, in which the DMR resides, had approximately 6,000 contracts with approximately 1,300 vendors (Peter Bates, personal communication, October 18, 1993). Boyce Slaymon, executive director of the Massachusetts Council of Human Service Providers, in January 1996 (27 months later) described a total of about 1,400 human services providers, approximately 200 of them being cities and towns and for-profit organizations (personal communications, January 4, January 26, 1996).

By 1996 the Massachusetts human service contracts were estimated to range between $4 billion and $5 billion annually. Boyce Slaymon (personal communications, January 4 & January 26, 1996) explains the calculations as follows. The lower figure is his: the higher comes from Governor William Weld. Slaymon focuses exclusively on community-based care, whereas the governor includes contracting for private mental hospitals and prison health care, for example. The reasons these estimate are higher than those previously cited is that they also include federal matching funds, as in Medicaid. Also, the press cites data only from the Office of Contracting under the Secretary of Administration and Finance (A&F). Slaymons and the governor's estimates include funds that come directly from the human services, aging, and education secretariats without the oversight of A&F.

In fiscal year 1992, some 67 of the 1,300 to 1,400 human services agencies received total contracts exceeding $4 million.* Collectively representing about 5% of the providers, they account for about one third of the state's expenditures through the Office of Human Services, or a mean of $12 million per "mega-vendor," a hyperbole, to say the least (Armstrong, 1993i, pp. 6, 14).

A CASE HISTORY OF CONTRACTUAL RELATIONS: THE MEDIA ATTACK

This tale begins on February 16, 1993 when the *Boston Herald*, a tabloid daily newspaper—after what it described as a 4-month investigation—began a page 1, 5-day, 12 part series headlined "Waste, abuse cast cloud over States's [*sic*]privatization program." Its page 1 headlines on successive days follow: "Soaring Exec. pay robbing the system," "State fails to drop shady firms," "Political ties is name of the game"; and on February

---

* The Massachusetts data, as reported by the several sources, may not be identical, but the diverse reports are reasonably consistent with each other and have face validity. Hard, unequivocal figures are often not available. Where there are clear inconsistencies, attention will be drawn to them.

20, day 5, the last headline read "All agree on need for privatization reform" (Armstrong, 1993m, p. 8).

The headlines caught well the flavor of the articles, which involved in some detail 8 of the 1,300 or so human services vendors then contracted by the state. (These eight constitute slightly more than 0.5% of the total number of vendors.) About 40 agencies were referenced in total; most were in the list of those with salaries exceeding that of the governor. The following discussion focuses on one of the 11 agencies alleged to have salaries higher than that of chief executive. Three of the 11 agencies had been dissolved some years prior to the articles, leaving 8 actually in existence at the time of the writing.

The Habilitation Assistance Corporation (HAC), the targeted case, is the only for-profit body among the group of eight, although its for-profit status is not at issue relative to this assault on privatization. For the most part the "exposé" focused on the salaries paid to the executive director (three cases); the use of expensive automobiles (two cases); the purchase of condos in Florida (two cases) and a house on Cape Cod (one case); the mismanagement of one program, an agency with what seems like good political ties (one case); and two past cases of what appears to be outright fraud.

Some agencies were accused of more than one misdeed. In one case three persons pleaded guilty to defrauding the commonwealth of $1 million. Their organization was closed, then reportedly reopened under a new name and charter, apparently with one or more of the three "guilty" parties as principals, although this was not clear from the press account. This agency closed shortly after the publication of the *Herald* series.

This leaves the one agency on which this chapter will principally focus, an agency about which the author coincidentally had access to information. In addition he was invited by the commonwealth to serve on an ad hoc committee monitoring a year of its activities (discussed below). The part of the series that dealt with the HAC is sufficiently brief to quote it in its entirety as follows.

> Hidden on a quiet side road off busy Court Street in downtown Plymouth is a nondescript brick storefront housing the offices of Habilitation Assistance Corporation, Inc.
> The for-profit company run by Alan Eddy of Duxbury, is one of the agencies highlighted in the unreleased state investigative report.
> Habilitation, which provides day programs for the mentally retarded, received $498,000 from the State Department of Mental Retardation last

year. There were no other bidders for the work performed by Habilitation, according to the DMR.

Eddy is a long time friend and business associate of Virga, the man indicted in Ohio and barred by a Superior Court order from doing business in Massachusetts. In fact, Eddy was the paid treasurer of the Ohio corporation used by Virga to allegedly pocket $1.7 million in funds earmarked for the mentally retarded, according to an Ohio Legislative report.

The Ohio corporation—Community Assistance Corporation—also operated programs in other states according to records. In fact, CAC contracts were terminated by authorities in Maryland, the District of Columbia, Louisiana and Florida, records reveal.

Eddy was also a principal in Human Services Resources Center Inc., a Cape Cod company run by Virga. The company operated group homes for the mentally retarded that were cited for poor client care, including inadequate food supplies and misuse of client funds.

The miserable conditions at the group homes and the company's severe financial problems led to the 1990 court order banning Virga from operating health service agencies. Eddy, however, was unaffected by the court ruling.

While Virga is prohibited from running his own business in Massachusetts, his old friend Eddy has been there to help out. He hired Virga as a consultant and placed Virga's wife on the Habilitation payroll after the court ruling.

The state report, meanwhile, highlights a number of Eddy's own problems at Habilitation, including:

Habilitation allegedly paid health insurance benefits in 1986 for individuals who were not employees of the corporation, including Virga.

Former employees alleged that Habilitation routinely bounced payroll checks and that employees were asked to misrepresent their titles, skills and the agency's operations during state and federal inspections. Eddy said he has never bounced a check.

An audit of the company's fiscal 1986 books found "several deficiencies in internal controls, unusual business practices and undocumented costs."

In an interview, Eddy acknowledged problems with companies he operated with Virga, but said any shortcomings resulted from poor business acumen rather than deliberate wrongdoing. "I don't believe anybody ever did anything inappropriate with any funds in any of the operations," he said.

Eddy also said he concentrates solely on operating his Plymouth company now, and that the state reviews of his performance have been extremely positive.

DMR Commissioner Philip Campbell said the department is satisfied with the performance of Habilitation. Campbell, who was appointed to his position in July 1991, also said that he was unaware of the June 1991 report recommending the state terminate all contracts with Habilitation.

"I know there have been allegations made," Campbell said. But he added, "I have seen no reports concluding we shouldn't do business with them." (Amstrong, 1993e, p. 14)

Missing from this *Boston Herald* February 18,1993, story about HAC is an essential point. In 1985, when a for-profit company operated by Charles Virga in Massachusetts lost its contracts, Alan Eddy established a new corporation that assumed most of the terminated contracts. In essence, the new principal was accused of past and continuing association with Charles Virga, at least into 1986. As noted above, Eddy continued to use the Virgas (husband and wife) during the transition. In some quarters that might be considered wise management. Those knowledgeable about the existing clients, programs, and contracts should be better able to facilitate the management transfer than someone without this prior experience. It might also be seen as a measure of a positive character. Friends are supported during crises. It may also be a measure of arrogance, stupidity, or lack of political sophistication.

Eight years after the fact, Eddy was still being criticized for his relationship with Charles Virga. To Susan Milton (1993b), writing in the *Cape Cod Times* following the *Boston Herald* series and some political action by supporters of HAC, the mismanagement of the mid-1980s "is coming back to haunt the program's managers and the people they serve in the 1990s" (p.A3).

Charles Virga (now Rev. Charles Virga) has become a near-legend in some circles. At one time he operated programs in six states and the District of Columbia, all with state contracts that ended some years ago (Associated Press, 1992; Franklin, 1993; Milton, 1993a). The last press reference to him was in April 1994, when he successfully appealed an Ohio conviction of nine charges of deception and one of theft against 11 group homes for the retarded (Armstrong, 1993m; Franklin, 1994). The prosecutor apparently failed to implement the terms of the plea bargain, and the judge refused to allow him to withdraw his plea of no contest. Presumably, a new trial is to take place.

Some HAC 1986 financial deficiencies and practices are also noted in the *Herald* series, then 7 and now 11 years after their occurrence. None was serious enough then or now to either bring formal charges or terminate the contracts.

Of all the agencies cited in the five-part series, the commissioner of the responsible department is quoted in response to only one, HAC. He had no criticism to make of it.

The series ended on Friday, February 20, 1993. The following Tuesday, February 23, Governor William Weld issued a directive to the relevant state agencies, including the DMR, to cease doing business with a small number of human services providers. One of these agencies was HAC, about whom a letter was sent by the DMR to parents with children in such programs. The letter noted that the administration of the programs would change (J. M. Brown to parents, February 24, 1993). It seems that the commissioner heard from his boss, the secretary of human services, by phone and was told to start the termination process. He was never asked whether the allegations had substance or were all of equal merit. He acted immediately in regard to the parents with children (all adults) in the programs. Communications to the affected organizations occurred later, if at all.

As will be noted later, the contract revocations were largely programmatically ineffectual but politically effective as a symbol. For a governor who had campaigned on a promise to privatize many state services, headlines about alleged scandals could be counterproductive. Thus, he acted quickly. His critics say he knee-jerked (Tong & Young, 1993). His supporters describe his behavior as assertive and forthright.

All of these examples demonstrate a current political value—act first, right or wrong; be preemptive and proactive. The facts can wait. It appears that these decisions were wise political choices, for none of them stimulated negative reactions equivalent to what would have occurred if a more studied response had been the choice.

It should also be noted that neither the governor nor the secretary has the authority to revoke the contracts, nor is the commissioner legally required to follow their orders to do so. The statutory authority is in the hands of the commissioner; only the legislature has the authority to change the enabling act.

The standard provisions in contracts required by the state for human services vendors provides that the commonwealth may terminate a contract in 60 days without cause. For a 30-day termination some due process is required. Agencies receiving these contracts are generally small and undercapitalized and often were formed to deliver specific services desired by the state. They might have been organized by parents or by disabled clients themselves. They often feel powerless in the face of the state's omnipotence. Thus, they sign contracts that deprive them of what is often considered fundamental rights, the prerogative to be informed of the charges made against them and the right to defend themselves. Certainly, the state does not require such provisions in their purchase of goods from such companies as General Motors or IBM, for these vendors are usually strong and politically skillful, with access to the political system.

In fact, human services providers with a substantial consumer base are potentially very robust, for they usually have a strong middle-class base with well-established community organizing skills. They have access to their local legislators and the media. However, enlightened self interest is often not engaged.

If threatened sufficiently, action may well occur. HAC was not a passive observer. It did not fold its tent. The president, Allan Eddy, hired as legal counsel Robert Quinn, a former attorney-general, state legislator, and chairman of the Democratic State Committee. Eddy and his staff also wrote and phoned the parents and significant others of his retarded clients (he calls them consumers) in the four contracted programs. In large numbers they wrote, phoned, and were otherwise active in defending the programs with which they were familiar. The several state legislators in whose jurisdictions the programs were sited were among those asked to intervene, and some did so. Interestingly, HAC did not seek allies among the others who had been singled out in the *Herald* series.

Another of the agencies under attack, the Crystal Springs School, also responded, even more vigorously. Their officers charged politics in the press. They too hired a legal counsel. They demanded an independent arbitrator to examine the charges and promised court action failing a positive response by the arbitrator (Tong & Young, 1993), and such an action was initiated.

The Role of Medicaid

State contracts from the Executive Office of Human Services exclusively using state appropriations were not the primary source of income for the HAC. Massachusetts uses the federal–state Medicaid program to finance various community-based day programs for many multiply disabled adults who live at home or in organized group arrangements. Following federal guidelines, the state Medicaid authority is responsible for its own contracts, independent of the superordinate contracting service located in the executive office of the secretary of human services or of line contracting activities located in the individual departments. (The *Boston Herald* series did not refer to these contracts and were apparently unaware of them. For example, when the state financing of HAC was discussed, the articles mentioned $450,000 per year; in reality, in that fiscal year total contracting with HAC reached approximately $4 million.)

Medicaid is financed by a 50%–50% federal-state contribution in Massachusetts. Federally established Medicaid is governed primarily by federal laws and regulations. All state laws and regulations must be consistent with their federal counterparts, which are superordinate. To modify them the state must seek specific waivers, and they have not attempted to do so in respect to the awarding, monitoring, and contracting procedures using the Medicaid match.

Medicaid writes its own contracts, following federal contracting procedures, which provide full due process to all participants. The determination of whether the agency meets appropriate programmatic and personnel standards is the responsibility of the state agency, as is the monitoring of the services. Medicaid reserves to itself the monitoring of its fiscal practices. Thus, a gubernatorial order to a state official is not automatically followed by Medicaid. The Habilitation Assistance Corporation had and has a total of four contracts with the commonwealth; three of the four are covered by Medicaid, and only one was fully state-funded. Thus, when the DMR attempted to act in response to the orders of the governor, it had limited authority to do so, as it found out after the fact.

As noted earlier, letters from the DMR were mailed to parents and significant others of clients in all four programs. The contract closure announcements for three of the four programs had to be retracted. It was later understood that Medicaid might and could have acted in concert with the state had they been informed or otherwise knew that the services failed to meet the expected standards, but neither was the case. Medicaid was not informed, and all reviews of HAC programs were and continue to be quite laudatory. The criticisms were not considered substantive, and Medicaid was satisfied with its ongoing fiscal reviews.

Habilitation Assistance Corporation

But what of the agency? Are its finances in shambles? Is the program a disaster? The answer to both questions appears to be an unequivocal no. In talking to informed observers, the typical response to the *Boston Herald* series was that there was "no local problem," HAC "does a good job," the report was "old stuff." Parents of the clients in the several programs say,

"My daughter has gained considerably in the program," "the best she has been in"; whatever happens, "retain the staff." The typical parental response was positive.

Programmatically, the respondents were consistent. In regard to financial matters they were less sanguine. During the exchange of letters, the hiring of lawyers, and court sessions, the rumor mill was active. Staff morale was poor even after it was determined that the termination order had been revised to refer to only one of the four programs. It was noteworthy that staff turnover remained low. Some parents and significant others were generally of the opinion that HAC was not long for the arena. Others saw themselves as trying to save the programs and staff. There was an assumption that if wrongdoing was proclaimed in the press, there must be some substance to the claims even though their own experiences were satisfactory. There were also those who felt "you could not fight City Hall." Well, they could and did, and 4 years later the agency and each of its programs exists unchanged. The one program finally in question found its contract renewed for the standard 5 years. Much, however, occurred in the interim.

The official letter to the agency, as differentiated from the February 24 letter to the parents, was dated April 28, 1993 and gave notice of termination of the contract effective June 30, 1993, the same date the contract would have ceased in the normal course of events. Thus, the DMR began its standard request for contract approval, although delayed because of the *Herald* series and the several reactions to it. The usual practice is to have an ad hoc committee of state technocrats and consumer representatives review the proposals to make recommendations to the regional administrator, who has the final authority. Among the several proposals was a renewal one from HAC, still an eligible vendor despite the allegations. In the interim, HAC had also taken the state to court, seeking information about the charges against it.

As one of five bidders, HAC participated in a well-established bidding, review, and award process, which was altered for this particular bid. The local DMR staff knew the competing agencies and the clients served by the program and were deemed to be "in conflict of interest" by some superiors. Thus they were not permitted to participate in the evaluation of the vendors as required by the traditional process. Their collective conflict of interest appeared to be their failure to provide negative information about HAC and its programs. Similarly, parents with children in the program were also excluded from the process, again deviating from the typical review process. They too were seen as having a conflict of interest for apparently speaking favorably about the program serving their children. Instead, staff and parents were chosen from outside the region because they had no personal contact with HAC and the program under review. Nevertheless, the HAC proposal was considered the best of the five proposals, and it was awarded a 5-year renewal subject to a special review midway through the first year, as discussed below.

The Program

This section focuses on the Intensive Day Service (IDS) program of HAC. As noted earlier, although all four of the HAC programs received discontinuance notices, only in one, the IDS, was the initial action implemented, for it was the only one of the four free- standing units with an exclusive contract with the commonwealth. The other three contracts were with the shared federal–State Medicaid program, not subject to unilateral decisions by the governor or the commissioner.

Most of the more intensive analysis of the IDS contract that follows was derived from the special committee established to monitor the first year of the subsequent contract renewal. This writer served as a member of that committee and was thus a participant-observer in the process that followed the series of *Boston Herald* articles.

Committee Formation

The awarding of a 5-year renewal contract to the organization that was charged in the press and whose contract was ostensibly terminated unilaterally by the state on direct orders of the governor would appear to be a mark of extraordinary courage or a most ill-advised move by the DMR commissioner. However, there were not many options. The formal procedures for contract termination and their awards were followed very closely, and HAC won the contract renewal fairly in a competitive situation. The DMR, in collaboration with the Office of the Secretary of Human Services and with the agreement and participation of the provider, attached a series of conditions to the renewal contract. In essence a review committee was established, to be designated by the DMR, "which will monitor the fiscal and programmatic activities provided under this contract". In the agreement it also was specified that the draft "written report" of the committee would serve as the basis of a debriefing meeting with the administration of HAC. "The purpose of this meeting will be to provide feedback on the strengths of the program and to make recommendations for improvement" (attachments to the 1994 agreement No.25704570387 between the DMR and HAC).

Committee Membership and Procedures

The review committee was composed of three parents of consumers, three DMR staff members, and one representative of the Executive Office of Human Services. The committee was to select one of the consumers' representatives as its chairperson.

The charge specified that the monitoring should concern itself with matters provided under the current contract, which in effect meant that the committee was to examine fiscal and programmatic matters specific to the one Hyannis-based program in the current fiscal year. A series of conditions under which HAC would cooperate, including concerns about the confidentiality of HAC data, due notice, and the like, were spelled out. Following the draft report and its debriefing, HAC had the option of commenting on the recommendations. Upon submission of its recommendations to the commissioner and no later than May 1,1994, about 7 months following its formation, the committee was dissolved.

Each member of the committee had his or her own personal contacts with the IDS program in Hyannis, Cape Cod. Thus, the aggregation of observations was substantial. The experience of one of the committees' three volunteers who had no prior contact of any kind with the IDS program illustrates the range and variety of observations. Prior to the committee formation, this volunteer had never seen the IDS program, talked to anyone about it, nor possessed any information about it. He knew only vaguely that something existed in Hyannis under the auspice of HAC.

In pursuit of the charge to the committee, he first read the renewal contract proposal. He then talked to several people who had substantial personal contact with the program. One was a parent of a client in the program, who made frequent visits to the facility for various reasons. A second respondent was a client's van driver, who, by virtue of role and task, was at the program twice each day. Other conversations occurred with a manager of several group homes, some of whose clients were participants in the program; a staff member of another local retardation program with fairly frequent contact with the IDS; a volunteer member of the Human Rights Committee for the Cape; and members of the DMR regional and area staff. In addition, he made a planned site visit to the program and talked to several staff members. He also participated in discussions in formal meetings of the committee, in which the quality of the program was a major topic of concern.

In every contact he solicited personal observations from these several experienced observers. The first inquiry about the program focused on what was wrong and was followed by an inquiry about what was right. Without exception the comments were positive—about the staff, the program, and the facility. There were no negative personal observations, nor were there any negative anecdotal information from other sources.

The review committee took its responsibility seriously and sought information from a wide range of sources. Each member of the committee was responsible for his or her own data collection.

MONITORING

Some Operating Definitions of Monitoring

The committee followed the contract conditions in the 1994 agreement between the DMR and HAC, which set forth its responsibilities to "monitor the fiscal and programmatic activities provided under this contract" (contract No.25704570387).

Thus, following the above-cited contract, the committee attempted to monitor the fiscal and programmatic activities under the contract that dealt with a single unit of HAC: the IDS program in Hyannis for the 1994 contract year.

Monitoring was understood to be considerably less than that which might be subsumed under evaluation. The question was, did the provider comply with the terms of the contract? Concern was on the concrete, the current, and the practical. Processes and performance were the concern, rather than outcomes, and relative rather than absolute indices. The committee was satisfied that it was able to meet the terms of the contract in respect to the program of the agency in question. In regard to matters of finance, the simple separation of the Hyannis unit from its sibling units is not as readily accomplishable. However, the likelihood that funds were diverted from the Hyannis unit was dismissed. In fact, the resources are well used. They could easily use more and expend it well.

The review committee concluded that there were no substantive problems with the program at the IDS facility. Instead, it was found to be well managed, delivering useful service to a very needy population. Given its limited budget, it was a highly competitive program.

The Formal Monitoring System of the Commonwealth

Beginning with the prequalification requirement procedure and continuing through licensing and accreditation (as appropriate) and the substantial set of external and internal monitoring and evaluation procedures, it would seem that the state has more than adequate procedural safeguards. One comparative measure would be to contrast these with the procedures used by the state in its purchase of goods and other services. Another measure of comparison would be to compare the procedures used by the state when it provided some of the same or like services directly with its own employees.

The committee felt confident in concluding that the human services providers from whom the DMR now purchases services are much more closely monitored than those delivering services directly by public employees. In fact, because of the history of this agency, HAC was the most closely monitored provider in the region in which it operated.

The basis for ongoing evaluation is also substantial, as evidenced by the effort to implement performance-based contracting and by the consumer individual-service plan, with its twice-yearly client review managed by DMR professional staff and including the client, parents or parental surrogates, providers, and occasional outside specialists. The trend data indigenous to this model can have great power in determining the long-term effect of an intervention. From personal observation it is clear that the individual client plan is taken seriously and that the biannual review process can be a useful tool in upgrading the quality of care provided to clients.

The regular and frequent contacts of area staff members with the individual programs are substantial and likely supply a more than adequate formal early warning system to the DMR. It is likely that they have more information than the system can accommodate. If there are systemic gaps, they are to be found in the uneven procedure used to aggregate and analyze data for transmission upward to the DMR. These procedures are controlled centrally.

In addition to the activities of the local area staff, the regional staff may also find it necessary and appropriate to make personal visits to individual facilities, thus adding to the monitoring.

Fiscal matters, by definition, are supportive of the program. Thus, the several stages of fiscal review by the DMR must necessarily touch on the program, thus providing another set of skills and observations in the formal monitoring process.

The Legislature and the Courts as Monitors

The ultimate formal monitors in the American system of government are the legislators. The legislature first enacts legislation. The executive branch then implements the legislation. Finally, the legislature monitors implementation. This constant tension is another powerful impediment to excessive malfeasance or misfeasance.

The legal system has played an important role in the past 30 years in regard to human services. The policy implications of court decisions are extraordinary. They extend to governmental, constitutional, and business and commercial practices and to professional standards. They enhance the unity of the nation. They protect the individual.

The power, interest, and ideology of the three branches of government are not fixed but rather are in constant motion relative to each other. Thus, the Massachusetts legislature removed some of the governor's decision-making authority regarding the contracting of human services. It also changed the balance of power between two elected constitutional officers, the governor and the state auditor.

The Informal Monitoring System

The Parents. Parents and parental surrogates as monitors and advocates, individually or in organized groups, play a highly viable and effective role in retardation services. On an irregular, unplanned basis they are regular visitors to the several programs. The parent is at the facility to provide necessary transportation many times during the year and for a range of activities from medical and dental appointments to haircuts.

The Press. The press, too, has had and continues to play a significant role as gadfly to the public sector and its allies. Certainly, the *Boston Herald*'s weeklong front-page series was the stimulus for the formation of the ad hoc monitoring committee.

Public Employee Unions. The general formal anticontractual stance of public employee unions led by the Association of Federal, State and Municipal Employees (AFSME) creates a natural monitor of most public contracts. If it can be demonstrated that the contractual process is flawed, the funds used for contracts can be reallocated to hire more public employees, who will then become members of the appropriate unions. This tension is not necessarily dysfunctional. It adds to the informal monitoring and is a source of negative information about contracting for elected officials as contracting becomes politicized. The press, too, is always appreciative of stories about governmental mismanagement as cynicism about government grows.

Whistle-Blowers. Whistle-blowers are defined in the federal Civil Service Reform Act of 1978 (P.L. 95-454) as governmental employees who disclose fraud, waste, and abuse when they find it. In this matter, potential whistle-blowers would be former or present employees of HAC or of DMR. They are locally based professionals and paraprofessionals with a responsibility to their clients, their professions, their communities, and themselves, in addition to their employer.

Whistle-blowing is a well-established phenomenon in government and large corporations and is the best example of how employees can report irregularities. Their observations of their workplaces inevitably are communicated in the confidences of their family, friends, and neighbors. Cape Cod is a small community in many ways. Problems with a service provider will soon be known. Among the recipients of the information will be other private providers, who in some cases will or could be competitors.

Other Providers. As noted earlier, there are competitors too, some of whom are ready to expand their offerings. The retardation, mental health, social service, and rehabilitation network is relatively small, made up mostly of a series of small not-for-profit agencies. The employees move from one agency to another and from one field of service to another. In some cases, because of the low level of salary, they may moonlight and be employed in more than one agency, usually on a part-time basis.

Thus, their level of knowledge about how their competitors are functioning is generally quite substantial. It is in their self-interest to know how their fellow agencies are performing; they may well be competitors for future contracts, as they have been in the past. With a relatively flat appropriation for contracts over time, the growth of one agency must be at the sacrifice of another. Certainly, in such a competitive environment the vendors may find it to their advantage to monitor their rivals rather closely. Because of staff mobility and the closely knit character of Cape Cod, they are positioned to secure unfavorable information and to leak such information. But the monitoring committee was not the recipient of such negative feedback, nor did such information surface during the last bidding period, when five other agencies competed and this contract was renewed.

Observations about the Monitoring Processes

The volunteer members of the committee were most impressed by the extent of monitoring and evaluation of the contracts of the department, which occurs on an ongoing basis. They understood that some of the monitoring is of a generic nature, likely encompassing all state contracts, and that some is specific to the DMR and to HAC. They also understood that monitoring involves both organized, planned efforts and a substantial informal effort, as identified above.

Some of the monitoring and evaluations are size- and substantive-dependent. For example, the small group home, a shared apartment, or a foster home is unlikely to have the degree of oversight found in a large sheltered workshop or habilitation program. However, even in the former situation there are safeguards that undoubtedly need constant attention, given the fragility of the clients and the intimacy of the living situation. Some of the formal state monitoring of the larger programs might well be more effectively directed to the foster-home-shared apartment arrangements.

In respect to the IDS program operated by HAC in Hyannis, there were no reservations about the comprehensive and thorough nature of the program oversight, both subsequent to the *Boston Herald* series and before it appeared. The earlier history of the company placed it in a unique spotlight. As one example, several staff members of the Office of the State Auditor spent a number of months examining the financial and other records of HAC. In addition, the contracting office of the state's Executive Office of Human Services was sensitive to the history of the agency and ever alert to possible problems. It is likely that, controlling for contract size, HAC has been more carefully monitored than almost any agency from which the commonwealth purchases services.

Recommendations

In addition to monitoring, the contract provided that the review committee would do the following: (2) "provide feedback on the strengths of the program and . . . make recommendations for improvement" and (3) "provide a written report" The committee had to stretch to find useful and practical recommendations that the two agencies had not already considered. They were few in number and as many of the recommendations had to do with the DMR as with the provider organization.

For-Profit Status

One recommendation had to do with the organizational charter of the agency. In a world composed almost exclusively of not-for-profit organizations, the for-profit status of HAC is an anomaly. The reason for this status stems from its formation and is not necessarily a justification for the continuing status. It was noted that HAC's president was the sole proprietor of the corporation, without a board of directors.

The lack of an outside board of directors with ultimate responsibility for the organization and the standard of public accountability and reporting to the secretary of state in a context in which almost all other comparable bodies are organized as not-for-profits can be the basis of a continuing public relations problem for HAC.

The Allegations

Another matter of potential generalizabilty was the influence of sensational and negative stories in the press referring to earlier state studies, including that of the state auditor, threatened contract cancellations and litigation. The committee was limited to the previously referred to *Boston Herald* series. Its very existence as an ad hoc committee was in response to these events, yet it was not provided with any of the other documents, even though some must have been in the public domain. Further, their observation, as defined by the contract amendment, was limited to the single HAC unit in Hyannis, the current contract year and contract, and a limited scope of recommendations. Thus, much was left undone, allowing several allegations to continue to plague the state, the provider, their employees, and most important, the clients and their parents.

THE OTHER SEVEN AGENCIES

The continuing experiences of HAC and the other seven alleged culprits have been followed from the original *Boston Herald* stories in February 1993 through mid-January 1996, a total of almost 3 years. Several data sources were examined. The monthly index of the *Boston Globe*, beginning in January 1991 and continuing through November 1995 was searched for the names of the agencies and their chief executives, as were two general headings: privatization and contracting by government. The *Boston Herald* does not have a comparable publicly available system, but the librarian at the *Herald* checked the files in mid-1994 and found no follow-up articles on the eight agencies featured in their February 1993 series. Subsequent to that search, this author has spot-checked the *Herald* a few times a month from July 1994 to November 1995. Only one article connected with the negative series was found, and that was a laudatory article on one of the eight agency executives (Jones, 1996).

On two different occasions, the final time in 1996 as this chapter was completed, the executive director of the Massachusetts Council of Human Service Providers, Inc., and a senior official of the DMR were contacted to follow up on the current status of the "unholy eight." The DMR official could not be informed of all of the department's contracts, but he was familiar with all but one of the eight agencies of concern here and is very conscious of any scandal tainting any contract. The Massachusetts Council of Human Service Providers is a coalition of private human service providers. Its executive, Boyce Slaymon, was not familiar with the Rhode Island agency and one of the Massachusetts agencies, nor a member of their association (personal communications, January 4, January 26, 1996).

In regard to HAC, in addition to the data sources described above for all of the eight agencies, there were continuing ad hoc contacts with the agency and with some parents of the clients, providing a continuing responsible information baseline. The three consumer representatives have met informally each year since the review and continue to feel positively toward HAC.

In the nearly 3 years following the original series, the press has not been particularly vigorous in its continuing inquiries about the purported offenses of the "transgressors," but such an appraisal must be placed in context. How interested is the media in the larger private human services industry in general? With a potential pool of about 1,200 private and 200 public human services vendors contracting with the state, how do the 8 compare to the other 1,400-plus in respect to continuing interest? The *Boston Herald*, as best as can be determined, has revisited one. The *Boston Globe*, its successful competitor, after hiring away David Armstrong, the author of the *Herald* series, continues to cover the privatization of human services on an occasional and limited basis, mostly concerned with negative findings.

The nearly 3-year scanning found that one of the eight agencies had dissolved, and three others were the subject of press scrutiny, a very high ratio of coverage compared to the universe. One of the accused agencies, Integrated Services Associates, North (ISA), closed its doors within a few months of the *Herald* series and the receipt of the contract-closing letter.

Of all of the then operating agencies reviewed in some detail, this one seemed to be the most tarnished. According to the *Herald*, this organization had previously existed as Servess, which closed its doors in 1989 and then reopened as ISA with one of the same executives in charge. In 1992 the two founders and one other employee had pleaded guilty in federal court to defrauding the state of one $1 million. In its most recent financial filing for 1991, it showed a deficit for the year of $57,000 (Armstrong, 1993a). Although no longer officially in business, it is still engaged in adverse negotiations with the Office of the State Auditor.

Reportedly, this agency was offering very competent services to multiply disabled clients; its closure caused complications in client care as the DMR had to work with a less experienced provider. Now, more than 2 years later, the service appears to be competitive again.

A second agency, Work Inc., reimbursed the commonwealth for $588,000 (Armstrong, 1994b). The executive directors of Vinfen and the Greater Lynn Mental Health and Mental Retardation Association, Inc. (GLMHMRA), continue to find their salaries of interest to the *Boston Globe*. The *Herald* finds many positive things to say about the Vinfen executive and some about its program (Jones, 1996).

The remaining agencies appear to have kept a low media profile in the ensuing period. They are the Center for Human Services, Crystal Springs School, the New England Residential Services, Inc., and HAC. Despite the low press threshold, Crystal Springs, which has initiated litigation against the state, continues to press its case, one part of which has been settled to its satisfaction. As noted earlier, HAC also sued the state, which generally means action against the governor, the secretary of health and human services, and the appropriate commissioner. As long as sovereign immunity is not operative, it is likely that litigation against the sovereign, the state, will be increasingly popular.

In regard to Work Inc., as with most of the negative allegations, the state auditor, an elected official, led the way. He is quoted as follows: "This audit demonstrates that the state's purchase-of-service system is broken and in need of repair" (Benning, 1993b, p. 33). In denying the accusations, the attorney for Work Inc. described the state audit as "incompetent and unprofessional" (Benning, 1993b, p. 33).

Fifteen months later the parties had agreed to the $588,000 repayment cited above, to be paid during a 4-year period by the provision of free services and by deductions from future state payments. Work Inc. continued to deny that they had overbilled the state; rather, the dispute was a function of varying interpretations of state accounting procedures.

Good-faith differences were noted. The DMR and the state auditor came to an agreement because it appeared to be cost-effective, the criteria for many such conclusions. (The auditor still maintained that there was an overbilling of $1 million.) Legislative critics of privatization wanted the agency banned from continued state contracting. The DMR, noting the 25 years of quality service by Work Inc. and participation in the agreement, planned to continue its contractual relation with the vendor (Armstrong, 1994b).

The *Herald* series found Work Inc. at fault for two reasons. The executive drove a $43,000 BMW, and that executive and one other served as consultants to organizations with ties to Work, Inc.(Armstrong, 1993a).

The second agency receiving some continuing publicity was Vinfen (Armstrong, 1995b, 1995c). Its 1993 claim to fame was twofold. The secretary of administration and finance under Governor Weld had been a board member of Vinfen before joining the administration. Its second offense was that some state Department of Mental Health employees were on the Vinfen payroll. This latter practice goes back to the 1950s as a component of the then partnership clinics and the state-Harvard collaborative operation at the Massachusetts Mental Health Center. The idea was to help the state agency be more flexible and to recruit people who would otherwise be difficult to secure. The practice left room for criticism then and continues to do so. Vinfen itself is a direct spin-off of this long-standing state-Harvard mental health–psychiatry collaboration.

The 1995 complaint (Armstrong & Phillips, 1995) is about the salary and fringe package of the chief executive. It is too high, and the salaries of the line workers are too low according to the *Boston Globe*. The executive defends his salary, noting that the job is complicated and requires someone with skills and talent. He fully agrees that the line workers are underpaid and that the state should fund adequate salaries for them.

In 1993, Armstrong identified $24 million in state contracts with Vinfen. In 1995 he described the agency's budget as $40 million. The proportion of the budget from contracts was not provided, but probably most of the 1995 budget was from state contracts, as it was in 1993. Given the public criticism, the growth of the budget is impressive or at least interesting.

The Greater Lynn Program, like Vinfen, has most recently been criticized for the salary of its executive director. Unlike the Vinfen executive, no comments were reported from Greater Lynn (Armstrong & Phillips, 1995). In 1993 the condemnations were threefold (Armstrong, 1993a, 1993c): (1) the salary of the executive, (2) the hiring of a former state employee who had been a contract monitor a year after she left state service, and, (3) the 1988 purchase by a subsidiary of a $105,000 three bed-room condominium in Florida with nonstate funds.

The two state agencies principally involved in these assertions have cho-sen to continue their contractual relationship with seven of the eight agen-cies criticized in the *Herald* series and to a lesser degree in the continuing *Globe* stories. The state agencies have considerable power, as noted ear-lier. With a 60-day notice, they can unilaterly terminate contracts without citing a cause.

A NOTE ON POLITICS AND THE PRESS

The *Boston Herald* series lent itself to politicization, and the governor responded in kind. He unilaterally and immediately canceled the con-tracts of the alleged offenders without discussion with any of the knowl-edgeable actors in his own administration and without due process for the accused. The source of the stories was most likely the state auditor, according to well-informed observers: the auditor is well cited through-out the series. An additional source for a negative evaluation of contracting would be the state employees' unions. Both the auditor and the unions are adversaries of privatization. The auditor, an elected official, is a Democrat. In an address to the Democratic State Convention in mid-1994, he is quoted as criticizing the Republicans for "their commitment . . . to privatize state government," adding, "They believe that I stand in their way" ("DeNucci not reticent," 1995, p. 32). In the same article The *Boston Globe* suggests that "they" were right. The unions see contracting as threat-ening their membership, by either actual job loss or a flat growth rate.

Public auditors typically function in the public eye. They are politicians first. They may release their reports to the press at the same time the "offending" agency receives it. There is a certain ritualistic dance that occurs. The hapless agency first replies by noting that it has just received the document and has no comments. Later it offers one or more of sev-eral defenses: (1) it is innocent, (2) the audit missed important items, (3) the faults have long since been corrected, and/or (4) fault is acknowl-edged. In any case, they are generally in a lose-lose situation. The head-lines last only as long as the accusations, not the responses.

What is different when the accusations are against the private sector is that the latter may fight back with equally negative accusations and well-connected lawyers. One oddity of the *Herald* series is that the *Herald*, then owned by Rupert Murdoch, was staunchly Republican and a supporter of the governor. The alliance with the Democratic state auditor seemed anomalous. Thus, the governor, the privatization movement, and the named agencies all suffered. It perhaps suggests that, for some in the press, circulation and economic survival override political ideology.

The curious romance was but a brief respite. The *Herald* denounced the auditor in a no-holds-barred set of front-page stories in October 1995 (Battenfield, Meyers, & Sciacca, 1995a–1995d). The political scenario plays out. The governor garnered nominal plaudits for his immediate actions in canceling the contracts of those accused. He certainly would have been criticized if he had failed to act.

Responses

In Massachusetts, early in 1993, the majority Democrats seized the initiative on privatization from the governor. Legislation was proposed to require that, prior to contracting, the administration demonstrate that contracting would uphold state standards and prove that the savings to the commonwealth would be greater than program management and service delivery by state employees. The final determination was to be made by the same state auditor who continued to voice opposition to what he described as privatization. Other provisions required that all vendor fiscal transactions be reported to the state, that salaries for administrators could be controlled by the state, and that when state reductions occur, those same managerial salaries could be the first to be cut (Aucoin, 1993b). Other provisions in the legislation are cited elsewhere in this chapter.

The Democratic chairman of the Senate Ways and Means Committee was quoted as saying, "The bill we have before us is truly the most modest anti-privatization bill. . . . Yet you have a lot of zealots of the administration who are on a holy war to privatize at any cost . . . dismantling state government." Other Democrats were also willing to exchange with the Republicans. "Profiteering and fraud" by private firms was the allegation (Aucoin, 1993a, p. 23). For a brief period some bankers tentatively entered the fray, encouraged by the administration. These private agencies are often mortgage-and-cash poor and the recipients of substantial letters of credit from the banking community. Any drastic change might make the borrowers very vulnerable.

In addition to the standard problems that can occur when vendors lose contracts, the legislation included special provisions for the return of equipment purchased with state funds and the return of state funds spent in the purchase of real estate (Howe, 1993).

As noted above, the Democrats succeeded. A modified statute limiting privatization was enacted in mid-December 1993 with an override of the veto by the governor. The major advocates for the restrictive legislation were the public employees' unions and the parents of children placed in the Paul A. Dever State School for the Retarded, slated for closing by the Weld administration (Wong & Aucoin, 1993). The chief sponsor, Democratic Senator Marc Pacheco, saw contracting for human services as "about changing the status quo; back-room deals, insider deals, revolving doors. This is about having responsibility when we spend tax payer dollars" (Aucoin, 1993c, p. 46).

A selected segment of the Massachusetts *Boston Herald* tale was renewed less than 2 ½ years later by the same author, David Armstrong, this time with a collaborator, Frank Phillips (1995), both now at the *Boston Globe*. Instead of focusing on those with salaries exceeding that of the governor, as in the *Herald* exposé, this time they examined the salaries and benefits of the chief executive officers (CEOs) of the 10 largest human services providers contracting with the state (out of a pool of 1,200–1,400). They found a range of $56,300 to $185,000, which, not unexpectedly, led one indignant legislator opposed to privatization, Representative Marie Parente, to complain publicly. She justified her hostility on two responsible grounds. The 60,000 private direct-care workers had not received an increment in 4 to 6 years, although the CEOs averaged a total 20% increase for the same 3 years. (The commonwealth violates many of the principles of sound purchasing practices; it sets standards for its human services vendors, including salary levels, and has not increased them in several years.) The CEOs are limited to $87,000 from state funds. The implication of the *Globe* story is, of course, that their salaries are symptomatic of something untoward— at the best, very poor judgment if not some illegal action.

The number of private human services workers employed under state contracts is also subject to uncertainty. In 1993, Armstrong was citing state officials who reported that between 40,000 and 45,000 people were found in such positions. More recently, it has cited the number as 60,000, although the growth of contracts has stabilized in recent years. Nor do we know whether these are full-time equivalents or totals or both full- and part-time employees. We also don't know whether this includes or excludes the Medicaid-supported contracts or other comparable contracts not under the control of the secretary of human services.

As far as the move to purchase human services by the commonwealth is concerned, the media appear to have missed the major stories as they search for headlines and scandal. Curiously, on the op-ed page of the *Boston Globe*, several well written, analytic, thoughtful pieces on purchase of services (POS) have appeared, all written by outsiders, largely in response to the *Globe*'s narrow parochial focus (Christenson, 1993; Johnston, 1993; Rios, 1994). The *Globe* has not responded to these challenges.

James Fallows (1996), an editor of the *Atlantic Monthly* and a National Public Radio commentator, is highly critical of his profession in a 1996 book, *Breaking the News*. He sees much of the public disconnection from the major institutions as related to its alienation from the press. The medium is the message. It is trivial, arrogant, and cynical. The distorting television news is the principal culprit (Fallows, 1996; Rich, 1996). To Jenkins (1996), reporters from all the media are equally seduced by trends, especially those possibly sensational in nature.

About the only positive note in this review of the press is that to date, to the knowledge of this author, television has yet to focus on POS/privatization. The potential distortion of the underlying issues is more than this futurist can forecast.

Recapitulation

The eight agencies that were the objects of a singular focus in the *Boston Herald* series became seven as one with a tainted past closed up shop. The others all continued contracting with the commonwealth with no untoward changes. However, three of the remaining seven found themselves in the *Globe* for renewed attention.

The time between the February 1993 *Boston Herald* series and November 1995 was fully occupied with human services privatization activities in Massachusetts. The Democratic legislature enacted laws placing substantial limits on the ability of the executive branch to act. Some important members of organized labor demonstrated a willingness to consider alternative approaches to the delivery of services by the private sector.

The state auditor and the chairwoman of the House Federal Financial Assistance Committee, Representative Marie Parente, continued their determined attacks on POS. The state employees' unions, of which there are several, became less publicly verbal in their opposition.

The *Boston Herald* dropped out of the privatization attack mode but added the state auditor to its hit list, engaging in a scathing attack on him (Battenfield, et al., 1995a–1995d; Sciacca, 1995; Carr, 1995; Meyers, 1995; "Watching the watchdog.", 1995).

The *Boston Globe* reengaged itself in an expose of POS. In 1991 it had a major "Spotlight" series on the Center for Humanistic Change (Wen & O'Neil, 1991a, 1991b). It revisited its pursuit in 1992 (Howe, 1992; Malone, 1992), four times in 1993 (Benning, 1993a, 1993b; Howe, 1993; Locy 1993), and finally in 1994 (Armstrong, 1994b, Rakowsky, 1994), the last two subsequent to the *Herald* series.

The *Globe* has concluded that at least one medium-size state institution for the retarded and one small private facility using aversive therapy, including shock therapy for the retarded, are both necessary and appropriate facilities for some citizens of the state and has written vigorously to these ends in both news stories and editorials. It also appears to be supportive of cries for the resignations of the three major purchasers of human services, the commissioners of the departments of retardation, mental health, and social services.

The public bureaucracy continues to plod along with little support from the public, the press, or the administration. It can and does move with the criticism, perhaps even bends somewhat, but basically holds to its fundamental beliefs. Government is such a continuing scapegoat that it has developed a Teflon-like quality.

1,200-plus private, mostly not-for-profit agencies remain very vulnerable. It is clear that, given the politicization of their role and the unyielding need of the press for fresh scandal, they must be above reproach. If they are to serve their specialized populations effectively, and most are so committed, it is in their enlightened self-interest to fight for those things they feel are essential to effective operation. They have to be able to pay adequate salaries and benefits free from the rigid job descriptions and anachronistic budgeting systems of government. They must have rational operational freedom with appropriate outcome monitoring. If they are to be merely miniature versions of the state government, the contract mechanism is hardly necessary.

The governor who first politicized POS in Massachusetts was reelected on a plank that still included privatization as a goal but without the vigor expressed earlier in his political career. He also unsuccessfully ran for the U.S. Senate with downsizing of state government as a major objective.

LESSONS LEARNED

Yes, there is politics in contracting. It is not likely to go away. The case(s) just described deal with matters of ethics, the role of the press in a democracy, muckraking, how controversy is addressed, management of both public and private agencies, monitoring, and how agencies function in a turbulent contracting environment.

Matters of poor public relations skills and poor judgment are evident. That the not-for-profit sector has some fence mending to do is becoming increasingly evident to some of its leaders. Thus, an occasional note of advice will appear at conferences or in literature. An example is to be found in *Children's Voice*, the magazine of the Child Welfare League of America, "When Bad Press Happens to Good Agencies" (Layton, 1995). The article suggests that the agencies must be proactive, and concrete examples are given. How to cope with the varied scrutiny of the public bureaucracy, the state auditor, the legislature, the press, parents, and parental surrogates is a lesson to be learned. Buying condos in warm climates or vacation areas or BMWs in any environment, even with the agency's own budget, would seem ill-advised, no matter how pure the motivation. If programatically advisable, a separate corporation might be the appropriate vehicle.

When egregious behavior is found, the boards of the agencies bear an important responsibility to the public. As governmental funds, rules, and regulations require increasing bureaucratization of the voluntary sector, the roles that board members play must change if the organizations are to retain their relevance. They will still raise money, even as its proportion of the total continues to decline. Their flexibility may become even more vital. They will continue to play technical advisory roles, but as the agencies grow, these activities will increasingly be filled by full- or part-time staff. The trustees' policy role will be delimited by governmental and third-party statutes and practices. Following the health industry, managed social services is next.

Growth in board member responsibilities will be found in several areas. They will need to be more vigorous in establishing standards and monitoring their implementation. They must provide a more effective bridge from the consumer/client and community to their management technocrats. Contrariwise, they will have to represent their clients and their agency to the larger world of politics and the press. Their principal role may be to act as an early warning system to prevent their institution from succumbing to the natural organizational tendency to inflexibility and dehumanization (Demone, 1978). Philip Johnston, in chapter 3 of this volume, recommends that the board members organize statewide. He suggests that they would make a very powerful public interest group.

Should the voluntary not-for-profits and government be managed as if they are for-profit organizations? Is profit making their primary purpose, and if not, what role does it play? Are we willing to sacrifice some efficiencies for other objectives, such as altruism, equity, fairness, entitlement, and voluntarism? The not-for-profit organization as a minimum matter of purpose must demonstrate a high degree of ethical behavior. How do we maintain the innovative capacity of the voluntary sector during its increased politicization? Do contracts make a difference? These questions demand exploration and, ultimately, resolution.

REFERENCES

Armstrong, D. (1993a, February 16). Waste, abuse cast cloud over state's privatization program. *The Boston Herald,* pp. 1, 6, 20.

Armstrong, D. (1993b, February 16). Payroll allegiance blurs for 2 state officials. *The Boston Herald,* p. 6.

Armstrong, D. (1993c, February 17). Soaring exec. pay robbing the system. *The Boston Herald,* pp. 1, 12, 20.

Armstrong, D. (1993d, February 17). Non-profits soak up sun with Fla. property. *The Boston Herald,* p.20.

Armstrong, D. (1993e, February 18). State fails to drop shady firms. *The Boston Herald.* pp. 1, 14, 22.

Armstrong, D. (1993f, February 18). Clergyman's track record one of the worst. *The Boston Herald,* p.22.

Armstrong, D. (1993g, February 19). Political ties is name of the game. *The Boston Herald.* pp. 1, 12.

Armstrong, D. (1993h, February 19). Response to probe: Circle the wagons. *The Boston Herald,* pp. 15, 24.

Armstrong, D. (1993i,February 20). All agree on need for privatization reforms. *The Boston Herald,* pp. 1, 6, 14, 20-21.

Armstrong, D. (1993j,February 20). State review raises questions about fiscal oversight of private vendors. *The Boston Herald,.* p. 12.

Armstrong, D. (1993k,February 20). State ignores evidence, helps school carry on. *The Boston Herald,* p. 12.

Armstrong, D. (1993l February 20). Irregularities alleged in previous Young venture with state. *The Boston Herald,* p. 13.

Armstrong, D. (1993m, April 9). Priest in fraud case gets suspended term & must repay $1.5M. *The Boston Herald,* p. 8.

Armstrong, D. (1994a, May 4). State union to recruit from private agencies. *The Boston Globe,* pp. 31, 37.

Armstrong, D. (1994b, June 10). Overbilling settlement set for DMR. *The Boston Globe*, p. 1.

Armstrong, D. & Phillips, F. (1995, June 5). State health-care work pays off for executives. *The Boston Globe*, p. 1.

Associated Press. (1992June 25). Mass. man convicted of stealing over $1.7 in federal funds. *The Boston Globe*, p. 7.

Aucoin, D. (1993a, November 9). Antiprivatization bill nears final OK. *The Boston Globe*, p. 23.

Aucoin, D. (1993b, November 16). Bill to curb privatization hits fast lane in Mass. House vote. *The Boston Globe*, p. 31.

Aucoin, D. (1993c,November 17). Senate softens on curb of Weld. *The Boston Globe*, p. 33.

Battenfield, J., Meyers, J. & Sciacca, J. (1995a, October 24). Auditor ignores his own problems. *The Boston Herald*, pp. 1, 6.

Battenfield, J., Meyers, J. & Sciacca, J. (1995b, October 25). Absences are par for auditor DeNucci. *The Boston Herald*, pp. 1, 5.

Battenfield, J., Meyers, J. & Sciacca, J. (1995c, October 25). Auditor's aide runs errands at state taxpayers' expense. *The Boston Herald*, p. 5.

Battenfield, J., Meyers, J. & Sciacca, J. (1995d, October 26). Pals, pols see shaky future for DeNucci. *The Boston Herald*, pp. 1, 23.

Benning, V. (1993a, February 13). Quincy agency bilked the state out of at least $1 m, audit says. *The Boston Globe*, p. 33.

Benning, V. (1993b, February 2). State to sever contracts with provider of services to retarded. *The Boston Globe*, p. 46.

Butterfield, F. (1996, January 31). Killing of the nune prompts questions of mental care. *The New York Times*, p. A10.

Carr, H.(1995,October 25). No-show Joe's excuses just par for the course. *The Boston Herald*, p. 4.

Christenson, D. M. (1993, March 17). The value of privatization. *The Boston Globe*, p. 15.

Demone, H. W. Jr. (1978). *Stimulating human services reform.* Washington, DC: U.S. Department of Health, Education and Welfare, DHEW No. OS-78-130.

DeNucci not reticent on feelings about Weld's privatization effort. (1995, March 5). *The Boston Globe*, p. 32.

Fallows, J. (1996). *Breaking the news.* New York: Pantheon Books.

Franklin, J.L. (1993, December 2). Convicted cleric finds home. *The Boston Globe*, p. 1.

Franklin, J.L. (1994, July 13). Priest's conviction overturned. *The Boston Globe.* pp. 1, 20.

The Healey case . . . allowing individuals to live in the community. (1995, May). *Mass. Advocate*, p. 4.

Hicks, J.P. (1995, March 8). Attacks on youth agency called unfair. *New York Times*, p. 33.

Howe, P.J. (1992, April 10). Group home contractor raided. *The Boston Globe*. p.23

Howe, P.J. (1993, December 5). Banks fear bill clause may hurt loan deals. *The Boston Globe*, p. 41.

Jenkins, P. (1996). *Pedophiles and priests*. New York: Oxford University Press.

Johnston, B. (1993, November 6). Weld's magic bullet for solving fiscal problems is on the verge of collapse. *The Boston Globe*, p. 11.

Jones, S.P. (1996, January 1). Vinfen aids disabled adults. *The Boston Herald*, p. 20.

Krauss, M.W., & Seltzer, M.M. (1995, November 25). Mentally retarded benefit more in community-based settings, not institutions. *The Boston Globe*, p. 11.

Layton, M.J. (1995). When bad press happens to good agencies. *Children's Voice, 5* (1), 16–18.

Locy, T. (1993, August 4). Probed firm to regain role. *The Boston Globe*, p.29.

Malone, M. E. (1992, June 26). Mass. renews contract with suspect vendor. *The Boston Globe*, p. 18.

McGovern, P. (1989). Protecting the promise of community based care. In H.W. Demone Jr. and M. Gibelman (Eds.). *Services for sale: Purchasing health and human services*(pp.251–280). New Brunswick, NJ: Rutgers University Press.

Meeting the needs of the retarded. (1995, October 31). *The Boston Globe*, p.18.

Meyers, J. (1995, November 2). Concerned donors fill auditor's war chest. *The Boston Globe*, p. 18.

Milton, S. (1993a, April 1). Night on the town gives clients reason to dance. *The Cape Cod Times*, p. A3.

Milton, S. (1993b, April 1). Private agency stands to lose state contracts. *The Cape Cod Times*. p. A3.

Nordheimer, J. (1995, May 16). Senate to consider bill on release of mentally ill. *New York Times*, pp. 1, 16.

Pamler, T. C., Jr. (1993, December 12). Weld aides fault antiprivatization. *The Boston Globe*, p. 42.

Pamler, T. C., Jr. (1994, March 15). Sloganeers try to stay one word ahead of critics. *The Boston Globe*, p. 17.

Preer, R. (1993, October 3). Union vote is set at privatized hospital. *The Boston Globe*, pp. SW 1, SW 3.

Purnick, D. (1995, March 9). Months after the tar, A feather in his cap. *New York Times*, p. B3

Rakowsky, J. (1994, June 28). Health providers admit to fraud. *The Boston Globe*, p. 1.

Rich, F. (1996, January 13). The capital gang. *New York Times*, p. 23.

Rios, N.M. (1994, October 30). After the Ventura case: The challenge of a new partnership. *The Boston Globe*, p. 75.

Sciacca, J. (1995, October 24). Phone bills don't apply to his office. *The Boston Herald*, pp. 1, 6.

Tong, B.Q.M. & Young, M. (1993, March 7). School for retarded youths backed. *The Boston Globe*, p. 33.

Watching the watchdog. (1995, October 24). *The Boston Herald*, p.30.

Wen, P. & O'Neill, G. (1991a, May 5). Profit in hidden interests. *The Boston Globe*, p. 152.

Wen, P. & O'Neill, G. (1991b, June 14). Springfield center under audit for use of state funds. *The Boston Globe*, pp. 1, 17.

Wong, D.S., & Aucoin, D. (1993, December 16). Senate rejects Weld on privatization. *The Boston Globe*, p. 35.

6

Contracting as a Strategy for Organizational Survival

Barbara Bailey Etta

This chapter focuses on the forces, factors, and strategies utilized and developed to maintain the viability of St. Ann's Infant and Maternity Home, Washington, DC, when other child welfare agencies in the same general area were not able to adapt. The history of St. Ann's Infant and Maternity Home in regard to its contracting for services is discussed; the impact of purchase of service (POS) on organizational adaptation, change, and survival is highlighted; and finally, variables are identified that are instructive and generalizable to other organizations during periods of crisis. In discussing the involvement of St. Ann's with POS contracting, crisis and responses to crisis are presented in their historical context.

Data sources analyzed were board minutes and other documents from the archives of St. Ann's, such as case records, log books, and agency files. In addition, media coverage of the organization was reviewed, as well as relevant Congressional records and oral history interviews with contemporary staff, former staff, and significant persons within the Catholic church and the community. Other data were drawn from the U.S. Decennial Manuscript Census for 1870, 1880, 1900, and 1910.

During the past century a significant number of Washington area child welfare institutions have closed. This has occurred within the context of changes and developments in the total child welfare movement nationally and locally (J. Theban, Personal Communication, August 19, 1987; J. Schreiber, personal communication, August 8, 1987). The primary reasons that the sectarian and nonsectarian child welfare institutions across the country closed are changing community needs, attitudes toward congregate care, and resulting social reform movements in child welfare.

Currently, child welfare practitioners and policymakers are focusing on permanency planning, which includes reuniting children with their biological families whenever possible and adoption placement when family reunification is not possible (Leashore, McMurray, & Bailey, 1991). Congregate care remains a placement option only when absolutely necessary.

In Washington, DC, at least seven institutions for children have closed during the past century, primarily because of insufficient funding and/or changes in the social climate (e.g., Merriweather Home for Children, St. Vincent Home, St. Joseph's Home, and Junior Village Child Care Institution for Children). However, St. Ann's, a Catholic child care institution under the aegis of the Daughters of Charity of St. Vincent de Paul Society, which was established more than 130 years ago, has remained open and gives testimony to institutional survival (Etta, 1988). Currently, St. Ann's remains the only private or public institution for the care of neglected and abused children in Washington, DC. It is in the process of building and developing a residence for teenage mothers and babies so that the mother can more effectively care for her child.

AGENCY BACKGROUND

St. Ann's was established in August 1860 in response to the care and placement needs of abandoned (neglected) children and foundlings of "prostitutes." Although there has been an expansion of goals, the original purpose of the institution has not changed over the 135 years of its existence. The agency has met the needs of its community, and its use of technology has improved (Sister G. Kureth, personal communication, August 25, 1987; Hayes, 1949; Sister Josephine Murphy, personal communication, August 25, 1994).

Chartered by Congress in February 1863, St. Ann's has remained a "corporate sole" while maintaining its affiliation with the Archdiocese of Washington and related human services agencies. What began as a home for children of prostitutes evolved into a modern complex organization with a multiplicity of programs and contractual liaison-collaborative relationships with federal, state, and city governments and private and community organizations.

St. Ann's earliest programs provided residential care for dependent and abused children and pregnant women. The offerings have been expanded to include a prenatal program, an adolescent mother–baby program that stresses family counseling and educational services, and a day care program. Finally, an important goal of St. Ann's has been to collaborate with and relate to other human service agencies in providing child welfare services and receiving and making referrals.

ADAPTATION THROUGH CONTRACTING

Throughout this institution's 137 year history it has made an important contribution to the well-being of children and families. In addition, St. Ann's has shown a remarkable ability to change and expand its program thrust consistent with the social welfare movement in the United States and the Washington, DC community. The context of St. Ann's adaptation is a period of retrenchment and withdrawal of funds by the federal government and other sources. Part of this adaptation and consequent organizational survival concerns St. Ann's involvement in POS contracting.

St. Ann's has had contractual or POS relationships with child welfare agencies affiliated with the governments of the District of Columbia, Maryland, and Virginia since 1923. The federal and district governments provide administrative licensing and child care standards and oversight to St. Ann's through approval of grants and contracts. In addition, the District, Maryland, and Virginia governments provide the basic core of St. Ann's clients through referral. Clients are referred to St. Ann's by the various jurisdictions. The referral process includes psychosocial data, medical information, and other data, which are reviewed and evaluated by the admissions staff composed of a social worker, psychiatrist, psychologist, and nurse.

To deliver services to clients, the agency first had to acquire necessary resources. This was not always easy; at times the agency was faced with extreme difficulties in maintaining a sufficient flow of resources. Initially, St. Ann's had no stable source of income to defray its expenses. Instead, it relied on fund-raising activities, bequests, legacies, real estate transactions, and Congressional appropriations. However, consistent with the child welfare movement locally and nationally, the agency began to negotiate for public funds vis-à-vis contracting in its search for financial stability beginning early in the 20th century. Contracting or POS has steadily increased for more than 60 years and now comprises more than 90% of the budget for program services (St. Ann's financial statements, June 30, 1994). St. Ann's response to funding crises and the resultant use of POS as a survival strategy is outlined below.

Congress Supplements an Uncertain Resource Base: The Earliest Days

The Daughters of Charity assumed responsibility for financial maintenance of St. Ann's from the beginning of its existence on August 15, 1860.
The organization was incorporated by an Act of Congress on February 27,
1863, and the charter was signed by President Abraham Lincoln on March
3, 1863 (board minutes, March 26, 1863).

The Daughters of Charity have been reported to be the largest community of women in the world (Sister G. Kureth, personal communication, August 25, 1987; Dion, 1961; O'Grady, 1930). They address the social
and medical needs of children, the sick, and the aged. Two programs that
have been operated at St. Ann's since the 1860s were the neglected child
program and the unwed mother's program established for the foundlings
of prostitutes (board minutes, March 26, 1863; Etta, 1988, Hayes, 1949;
Mulholland, 1947).

Sisters were primary program managers until the 1970s when a decline
in the number of women entering the Daughters of Charity necessitated
the increased use of other staff. Initially, in 1860, there were three staff
members. Currently, there is a staff of 171 persons: 7, management; 28,
professional (social workers, nurses, psychologists, a psychiatrist, infant
development specialists, physical therapist); 101, child care; 8, office and
clerical; 7, laborers and craft staff; and 20, kitchen and maintenance.

The contracts for the children's residential program stipulates that St.
Ann's will serve 57 children in the residential program, 58 clients in the
prenatal program; 14 in the adolescent mother-baby program, and 80
clients in the day care program. Ninety percent of the cost of care for the
children's residential and prenatal programs are paid for through POS
contracts. The day care program is not government-funded but is privately
run on a fee-for-service basis.

St. Ann's response to the challenge of finding sufficient funds to maintain the organization included private fund-raising activities and, eventually, effecting a financial relationship between church and state that
evolved into POS contracting. The original charter did not specify that
there was to be any public funding for the organization, leaving the burden entirely to the Daughters of Charity. For the first 13 years, the sisters
managed to survive with proceeds from entertainment, fairs, and festivi-
ties that helped pay a portion of the debt for operating its building (Hayes,
1949). However, they had no stable source of income (Mulholland, 1947).

In 1877, St. Ann's decided to petition Congress for an appropriation of $20,000 to allow it to continue its work (anonymous source, 1877, board minutes, March 29, 1878; Hayes, 1949; Mulholland, 1947; Archives, St. Ann's). St. Ann's received $5,000 from Congress in 1877. This same amount was also received in 1888, after which the sum was increased to $6,000 (Hayes, 1949). However, funding was variable by year and somewhat unpredictable. St. Ann's received $7,079 in 1892; $6,500 in 1893, and $3,840 in 1895. There was an increase in the Congressional appropriation—to $5,400—in 1894 following the recommendation of the superintendent of charities in Washington, DC

Congress passed a law in 1890 creating the position of superintendent of charities, and this office was vested with the responsibility of visiting, inspecting, and supervising all charitable institutions supported partially or fully by funds from Congress (Hayes, 1949). Although there was great opposition and hostility about giving public funds to private institutions under sectarian or church control, the sisters were quite resourceful in petitioning Congress directly or indirectly to continue their appropriations.

The 46 years of Congressional appropriations to this private Catholic child care institution are evidence of the high level of skill of the organizational leaders in relating to their political-economic environment, particularly in regard to frequently sensitive issues of church-state relations in American society. However, Congressional appropriations were terminated in 1923 because there was broad and generalized antipathy about private agencies receiving public funds. The loss of public support signaled another era of financial challenge for the organization.

Searching for Funds: 1923–1960s

After the withdrawal of Congressional funding, St. Ann's continued to raise funds through entertainment functions, fairs, bequests, legacies, and real estate transactions. However, the agency encountered difficulty in obtaining sufficient money for food and clothing for the children under its care (anonymous source, 1918; Hayes, 1949; Mulholland, 1947; Archives, St. Ann's). Various private individuals and charities responded, as exhibited by benefit concerts and initiation of the use of volunteers. St. Ann's also joined the Community Chest, a consortium of private agencies, in 1929 as a survival strategy.

In 1942, Congress approved an amendment to the charter expanding the limitation on assets of the corporation of St. Ann's to $1 million. This

action illustrates the overlapping technical, political, and social processes
to enhance change and growth that proved necessary to achieve the physical improvements required by a new law passed by Congress in April 1944.
This law mandated the licensing of all child-placing agencies under the
Washington, DC Board of Public Welfare (Hayes, 1949: Tichey, 1980).
Thereafter, licensing requirements (i.e., external controls) increased the
quality of care and the standards of the institution's programs (Hayes,
1949). As of 1949, as a result of these pressures, the physical facilities had
improved, and there was a broader range of skilled staff and types of programs (Hayes, 1949).

A day care program for children placed in St. Ann's and for children
from nearby embassies was started on December 12, 1949. Day care was
not only a response to community need: it became an extremely important element in establishing connections with powerful segments in the
Washington, DC community that could help the agency (Sister R. Gerace,
personal communication, June 8, 1987). At the time the day care program
opened, it was located in a well-to-do neighborhood that included several
embassies. Children brought into the day care program thus came from
the upper strata of Washington society. This earlier development of a day
care program was a precursor of St. Ann's use of contracts to enhance its
resource base.

In 1929, when St. Ann's joined the Community Chest (now United
Way), it extended its involvement and collaboration in more formalized
relationships with other human services delivery systems and concurrently
sought to regularize part of its resource base. The Community Chest provided social and financial support to St. Ann's (board minutes, December,
1929; Hayes, 1949; Mulholland, 1947).

During the period 1923 to 1960, St. Ann's made increasing use of POS
contracts with state government (i.e., Washington, DC, Maryland, and
Virginia). These contracts produced board payments for the cost of care
for children and unwed mothers. The dependence on public contracting
became increasingly significant after 1940, with a large and growing proportion of St. Ann's funds based on contracts.

Challenge of Deinstitutionalization: 1960s–1980s

Undoubtedly, one of the most serious threats to this institution's continued existence in all of its history resulted from the wave of deinstitutionalization that occurred from the 1960s into the 1980s (personal

communications: J. Theban, August 19, 1987; J. Schreiber, August 8, 1987; M. Mc Grory, June 30, 1987; L. Donaldson, June 25, 1987; B. Byrams, June 20, 1987; Sister E. Staab, June 2, 1987). Nationwide, legislators, politicians, advocates, and practitioners came to view residential placement as an ineffective and often damaging form of social control rather than a true social treatment alternative. Reformers saw children as languishing in institutions without effective alternative placement plans (McGowan & Walsh, 1985).

Tremendous pressure was generated to diminish the population of public institutions and close as many of them as possible. Private institutions, too, were affected by this nationwide support for deinstitutionalization (Costin, Bell, & Downs, 1991). Moreover, laws were passed stipulating that children be placed in more appropriate settings, meaning, in most cases, noninstitutional placements.

In the 1960s the DC government greatly reduced the number of institutional beds for children and unwed mothers it had heretofore funded through contracts. This posed a very serious threat to St. Ann's, which had come to rely heavily on DC government contracts. Concomitantly, the United Way budget deficit from 1966 to 1968 necessitated a reduction in funding to St. Ann's.

Many public and private children's institutions in the Washington, DC area closed during this period (1960–1971): St. Joseph's, St. Vincent's, Meriweather Home, DC Junior Village, and DC Children's Emergency Screening Center. The primary reasons for the closing of these institutions were lack of viable funding; inability to creatively adjust their programs to the needs of the community; and the pervasive belief in the community about the problems inherent in congregate care (e.g., lack of individualism, bonding issues, need for a family-like setting).

The responses of St. Ann's to these challenges were multiple and varied. It remained available to take children needing placement and adjusted its programs accordingly. It agreed to accept children on a 24-hour basis, making it the only children's institution in Washington, DC to accept children around the clock. Further, it agreed to accept older children with special physical, emotional, and educational needs who could be cared for in an institutional setting (personal communications: Sister G. Kureth, August 25, 1987, J. Carey, Esq., June 26, 1987; Monsignor R. Montgomery, June 9, 1987; Sister M. Edelin, June 8, 1987; Sister E. Staab, June 2, 1987). In addition, St. Ann's developed a respite care program for children with handicapping conditions; reopened the day care center, which further enhanced its strategy to respond to community need; and opened an infant day care program (personal communications: Sister G. Kureth, August 25, 1987; J. Carey, Esq., June 26, 1987; Monsignor R. Montgomery, June 9, 1987; Sister M. Edelin, June 8, 1987; Sister E. Staab, June 2, 1987).

Thus, as contract funding was threatened, St. Ann's continued to effectuate survival strategies and rapidly modified its service programs to retain as much POS funding as possible. It responded to the needs of the community and established service programs that were needed and not available elsewhere in the community.

Kettner and Martin (1985) posited that among the salient reasons government agencies purchase services is that the purchase agency may provide greater quantity, quality, and flexibility of services and talent that is not always available to clients of public human service agencies. St. Ann's responded to the various crises by providing different and more creative services, which served not only the needs of the community but also helped secure its financial viability.

St. Ann's responded to community need by initiating and maintaining ongoing residential placement for children and sustaining a prenatal program for unwed mothers and a residential after-care program for mothers and their newborn babies. In addition, it is now building and developing an apartment complex for mothers and babies to assist them with their growth, development, and adjustment in society. The initiation of these services tailored to community needs has further enhanced St. Ann's ability to provide contracted services.

An extremely important element in surviving the deinstitutionalization threat was the use of powerful social and political connections. For example, Mary McGrory, syndicated columnist for the *Washington Post*, whom Phil Gailey, columnist for the *New York Times*, described as being better known for her "journalistic floggings" of the city's politicians and bureaucrats, approached the DC government about continuing its contractual arrangement with St. Ann's. Her influence succeeded in swaying opinion, and St. Ann's enhanced scope of POS contracting was striking at a time when institutions across the country were going out of business as result of deinstitutionalization (personal communications: Sister R. Gerace, June 8, 1987; Sister E. Staab, June 2, 1987; Bielawski & Epstein, 1984).

Moreover, incidental to the period of deinstitutionalization, the trend of unwed mothers to remain in the community and keep their babies exacerbated the pressures on institutions such as St. Ann's. The effect of contract setbacks was therefore magnified (Sister E. Staab, personal communication, June 2, 1987). A response to this challenge by St. Ann's was the creation of a residential program in which mothers and babies could remain together for an habilitative-rehabilitative period (personal communications: Sister J. Kureth, August 25, 1987; Sister E. Staab, June 2; 1987). Changing philosophies and values regarding appropriate services to human need affected St. Ann's program priorities.

The ramifications of deinstitutionalization extended through the 1980s, by which time the child welfare movement was directed toward permanency planning, that is, placement with parent or relative (family reunification) or adoption planning for children who were not able to return home, as mandated by the Adoption Assistance and Child Welfare Act of 1980 [P. L. 96-272]). Among other safeguards, the law specifies that states and localities conduct periodic case reviews at least twice a year on all children in foster care as a prerequisite for receiving federal financial reimbursement. The child welfare system was required to develop goal-directed case plans designed to achieve permanence in the least restrictive, family-like setting available, in close proximity to the parents and consistent with the best interest and special needs of the child.

The focus of the child welfare movement in the 1990s remains that of permanency planning. Notwithstanding, POS contracting between local governments and St. Ann's has continued to increase because of social needs and changing philosophies and values regarding the use of POS contracting. Also of importance is the consistent use of St. Ann's as a contract agency is its established reputation as a provider of high-quality services and its proven track record in this regard.

In summary, when the District government sought to reduce the POS beds at St. Ann's, St. Ann's responded by using its political connections to intercede with the government, thereby expanding its programs and resource base. This was effectuated by opening a mothers and babies program; starting a respite care program for children with handicapping conditions; reopening the day care center, and opening an infant day care center (personal communications: Sister M. Doyle, September 29, 1987; R. Carey, Esq., June 26, 1987; Bishop E. Herman, June 24, 1987; Sister E. Staab, June 2, 1987). These programs were financed through a combination of private contributions, client payment for services, and POS contracting.

Organizational Response to Racial Diversity

On a formal level and from its beginning, St. Ann's stipulated that its policy was not to discriminate according to race, creed, or sex. However, it seems clear that on an informal level the selective pattern of placement

of Black clients through the years was consistent with the racial discrimination patterns of the Catholic church and societal norms. When the political climate became more conducive, migration patterns changed, the
Black population in Washington, DC, increased, and the threat of deinstitutionalization emerged, it became more vital to accept a broader client
base. In addition, this change occurred during a significant period of
social welfare history, as exemplified by the Civil Rights Act of 1964.
Moreover, contract stipulations mitigated against discrimination by race,
sex, or handicap after the Civil Rights Act was passed. Purchase of service
contracting might have facilitated antidiscrimination because of its regulations and because clients who lived in St. Ann's geographical area were
referred. Thus, clients requiring services were increasingly members of
the minority population.

LESSONS

A key characteristic of not-for-profit human service organizations is their
dependence on donors and positive relationships with their environment
(i.e., federal and state funding agencies and private charities) for a steady
flow of resources and support (Hasenfeld, 1983; Johnson & Schwartz,
1994). Furthermore, because organizations depend on communities for
legitimization and clients, they are also influenced by the norms and socio-
cultural and economic characteristics of the community (Hasenfeld, 1983).

   To survive, programs must change to meet the needs of a changing society, and the continued adaptive pursuit of good public relations is imper-
ative (G. Kureth, Sister, Daughters of Charity, personal communication,
August 1987). The initial goal structure and program of St. Ann's reflects
its response to community need as well as its dependence on the political
environment (i.e., Congress and the president of the United States) for
sanctioning. St. Ann's was able to continue its program operations through
creative use of organizational-environmental relations that facilitated POS
contracting.

   Currently, fiscal problems in Washington, DC are severely threatening
POS contracting. However, the basic goal of any organization is to survive
without immobilizing itself, frustrating clients, and antagonizing staff
(Perlmutter, 1984). Survival includes the ability to understand and adjust
to the political and economic environment and differences in the national
and local political and economic climate. Although St. Ann's POS contracts for the children's and prenatal program have not been renewed,

the institution is receiving payments for services rendered on a case-by-case basis. This allows continuous delivery of services.

Present anxieties and tensions are reflective of the cyclical nature of child welfare service delivery during times of crisis. St. Ann's survival as an organization has been based on altering its program to meet the needs of the community, the use of organizational-environmental relationships, and creative resource-acquisition strategies. Given the history of St. Ann's and its ability to survive throughout its 137 year history, it remains at the vanguard of initiating and maintaining programs consistent with community needs.

Demone and Gibelman (1989) saw POS as reflective of and integrally related to changing conceptions of the roles of the public and private sectors of this society. The history of St. Ann's verifies this assertion as, for this agency, prevailing societal and professional attitudes and opinions have defined its strategies and programs.

Despite the current fiscal problems in Washington, DC, which have severely threatened POS contracting, the political, social, and legal climate mitigates against reducing POS contracting. Currently, the Washington, DC child welfare program is under a U.S. District Court order to improve service delivery. One tool to accomplish this goal was the appointment recently of a general receiver to ensure program improvement. Therefore, in all likelihood, POS contracting will increase due to prevailing opinions that public sector services should decrease, that private sector services are superior, and that contracting is more cost-effective and efficient.

REFERENCES

Biclawski, A., & Epstein, I. (1989). Assessing program stabilization: An extension of the differential evolution model. *Administration in Social Work, 8,* 13–23.

Costin, L. B., Bell, C. J., & Downs, S. (1991). *Child welfare policies and practice* (4th ed.). New York: Longman.

Demone, H. W., & Gibelman M. (1989). The evolving contract state. In H. W. Demone, Jr., & M. Gibelman (Eds.), *Services for sale: Purchasing health and human services* (pp. 17–57). New Brunswick, NJ: Rutgers University Press.

Dion, P. E. (1961). The Daughters of Charity: Their early United States history. In A. E. Kovacs (Ed.), *Saint Vincent DePaul* (Vol. 9, pp. 92–119).

New York: St. John's University Press.

Etta, B. B. (1988). *Political economy strategies for institutional survival: A case study of Saint Ann's Infant Asylum.* Unpublished doctoral dissertation, Howard University, Washington, DC.

Hasenfeld, Y. (1980). The implementation of change in human service organizations: A political economy perspective. *Social Service Review, 54,* 508–520.

Hasenfeld, Y. (1983). *Human service organizations.* Englewood Cliffs, NJ: Prentice-Hall.

Hayes, A. M. (1949). *History of St. Ann's Infant and Maternity Home, June 1949.* Unpublished masters thesis, Catholic University of America. Washington, DC.

Johnson, L. C., & Schwartz (1994). *Social welfare: A human response to need.* Boston: Allyn & Bacon.

Kettner, P. M., & Martin, L. C. (1985). Issues in the development of monitoring systems for purchase of service contracting. *Administration in Social Work, 9,* 69–82.

Leashore, B. R., McMurray, H. L., & Bailey, B. C. (1991). Reuniting and preserving African American families. In J. E. Everett, S. S. Chipungu & B. R. Leashore (Eds.), *Child welfare: An Africentric perspective* (pp. 246–265). New Brunswick, NJ: Rutgers University Press.

McGowan, B. C., & Walsh, E. M. (1985). Social policy and legislative change. In J. Laird & A. Hartman (Eds.), *A handbook of child welfare: Context, knowledge and practice* (pp. 241–268). New York: The Free Press.

Mulholland, C. L. (1947). *The administration of St. Ann's Infant Asylum and Maternity Home.* Unpublished master's thesis, Catholic University of America, Washington, DC.

O'Grady, J. (1930). *Catholic charities in the United States: History and problems.* Washington, DC: National Conference of Catholic Charities.

Perlmutter, F. D. (1984). *Human services at risk.* Lexington, MA: Lexington Books.

Tichey, N. M. (1980). Problem cycles in organizations and the management of change. In J. R. Kimberly, R. H. Miles, & Associates (Eds.). *Organizational life cycle.* San Francisco: Jossey-Bass.

7

Contracting for Child Welfare and Related Services in the District of Columbia

Margaret Gibelman

This chapter explores the recent history of the purchase of social services in the District of Columbia within the context of the city's growing fiscal crisis and changes in prevailing views about the merits of social welfare programs. The chapter begins with a discussion of the stimulus to enlarge the scope of contracting in the District to meet court-ordered mandates to revamp the child welfare system. The expansion and later retraction of contracting for related human services, such as AIDS education and prevention programs, special education, and substance abuse services, is also discussed.

In this case study, political decisions about how to address the city's fiscal woes highlight the sometimes precarious nature of contractual relationships. The problems that can arise for contracted agencies when budgets are tight are exemplified in this case study of the nation's capital. Extrapolating from the experiences of the District of Columbia, contracted services may be highly vulnerable to the budget ax as municipalities across the country seek to reduce expenditures.

This author served as an administrator reviewer for the District of Columbia Department of Human Services (DHS) during the period under discussion (1991–1995). From this vantage point, the author had the opportunity to meet frequently with social workers employed by DHS, as well as those working in contracted voluntary agencies. The *Washington Post* proved to be a rich source of information about the status of contractual relationships in its frequent reports about the city's response to its fiscal crisis.

EXPANDING THE USE OF CONTRACTING
IN CHILD WELFARE

The District of Columbia, like many other state and local governments, embraced contracting for services for a number of ideological and practical reasons. Similar to other municipalities, the District's government has, over the years, grown exponentially. The District has, in particular, been chastised for the growth in the size of its public work force. Although it is difficult to determine exactly how much money is saved by contracting out, the *appearance* of substantial cost savings serves important symbolic purposes. Contracting is one way to circumvent negative public sentiment about the District government's size and role.

Contracting for human services also addresses the perceptions of an inept bureaucracy unable to bring about needed reforms in the provision of child welfare and related services. In 1969, following revelations of widespread neglect and warehousing of children in residential care, the District closed its large Junior Village residential facility. The District government reached out to voluntary agencies to ask them to establish a system of foster care services to provide an alternative to residential care. The agencies responded affirmatively, beginning an era of public-private collaboration to remedy the many documented defects in the public provision of social services to children and families (E. Manning, personal correspondence, April 1996). Concurrently, however, the DHS also expanded its own foster care system to address the expanding needs for out-of-home placements.

The Child Welfare System in Crisis

In 1989 a class action suit, *LaShawn v. Barry*, was brought on behalf of children in foster care in the District of Columbia by the American Civil Liberties Union. As a result of this suit, the District was mandated to revamp its child welfare system to ensure that families receive the intensity and level of services necessary to preserve family relationships, prevent additional abuse/neglect, promote better parental care, and assure good care for children (Greene, 1992). The final court order details the types of services that must be available, either directly or under contract with private agencies (Center for the Study of Social Policy, 1991). Such services include intensive home-based crisis intervention services, homemaker services, parent education/counseling, mental health services, substance abuse programs, housing assistance, respite care, day care, emergency cash assistance, access to other public benefits; and less intensive family services (ACLU, 1991). Thus, the full breadth of community services can be considered part of the child welfare response.

Although the DHS had, like most state and local governments, initiated contractual relationships with not-for-profit and for-profit entities prior to the LaShawn order, the 1991 court mandate to correct the deficiencies in the foster care system provided the stimulus for a substantially expanded purchase of service (POS) system. Several of the voluntary agency providers in the District of Columbia had already proved their reliability as providers of high-quality services.

Contracting as a Multifaceted Solution

Contracting in the aftermath of the LaShawn order met two different agendas. First, the DC government was in a fiscal crisis and was concurrently under pressure to reduce the size of its city work force. Contracting for services made it possible to decrease direct personnel expenses by transferring personnel costs to contracts for services.

Second, the District was encountering difficulties in recruiting professional social work staff. Purchasing services provided a ready mechanism to meet this mandate, a possibility recognized in the final implementation order (Gibelman, 1996). The DHS was instructed to "develop policies and procedures specifying the criteria for the provision of family services and for the referral of families to any private agencies with which the Department contracts for such services" (ACLU, 1991, p. 9). It chose to address some of the LaShawn mandates in part by contracting out to the extent feasible.

To attract social workers into city government employment, salary levels were set for these public employees substantially above those offered by the voluntary sector. In 1995 the starting salary for a social worker in the DHS was about $34,000, compared to $27,000 for a beginning social worker in a not-for-profit child and family agency (personal communications: L. Kuzma; A. Robinson, February 1996). In a twist of circumstance, the elevation of public sector salaries made contracting out more attractive: the DHS could purchase services for a lower dollar amount than it would cost to directly provide them directly. It was also easier to comply with mandates to reduce caseload size outside the bureaucracy. Caseload size became part of the negotiating items with voluntary agencies.

From the District's point of view, contracting with existing community agencies held the key advantage of quick start-up time without the necessity of a long-term fiscal commitment. The District was under constant Congressional scrutiny to diminish the size of its public labor force. At the same time, the provision of child welfare services, including its related components of family preservation, foster care, and/or adoption, had to be expanded to meet the rising tide of child abuse and neglect—at least in part a reflection of the growing problem of substance abuse. From the viewpoint of the voluntary agencies within the District, contracting provided a way to expand services and meet a real community need.

Contracting for service provision for those cases confirmed as abuse or neglect also served an important role delegation purpose. By law, only the public agency can investigate allegations of child abuse and/or neglect; the protective services component of child welfare cannot be contracted out. Public agency personnel began to specialize in intake and investigative functions rather than ongoing direct service (Gibelman, 1996). Public sector social workers could also maintain their social control functions, such as removing children from abusive homes and conducting investigations of alleged abuse without being encumbered with the dual and perhaps contradictory task of also serving as helper and supporter of these same families. Many of these latter functions were delegated to voluntary agencies through contracts. For example, children in foster care because of suspected or confirmed abuse or neglect would be assigned to a contracted agency for ongoing service. The result of role delegation ideally would be to increase specialization, decrease duplication of services, and allow each sector to do what it does best.

Early Contracting Problems

These contracts, however, were not without problems for the voluntary agencies, even from the outset. One such problem concerned the specificity of the contracts. The DHS could only enter into contracts that included specific performance standards, and contracts could be renewed only if there had first been an evaluation and review of services rendered under the previous contract, concluding in a determination that the services had been performed satisfactorily, as measured by fulfillment of the contract performance standards (ACLU, 1991). Further, contracts require that agencies must accept for service all clients referred by the DHS.

These types of requirements had the longer-term effect of altering the manner in which voluntary agencies conduct business.

To assist the District in meeting its child welfare mandates and to promote effective bargaining positions in contract negotiations, 10 voluntary agencies joined together in the late 1970s to form the consortium for Child Welfare. The goal of this Consortium was to improve services to children and families through such means as increased collaboration and coordination, the initiation and conduct of research and demonstration projects, and improved public-private ventures. The size and diversity of these agencies showed considerable variation, but all shared in common a history of contracting with the District.

Although the consortium has been highly successful in some of its advocacy and special project initiatives and continues to increase its span of influence, it has thus far not functioned as a collective unit for negotiating contracts with the District government. This failure to present a unified front in negotiations is understandable. Given the ongoing uncertainty about the amount of dollars available for contracting, some agencies, particularly the larger and stronger agencies that have established higher reimbursement rates than those of other agencies, were unwilling to give up their independent posturing. In fact, agencies were in competition with each other and operated from the position that there might not be enough contracts to go around (E. Manning, personal communication, April 1996). Thus, this potential mechanism for improving the collective bargaining strength of voluntary agencies was hampered by individual agency self-interest.

THE DISTRICT'S FISCAL CRISIS

The District has been plagued by long-term and mounting debt under the watchful eye of Congress, which has jurisdiction and ultimate authority over the District. The District is unique in its relationship to Congress and in the fact that, despite home rule, it has only "shadow" representation in the Senate (i.e., no vote). The close scrutiny of Congress into the affairs of the District relates not only to ongoing allegations of fiscal mismanagement but also to various scandals that have emerged in city government, foremost among these being Mayor Marion Barry's arrest and conviction on drug charges in 1989. Congress wields significant power over the fiscal affairs and management practices of the District through its appropriations process.

The District was faced with the need to cut expenses. DC's problem is relatively straightforward: it spends more money than it takes in (Henderson & Cohn, 1994; Henderson & Vise, 1994). This problem has transcended mayoral administrations. Faulty revenue and expense projections have taken their toll; several years of deficit spending led to a revision in the city's credit rating to that of "junk bond" status. Medicaid expenses, among other programs, have run about $20 million more than projected. Shortfalls in projected revenues of $20 million from a newly instituted public safety fee also contributed to a worsening financial crisis, and the city faced the prospect of running out of cash (Henderson & Vise, 1994).

In response to its fiscal crisis, Mayor Barry initiated several cost-cutting steps, among which are deep cuts in social service programs. Human services make up the largest part of the District's budget (Goldstein, 1994b). The DHS was informed that it must trim $68 million from its billion-dollar budget. The response on the part of the department was to slash or terminate many of its contracts with service providers (Schneider & Vise, 1995a). The effect on voluntary and for-profit contracted agencies and the people they serve was immediate and dramatic.

Delayed Payments

The demand to do more with fewer resources can pose insurmountable obstacles, particularly when the response to fiscal crisis is, in effect, to cut back the very services that have been mandated. This paradox of fiscal retrenchment and mandated service expansion highlights the vulnerability of contracted services.

One cost-savings mechanism initiated by the District is to delay paying contractors. This strategy has resulted in dire financial circumstances for the affected agencies, including those contracted to provide child welfare services. When the city stopped paying its bills, the contractors also found themselves unable to pay their bills. Agencies such as Family and Child Services, one of the oldest voluntaries in the metropolitan area, have been able to weather the delay in payments, relying on reserve funds and contributions from other sources, such as United Way of America, to keep afloat. Others have been forced to negotiate bank loans, miss payrolls, and lay off staff (Loeb & Wheeler, 1995). Particularly hard hit were family day care providers without benefit of agency backup resources. For these providers, payment delays meant personal insolvency.

To meet its LaShawn mandates, the DHS had also contracted for a temporary work force within its own offices. But in October 1995, 65 of these temporary DHS employees were removed from their positions by the firm contracted to provide the work force because the firm had not been paid. Similarly, DHS's main office was no longer being cleaned because the city hadn't paid the rent (Loeb & Wheeler, 1995). The cars leased by DHS for use by social workers in home visits and child placements were repossessed (A. Robinson, personal communication, February 1996).

Agencies Hard Hit

Many of the children under the care of the city's child welfare agency receive ancillary services, ranging from educational to psychotherapeutic, from a large number of agencies. Thus, a range of contracted providers of human services have been similarly affected. The Chelsea School in Silver Spring, Maryland, which serves students with severe learning disabilities, threatened to lay off its teachers and send back to the DC public schools the 40 children attending under DC contract. In response to the threat, the District government made an $81,000 payment against its debt of almost $400,000 (Loeb, 1995b). However, all of the approximately 30 private schools providing special counseling and instruction to DC students have been subjected to late payments.

A class action suit against the District's school system, responsible for paying the tuition for students needing special services, was brought by six special education students who alleged that the slow payments violated their right to a free, appropriate education (Fletcher, 1995a). The suit also suggested that there are long-term consequences for the affected children in that private schools and therapists, including those offering psychological, occupational, and speech therapy, are turning away District students for nonpayment and/or are no longer willing to accept students referred by the city (Fletcher, 1995a). Once again, public attention and pressure resulted in the city's making partial payment to several schools. The court later ruled that the District must pay $2 million in back tuition owed to the private schools and therapists and that future payments be made on a timely basis (Fletcher, 1995b).

This was not, however, the end of the story. Despite the court order requiring the District to pay the tuition for approximately 1,000 students with special needs, the District gave notice that it would stop paying tuition prior to the end of the private schools' contracted period. The District's argument was that the contract termination period should coincide with the end of the public schools' last day of school, providing equal treatment to students in private schools and in public schools (Fletcher, 1995b). The motivation for this action was to save money. However, the court found the District in contempt and instructed the city to continue to support the students in private school.

Hundreds of city contractors found their demands for millions of dollars in back payments falling on deaf ears. By January 1995, the beginning of the second quarter of the fiscal year, the city owed $68 million in bills and had made a deliberate decision to conserve cash by slowing down the timetable for payments (Schneider, 1995). Some agencies have not survived; others totter on the brink of financial disaster. The largest methadone clinic in the District, Moving Addicts Toward Self-Sufficiency (MASS) shut its doors after the city government failed to meet its $240,000 in overdue payments. The privately owned company also shut down its AIDS education program, which was owed about $100,000 in back payments. Despite the acknowledged drug epidemic in the city and its relationship to other social problems, such as the spread of AIDS, the city has had to halt new admissions to methadone programs while concurrently seeking to locate new service providers for over 350 recovering addicts who were receiving treatment at MASS (Goldstein, 1994a).

Another drug and alcohol counseling center, in southeast Washington, was not able to meet its payroll and had its telephone disconnected as it waited for $50,000 in back payments from the District (Goldstein, 1994a; Wheeler, 1994). The Spanish Senior Center faced imminent shutdown as the result of overdue payments in the amount of $107,000. Of its $300,000 annual budget, $240,000 comes from city and federal funds channeled through the District's Office on Aging (Constable, 1995). The agency's clients staged a news conference in front of the office of the District's chief financial officer, demanding payment. The District responded with a check for $47,000, leaving the fate of the agency uncertain.

Parents of children in the child welfare system are frequently referred to community agencies for a wide variety of services to help strengthen the family unit. These services may include adult education, job training, and job placement. The District school system, however, was behind by almost a year in making contract payments to private, nonprofit adult literacy programs. One program serving one of the poorer communities in the District was forced to close for the summer; others were unable to pay staff salaries for weeks at a time (Leonhardt, 1994).

THE QUANDRY OF CONTRACTING FOR PROVIDER AGENCIES

Reliance on contracts has proved to be a double-edged sword. Although the advent of contracting led to a dramatic expansion in the types and breadth of services provided by voluntary agencies (often to populations heretofore outside their purview), agencies were ill-prepared for the downward spiral.

The list of examples grows. The Center for Youth Services, founded in 1982 as a one-stop educational job training, counseling and health center for youth aged 12 to 24, is now struggling to survive for the same reasons other nonprofit human service providers are in trouble. This agency initially relied on foundation support but in the 1990s came to depend mainly on government contracts. Contracting also provided the means to vastly expand the agency's programs. Between 1984 and 1990, its annual budget grew from $290,000 to $870,000. In 1984 only 11% of the center's income came from government contracts, but by 1990 contracts constituted 56% of the income. The growth attributable to burgeoning contracts, however, was not sustained. With the phasing out of the Jobs Training Partnership Act, the Center for Youth Services lost $68,000 of its contract funds in 1994. Soon after, the center's Turning Points program, an after-school recreational, tutoring, and counseling program for junior high school students, was terminated when the District paid only $102,942 of its $390,001 contractual obligation (Thompson, 1995a). The staff size is now 7, in contrast to 32 in 1991.

The Center for Youth Services was not totally dependent on contract monies, but it found itself in a situation of diminishing resources from all sides. Changes in United Way of America regulations to increase donor choice now allow greater flexibility in targeting favorite charities. In 1995 the center received $8,000 from the United Way campaign, whereas in 1993, revenues from this source were $72,450 (Thompson, 1995b). This United Way change has meant that an increasing proportion of dollars is going to suburban agencies and a decreasing proportion to less glamorous causes in the inner city (Thompson, 1995b).

In August 1995 the District government imposed a 2-month freeze on payments to Medicaid providers. One of the agencies hard-hit by this moratorium was St. John's Community Services, an agency providing services to developmentally disabled adults and children. The agency had been receiving about $500,000 a month from Medicaid. The executive director of St. John's Community Services, Thomas Wilds, heads a coalition of about 50 agencies that provide services to the mentally retarded. At a news conference called by the coalition in the aftermath of the District's announcement of the freeze on Medicaid payments, Mr. Wilds spoke to the inevitability of worker layoffs, service curtailment, and delays in purchases in order to conserve cash. All of these measures, he indicated, would adversely affect the ability of agencies to provide services to patients (Schneider & Vise, 1995c).

The August 1995 action was not the first against Medicaid agencies dependent on third-party reimbursement. In October 1994, reports of delayed payments to nonprofit vendors surfaced (Henderson & Cohn, 1994). Hillcrest Women's Surgi-Center, for example, then awaited payment of $25,000 for about 100 Medicaid abortions provided since June of that year. Planned Parenthood was owed $73,982 for providing prenatal care to poor pregnant women (Henderson & Cohn, 1994).

The precariousness of the situation for many voluntary agencies was highlighted in an October 1995 letter from Gracy Stephen, program director of the Sunshine Multi Service Center, a nonprofit agency that was contracted to provide care for 64 mentally retarded DC residents. That agency is owed $700,000 by the District. The letter, distributed widely to the media, outlined some of the concrete problems resulting from payment delays:

(1) We cannot take any more loans.
(2) We already missed staff payrolls to both counselors and consultants.
(3) All our payments to vendors are overdue.
(4) The food supply at home will be affected.
(5) We have never been in this desperate and delicate situation ever in the
     history of our organization. (quoted in Loeb & Wheeler, 1995)

CUTS FIT WITH POLITICAL CURRENTS

Nonpayment of contractual obligations allowed the city to continue its own operations and rely on the goodwill and innovativeness of the voluntary agencies to find ways to 'float' during the payment hiatus period. The view that the private sector can and will pick up the slack is echoed in the halls of Congress. However, a June 1995 report of the Independent Sector, a national coalition of about 800 nonprofit organizations, estimated that charitable giving would have to increase by 70% by the year 2002 if nonprofits are to develop the ability to offset government cuts. Other surveys of the Independent Sector suggest that the rate of charitable giving is on the decline (Thompson, 1995a).

The District, which has experienced substantial urban flight, has also experienced its own decrease in charitable donations. In 1992, for example, charities in the District received $4.8 million of the $22.5 million raised by the United Way of the National Capital Area. Two years later, District charities received $2.4 million of the $22.6 million raised (Thompson, 1995b).

The reduction in charitable giving and anticipated and actual cuts in federal money for human services, combined with the cancellation of programs by the District as a cost-saving measure and/or late payments for services rendered, have left agencies at the brink. Within the District of Columbia a dubious new industry has been spawned: financing firms have offered to "float" government invoices by providing immediate cash in exchange—but only at 80% of the value of the invoice (Loeb & Wheeler, 1995). Those not-for-profits needing an infusion of cash to maintain operations thus were forced to barter some of their contract funds. And despite assurances in late 1994 that the city was making efforts to catch up on its bills, contractors continued to struggle with partial or late payments through 1996.

Reduced Service Commitment

The decision to target contracts for the provision of human services as a way to address the city's cash flow problem also met another agenda. The city was under increasing scrutiny and attack from Congress because of its volume of social services spending. Representative Thomas M. Davis III (R-VA), for example, accused the city of being addicted to spending on social welfare programs, leading to a "dependency on government handouts" (Schneider & Vise, 1995b, p. D1). In Davis's view, a large portion of the city's financial problems were attributable to its level of social welfare spending (Schneider & Vise, 1995b).

The decisions of the City Council in regard to where to make cuts to meet the $140 million spending cut imposed by Congress during the summer of 1994 reflect significantly on prevailing political and public sentiment. The decision to dismantle or chip away at social programs is consistent with the view that government social welfare programs have been largely ineffective and that social programs are frills in a pared-down government (Schneider, 1994). Significantly, the decision to cut social programs carries less political flack than other options, such as basic city services (garbage collection, police, fire, etc.). The recipients of social programs, largely the underclass in this society (the poor, the homeless, the chronically mentally ill) are less organized and less verbal about their needs and demands; as a collectivity, they carry less political clout than do other groups. Cuts in social programs may also be more palatable to politicians because of the assumption that the private sector can and will pick up the slack. This view is both shortsighted and unrealistic.

The decision to cut social services was most easily actuated by terminating contracts, failing to renew contracts, delaying payments to contractors, or delaying contract renewal. Controlling cash flow through the delay of legitimate payments to vendors came to be an acknowledged policy decision. In September 1994 district agencies were directed by the DC chief financial officer to stretch payments to vendors to 45 days, deviating from the usual practice of paying bills within 30 days (Henderson, 1994). Although DC law allows the 45-day payment schedule, in actuality, payments to agencies were delayed by upward of 60 days.

The effect was hard-felt. The DC CARE Consortium, composed of 63 agencies providing HIV and AIDS services, was owed $200,000 in payments for services rendered, about half of which had been due for over 90 days. It faced the prospect of missing its payroll. The city had amassed a backlog of $500,000 in payments to the Whitman-Walker Clinic, one of the largest providers of HIV and AIDS services, much of which had been owed for over 45 days. This agency, too, faced the possibility of missed payrolls (Henderson, 1994).

Concurrent with the decision to slow down vendor payments was the order by the DC controller to halt the award of contracts during the final days of fiscal 1994. Delay in contract renewals proved to be a particularly onerous decision for voluntary social service agencies. District law prohibits payments to vendors without contracts. Many voluntary agencies, however, continued to serve their contracted clients, under the assumption that contracts would be made retroactive and/or that the city would find the means of compensating them. That the city would eventually renew seemed less in doubt, given the mandates of the LaShawn order.

However, the mayor's efforts to pay the voluntary agencies met with City Council resistance. The council was reluctant to give the mayor authority to relax procurement regulations. The council favored a case-by-case approach to paying those agencies that were without a contract but still providing services. City officials feared that some voluntary agencies would simply not be able to survive the delay. After certifying the validity of the bills and the fact that the services were necessary to comply with court orders, the DC administrator authorized payment of $34 million in bills to agencies without contracts (Schneider & Goldstein, 1995; Weil, 1995).

The explanations are largely political and perhaps irrelevant for the affected agencies. The Barry administration has sought to put a positive spin on the situation, citing the progress that has been made in paying some contractors. And the blame for the accumulated debt to vendors has been placed on the former mayor, Sharon Pratt Kelly, who, it is claimed, left incoming Mayor Barry with $322 million in carry-over debt, now reduced to $128 million.

The long-term prognosis is not positive for the contracted voluntary agencies. In early November 1995, Congress voted to cut an additional $256 million from the District's budget (Loeb & Wheeler, 1995), thus, in effect, reducing the District's already strained ability to pay its bills. Complicating matters was the federal budget gridlock in the fall of 1995 and spring of 1996, including appropriations to the District. By February 1996 the DC Financial Control Board was ordering additional cuts in human services, and the final scenario, as of this writing, is not yet clear (Vise & Loeb, 1996).

FIGHTING TO SURVIVE

In the earlier days of contracting, voluntary agencies were in a positive position. There were few if any precedents to follow; the public and voluntary agencies were partners in the effort to define and implement contractual arrangements. Voluntary agencies could propose and initiate the contracting process; they had the expertise that government sorely needed. However, given the magnitude of the District's need to beef up its service-rendering capacity, it was most often the public agency that stimulated the expansion of contracting. Voluntary agencies traditionally had maintained a diversified funding base; although contracts were an attractive source of revenue to expand services or fund new services, procurement of such funds typically was an issue of augmentation rather than survival (Gibelman, 1996).

The partnership relationship gradually but continually eroded as contract dollars came to represent a burgeoning proportion of total agency revenues. Year-to-year funding has created a degree of financial uncertainty that has taxed the ability of the agencies to engage in long-range program and fiscal planning and has left staff uncertain about their future employment. The cumulative impact of the contract relationship has been the development of resource dependence and potential or actual devastation for agencies when the contracts are reduced or terminated.

As an increasing proportion of the services these agencies provide came to be financed through POS contracts, the potential precariousness of their situation also grew. In the aftermath of the LaShawn decision, the District's impetus to contract out human services increased. Smaller not-for-profit community agencies have grown substantially as a result of contracting. Traditional agencies, such as the network of family service and child welfare agencies, are now offering services that heretofore were predominantly, if not exclusively, within the public purview. These include family preservation and foster care services. In some cases these new service programs now overshadow the agencies' more mainstream services, such as family counseling.

The impact of contracting has been far-reaching and in most cases positive in regard to who receives services by what types of agencies. However, the downside, from the perspective of contracted agencies, is readily apparent. Resource dependent voluntary agencies in the District are in trouble. The real dilemma occurs when and if the contract funds are cut back, canceled, or delayed. These agencies are left impotent in the face of the District's payment delays.

The District's public agencies have also not been immune to these impacts. Despite the LaShawn mandates, the DHS has not been exempted from contract payment delays or failure to renew contracts. And because the DHS had elected to meet many of its mandates to improve services through contracting with voluntary providers, the failure to pay contractors or to let or renew contracts meant an inevitable deviation from those improvements that had been made. To the extent that the DHS, for example, has divested itself of much of its direct service delivery role while increasing its contract management and oversight functions, the question now becomes how to rebuild, quickly, its service delivery capacity. An alternative is simply to redefine the agency's service priorities, serving only the very worst abuse and neglect cases. This option, however, has social justice, humanitarian, and practical implications. In the face of the LaShawn decision, doing less is simply an unacceptable alternative.

IMPLICATIONS FOR THE FUTURE

The current fiscal crisis in the District of Columbia has made apparent some of the weaknesses in the system of contracting for social services.

Contracts are among the first budget lines examined in the effort to reduce costs. Terminating contractual relationships is easier than trimming the entrenched bureaucracies and a unionized work force.

Despite repeated promises that the delay in payments to contracted agencies would be remedied, the situation has not only been ongoing but has grown worse. City Administrator Michael C. Rogers offered advice to contractors: "Get used to it" (as quoted in Loeb & Wheeler, 1995, p. B1). Ironically, concurrent with this debacle for contracted agencies, the District government is considering privatizing many city services. The impetus to consider privatization of city services, despite the mayor's earlier opposition, comes on the heels of a congressional mandate to balance the city's budget and the belief that private companies might more efficiently provide services now offered by city employees (Behr, 1995; Goldstein, 1996). The cost advantages to the city have been borne out during a cash flow crisis; voluntary agencies, on the other hand, may have a different view of the benefits of increasing the breadth of privatized city services.

In regard to the District's court mandate to remedy the deficiencies in its child welfare system, contracting had initially proved to be an efficient and effective vehicle of positive change. But contracting for child welfare services, despite court orders, fell victim to the stronger fiscal imperatives of managing cash flow. This relationship between the city's fiscal condition and its child welfare delivery system was summed up by Judith Meltzer, the court-appointed monitor in the LaShawn case. Testifying before the DC council, Ms. Meltzer, a senior associate at the Center for the Study of Social Policy, voiced her concern that the gains that have been made in the child welfare system were being jeopardized by the District's financial crisis. Staff furloughs have caused many newly hired social workers to look for other jobs, and the inability to pay nonprofit agencies and foster parents in a timely way has created new hostilities in the system (as cited in Loeb, 1995a).

Contracting for child welfare services was not likely to be a panacea under the best of circumstances. But the hiatus on payments to vendors, the failure to renew contracts, and the uncertainty surrounding future partnership arrangements diminished the capability of voluntary agencies to do their part in strengthening the child welfare system. On May 22, 1995, U.S. District Judge Thomas F. Hogan ordered the DC government to relinquish its authority over the child welfare system, citing the city's failure, after 4 years of limited judicial supervision, to properly care for and protect the abused and neglected children within its jurisdiction

(Locy, 1995). This is the first time any court has seized control of an entire child welfare system.

LESSONS

This case study highlights some of the political realities of contracting in an era of cost cutting. Contracting occurs within a sociopolitical environment. It is consistent with the perceived desirability of decreasing the size of government, increasing privatization, and fostering public-private partnerships. But the same environment that encourages the use of POS arrangements also produces the negative side of the equation.

In the District of Columbia, purchasing services proved to be an expedient and effective way of expanding the service network and the quality of services. The advantage of fast start-up capability of the voluntary sector, unencumbered by bureaucracy, was realized. Observations by insiders and outsiders, including the courts, validated the benefits of contracting. Nevertheless, the bottoming out of the District's coffers made contracts an easy target.

The District learned that it could withstand most of the pressure brought to bear against contract cuts and delayed payments by loosely connected voluntary agency networks and the press. Public sentiment was with speedy responsiveness to the fiscal crisis.

The lessons for the voluntary agencies were harsher. They learned that

- contract funds are not dependable;
- dependence on any one financial source is a mistake;
- government can be a harsh business partner;
- their negotiating position was poor to non-exist;
- recourses are few and time-consuming;
- the power of the purse rules.

There are also heavy costs in regard to public-private relationships. The perceived disregard for the plight of the voluntary agencies led the boards of some agencies to purposefully seek business in the surrounding jurisdictions of Maryland and Virginia. There was anger about shoddy treatment; both staff and board members felt unappreciated (E. Manning, personal correspondence, April 1996). For other agencies, choices were more limited. They simply went out of business.

The situation in the District of Columbia may be more extreme than in other localities—a worse financial situation, a poorer record of contract payments, and so on. But it would seem that differences are a matter of degree rather than kind, at least in an era in which the majority of municipalities are facing budget shortfalls, and the forecast of more cuts from Washington in 1996 and beyond are causing anticipatory retrenchments. Voluntary agencies are, of course, searching for options as they face the dual blow of reduced charitable giving and contract cutbacks. Some have created for-profit subsidiaries to increase their competitive edge and reach out to new markets. Others are initiating or increasing their requests for foundation support. Still others are urging board members to become more involved in fund-raising (Thompson, 1995a).

The future scenario will be affected substantially by changes now being contemplated by Congress in health, welfare, and human services programs. The welfare debate, for example, includes arguments that drastic cuts can be justified on the basis of an expected increase in private charity and voluntarism; this increase in charitable giving, it is believed, would be stimulated by the withdrawal of government funds. There is, however, no evidence to support this contention ("Giving", 1995).

With diminishing contract funds, increased competition for foundation grants, changes in United Way distributions that favor the more well-to-do suburban agencies, and a growing expectation by government that the voluntary sector will pick up the safety net it is now abdicating, voluntary agencies are indeed facing difficult times. Some will simply disappear, particularly the smaller agencies within inner cities that serve the least glamorous clientele. Others will continue the quest for funds for day-to-day survival, in the process making all possible cuts. Less crisis-ridden agencies will encourage more active involvement of boards of directors in contributing and raising funds and looking for longer-term solutions. Options may include a switch from non-profit to profit status and/or a rise in fee-for-service, effectively driving out those clients who cannot pay.

Although contracting has been found to be a viable system of service delivery that links public and private sectors into a more extensive and far-reaching relationship, prior predictions about the durability of these arrangements are now in question. From the vantage point of the voluntary sector, the impact of resource dependence is now abundantly clear. Yet at the same time, political currents suggest that contracting for services remains a popular means of reducing the size and scope of government payrolls and increasing the effectiveness of services. This latter goal can be achieved only to the extent that the contractual relationship is honored by both parties.

REFERENCES

American Civil Liberties Union and District of Columbia, Department of Human Services. (1991). *LaShawn A. v. Dixon: Final order.* Washington, DC: Authors.

Behr, P. (1995, April 6). Barry names task force on privatizing agencies. *The Washington Post,* p. C14.

Center for the Study of Social Policy (1991). *Implementation plan for improving child welfare services in the District of Columbia.* Washington, DC: Author.

Constable, P. (1995, November 30). Saving the senior center. *The Washington Post,* p. C3.

Fletcher, M. A. (1995a. February 11). D.C. crisis jeopardizes education of special-needs youths. *The Washington Post,* pp. A1, A13.

Fletcher, M. A. (1995b, May 17). D.C. told to keep paying special education tuition. *The Washington Post,* p. B5.

Gibelman, M. (1996). Contracting for services: Bust or boom. *Journal of Health and Human Resource Administration, 19*(1), 26–41.

Giving and the government [Editorial]. (1995, November 8). *The Washington Post,* p. A16.

Goldstein, A. (1994b, October 21). The strange case of the Karrick Hall closing. *The Washington Post,* p. D6.

Goldstein, A. (1994a, December 17). Methadone clinic closes after D.C. doesn't pay bill. *The Washington Post,* pp. D1, D4.

Goldstein, A. (1996, March 2). Barry moves to privatize D.C. General. *The Washington Post,* pp. A1, A13.

Greene, M. S. (1992, September 28). D.C. hires 94 social workers as child welfare load rises. *The Washington Post,* p. D3.

Henderson, N. (1994, September 23). D.C. cash crunch slowing payments. *The Washington Post,* pp. B1, B7.

Henderson, N., & Cohn, D. (1994, October 21). District's contractors feel the pinch. *The Washington Post,* pp. D1, D6.

Henderson, N., & Vise, D. A. (1994, October 20). D.C. faces shortfall of cash. *The Washington Post,* pp. A1, A14.

Locy, T. (1995, May 23). Federal court seizes control of D.C. child welfare system. *The Washington Post,* pp. A1, A7.

Loeb, V. (1995a, March 2). Conditions "shocking" for district children awaiting foster care. *The Washington Post,* p. B3.

Loeb, V. (1995b, January 18). D.C. cash crunch traps special-needs students. *The Washington Post,* pp. D1, D6.

Loeb, V., & Wheeler, L. (1995, November 6). Contractors pay the price of D.C. debts. *The Washington Post*, pp. B1, B4.

Leonhardt, D. (1994, July 3). Adult literacy funds delayed in the district. *The Washington Post*, pp. B1, B4.

Schneider, H. (1994, December 22). $280 million cut by D.C. council. *The Washington Post*, pp. A1, A14.

Schneider, H. (1995, January 20). D.C. sends in the clowns but not the cash. *The Washington Post*, pp. A1, A15.

Schneider, H., & Goldstein, A. (1995, May 5). Law keeps D.C. from paying bills. *The Washington Post*, pp. A1, A22.

Schneider, H., & Vise, D. A. (1995a, February 18). Barry's fiscal plan includes deep cuts in social services. *The Washington Post*, pp. A1, A17.

Schneider, H., & Vise, D. A. (1995b, March 3). D.C.'s "addiction" to social spending is at root of fiscal crisis, GOP says. *The Washington Post*, pp. D1, D6.

Schneider, H., & Vise, D. A. (1995c, August 24). Medicaid contractors berate D.C. *The Washington Post*, pp. C1, C5.

Thompson, T. (1995a, November 12). Growing need, shrinking funds. *The Washington Post*, pp. A1, A18.

Thompson, T. (1995b, October 2). United Way funding shifts from district to suburbs. *The Washington Post*, pp. A1, A12.

Vise, D. A., & Loeb, V. (1996, February 24). D.C. control board cuts schools, social spending. *The Washington Post*, pp. A1, A12.

Weil, M. (1995, May 10). D.C. to pay suppliers who had no contracts. *The Washington Post*, p. D5.

Wheeler, L. (1994, December 4). From City Hall to city streets, D.C. feels the fiscal squeeze. *The Washington Post*, pp. A1, A28.

8

Purchasing School Psychological Services

Andrea Canter

Mental health services in public schools, particularly the services of school psychologists, have historically been provided by credentialed professionals who are employees of the school district. Where such models are impractical and during times of budget and/or personnel shortages, school districts may consider alternatives to employing their own school psychologists, such as purchasing services from other public agencies or from the private sector or simply eliminating some of the services typically provided.

Particularly during a recession, private business is increasingly interested in and more aggressively seeking contracts with public agencies. School districts that have employed school psychologists may regard purchased-service options as a means of *expanding* current services or as a cheap means of *replacing* services of employees. It is essential that administrators, policymakers, and consumers give careful consideration to the potential impact of such arrangements in relation to both costs and service quality in order to make informed decisions (Canter & Crandall, 1994b; National Education Association, 1990). Because little empirical data exist comparing various models of mental health service delivery in school settings, decision makers must rely on current regulations, professional standards of practice, and experiential evidence.

This chapter provides an overview of service models, standards, and issues regarding purchased school psychological services. To illustrate the potential impact of purchased services, both positive and negative, several case studies are presented.

MODELS OF DELIVERING PSYCHOLOGICAL SERVICES IN SCHOOLS

Public School Employees

Psychologists have practiced in school settings throughout much of the 20th century and were directly hired by school districts as early as the 1920s (Fagan, 1995). Following implementation of the first federal rules mandating special education in 1975 (Education of All Handicapped Children Act of 1975 [PL 94–142]), there was rapid growth in the employment of school psychologists by the public schools; this remains the most common model of service delivery. These professionals are usually licensed or certified by their state education agency as school psychologists with a minimum of 2 years of postgraduate training. Their training meets specific standards (e.g., National Association of School Psychologists, 1994), which overlap but are substantially different from the standards for licensure as a clinical psychologist or private practitioner. In many cases, school psychologists' district contracts are negotiated by the teachers' or administrators' bargaining unit; tenure rights, retirement, and other employee benefits apply to school psychologists who are school employees. As do teachers and other school district employees, these school psychologists must follow set policies regarding their assignment and accountability.

School psychologists employed directly by a school district are typically asked to provide a wide range of services, although the specific nature of those services may vary from one district to another. Minimally, school psychological services include assessments and collaboration with members of multidisciplinary teams to determine eligibility for special education. Assessment in school settings is broadly defined to include not only the administration and interpretation of various tests but also direct observation of students, interviews with students and significant adults, and evaluative reviews of student progress over time and in response to specific instruction or training.

In many school settings, district psychologists are called on to provide a much broader range of services, including mental health consultation with school personnel and parents, design and implementation of specific instructional and behavioral interventions, crisis intervention, staff and parent training, program evaluation, and (less frequently) research. They may also be actively involved in administration of specific programs and/or development of school or district policy and curriculum. Many school psychologists are limited by funding rules to serving the at-risk and special education populations. However, some districts hire school psychologists to provide more specific services, such as social skills training or mental health counseling, and/or hire psychologists to provide preventive and crisis services to the general student population.

Contracts with Other Public Agencies

In some parts of the country, particularly rural areas, local education agencies (LEAs) might contract with a public cooperative services agency or special education district to obtain services that may not be practically or economically delivered by small individual LEAs. These are public services but somewhat removed from local control. The cooperative unit might employ school psychologists, who in turn provide services to one or more contracting districts. There is evidence that this model can be cost-effective and, in many situations, the only practical means of obtaining fully credentialed service providers (Fagan, 1985).

Private Contracts

Local education agencies may privatize through contracts that shift the delivery of services from the public to the private sector. Examples of privatization in school psychological services include contracts between a school district and one or more individuals or between a district and a private agency such as a private consulting firm or private mental health clinic. Both for-profit and nonprofit providers have been used. In most states such individuals or employees of the private agency would be required to hold a license for the independent practice of psychology but would not necessarily be required to hold a credential as a school psychologist, depending on the state's education rules. However, some professional standards promote school psychology credentialing for providers of contractual services in schools (National Association of School Psychologists, 1992a, 1993).

Independent contractors are frequently hired on an hourly or per diem basis to provide assessments as required by special education regulations. In some states, particularly where personnel shortages are significant, private contractors may provide full-time or part-time services to small districts where there is no employee available or where district size does not justify hiring a full-time employee (e.g., see Allen, 1993). A private agency might contract with several districts to provide only assessment services or a wide range of services as might typically be delivered by a school-based psychologist.

Co-Location of Services

Another independent contracting arrangement might exist when community services are co-located in the public school setting. In theory, such services represent *additional* services not otherwise available in the public school and are not used to *supplant* existing services. However, some LEAs have considered *replacing* school psychologists (and other support personnel) with service providers from community agencies who co-locate to the school setting. These providers are likely to be clinical psychologists rather than school psychologists.

Prevalence of Purchased Services Models

Although no systematic national estimates of the prevalence of purchased school psychological services have been published, professional organizations have conducted relevant surveys in recent years. Data from a survey of practitioners and administrators in Georgia (Canter & Dryden, 1993) suggest that independent contractors provide some assessment services to well over half of the state's school districts. The primary reason given for purchasing services was personnel shortages, with financial restraints also cited frequently. In Massachusetts a survey of work force trends in school psychology indicated that independent contractors had recently replaced some or all of the functions of school psychologist employees in at least 12 school districts (Kruger, Wandle, & Watts, 1992). In some regions (e.g. the state of Maine), psychological services in schools have historically been provided through purchased services. Rural districts in particular have often purchased psychological and other support services through cooperative public agencies, such as the educational cooperatives and intermediate districts in Minnesota, New York, and Colorado. In at least nine states, professional associations and/or government agencies have developed specific guidelines for the provision of purchased school psychological services (Mars & Canter, 1993).

From available data, it appears that diagnostic services, particularly testing, are the most frequently purchased services. School psychologists responding to a recent survey conducted by the National Association of School Psychologists (NASP) (Schwartz, Mars, & Pionek, 1995) indicated that over half of their districts purchase some services and that assessment accounts for most of those purchased services.

PROFESSIONAL STANDARDS AND CONTRACTUAL SERVICES

Standards for Comprehensive Services

One of the concerns regarding purchased psychological services for public schools is the potential reduction in the provision of "comprehensive" services. The *Standards for the Provision of School Psychological Services* (NASP, 1992c) underscore the importance of a "comprehensive continuum of services" (sec. 3.1) and state that "breadth or availability of services should not be dictated by the funding source" (p. 38).

Comprehensive psychological services are promoted as a means of preventing negative outcomes for students and improving social adjustment and academic performance (Franklin, 1995: NASP, 1992b; 1993). One of the most significant components of comprehensive service models is the emphasis on prevention and early intervention with at-risk students. Through staff and parent consultation and "pre-referral intervention" (providing assistance prior to special education evaluation), the severity of student difficulties and need for special education placements is often reduced (Bergan & Kratochwill, 1990; Graden, Casey, & Bonstrom, 1985; Harvey, 1992).

One of the shortcomings of many private contractual arrangements is the limited range of services provided. Often, districts threatening to eliminate employee positions in favor of contractors are concerned only with purchasing mandatory special education assessments, rather than the pre-referral consultation, classroom observations, and intervention planning that the LEA psychologists typically provide (e.g. Canter & Dryden, 1993; Davids, 1993; Kelly, 1994; Kruger et al., 1992).

Of course, school districts are not *required* to comply with NASP standards or other professional guidelines. But compliance will likely help protect the district from liability for failing to provide services in accordance with recognized professional standards. And vulnerability to litigation is likely to increase when services are not comprehensive and when individuals without adequate supervision or credentialing are hired on a piecemeal basis. For example, McKee and Barbe (1994) note that schools may be liable for "second opinion" assessments requested by parents, particularly if they cannot demonstrate the appropriateness of the school's evaluation.

The federal mandates of the Individuals with Disabilities Education Act (IDEA), formerly PL 94–142, require that the evaluation and placement of students with disabilities is comprehensive, multifaceted, and determined by a multidisciplinary team. This process stresses the need for educational specialists to work with each other in the educational environment and to gather input from numerous sources, including observation of the student within the learning environment, consultation with school personnel regarding educational performance, consultation with parents, and individualized assessment of the student's skills.

Standards for the Use of Contractual Services

Standards for the Provision of School Psychological Services (NASP, 1992c) include the use of contractual services under conditions that do not *supplant* existing services or compromise the quality of services.

> *Standard 3.4.1.* Contractual school psychological services encompass the same comprehensive continuum of services that are provided by regularly employed school psychologists. Overall, psychological services are not limited to any specific type of service and include opportunities for follow-up and continuing consultation appropriate to the needs of the student. Individual contracts for services may be limited as long as comprehensive services are provided overall. (p. 40)

If the district intends to hire independent contractors, professional standards demand that such "services are not to be utilized as a means to decrease the amount and quality of school psychological services provided by an employing agency. They may be used to augment programs but not to supplant them" (NASP, 1992c, p. 40). This provision is intended to ensure the comprehensive continuum of services to all students, which in some districts might not be possible without using some independent providers with specific areas of expertise.

> *Standard 3.4.6.* Contracting for services is not to be used as a means to avoid legitimate employee rights, wages, or fringe benefits.(p.41)

Unfortunately, this is precisely what many districts propose to do when they consider eliminating employee positions. Teacher unions will likely support the employees on this issue, and in some districts and some states, teacher tenure laws may make such actions illegal. The private provider may also have grounds for action against a contracting district if it appears that the district is using the contract to avoid employee benefits (see discussion below).

Developed jointly by the American Psychological Association (APA) Division 16 and NASP (1992a), the *Guidelines: Contractual Services in School Psychology* document essentially reiterates section 3.4 of NASP's *Standards* and portions of Internal Revenue Service regulations defining "independent contractor" and reaffirms the need for psychological services in schools to be comprehensive. This statement helps differentiate "part-time employee" from "independent contractor." Many districts try to save money by providing benefits only to full-time employees. If an individual meets the definitions of "employment" as set in law, that individual is entitled to the benefits of employment. Many districts likely violate the first provision of the *Guidelines* hiring individuals to perform services "on School Board property, using School Board supplies [test kits], and under School Board supervision." Furthermore, districts that do attempt to provide a wide range of services through individual private contracts may find themselves violating *all* of the provisions of these guidelines, as the contractors' services and working conditions will likely be indistinguishable from those of district employees.

Qualifications of Service Providers

Both NASP and APA recognize the specialized training in school psychology as different from the specialized training in other specialty areas, such as clinical and industrial psychology (APA, 1981; NASP, 1994). The independent contractor who is not a trained school psychologist may be a skillful clinician but lacks essential knowledge, expertise, and experience to gather appropriate data in the school context and to facilitate a collaborative, comprehensive approach with the other members of the educational team. When services are provided by individuals lacking sufficient training and appropriate experiences, students are denied their rights to a free and appropriate public education.

Each state establishes its standards for education licenses and for the independent practice of psychology. NASP and APA have also established training and credentialing standards; the Nationally Certified School Psychologist (NCSP) credential is now recognized by a number of states as the appropriate minimum qualification for licensure as a school psychologist (Prus, Draper, Curtis, & Hunley, 1995). In addition, publishers of psychological tests usually specify the standards for training and credentialing of those professionals qualified to use the tests. Such standards generally describe the typical training of school psychologists.

If the LEA is considering contracted services, administrators need to examine the *qualifications* of the contractors. Will positions be eliminated and services replaced by contractors, or are the contractors augmenting the current level of staff? Again, vulnerability to litigation and due process hearings must be considered if contractors prove to be *less qualified* than LEA employees, particularly because independent contractors by definition are usually not provided with any professional supervision by the district. For example, a clinical psychologist may be appropriately credentialed for independent practice but less intensively trained to address developmental issues, school organizations, and/or special education eligibility, compared to a credentialed school psychologist.

In the case of independent contracting, Standard 3.4.2 of NASP's (1992a) *Standards for the Provision of School Psychological Services* supports hiring of *credentialed* school psychologists to provide services, noting that in limited circumstances a psychologist with a different area of training and expertise, such as clinical psychology, might be hired to supplement existing services.

COST-EFFECTIVENESS

Cheaper Services?

Purchased services, particularly those from independent contractors, are often regarded as more cost-effective than the services of public employees (e.g., Gibelman & Demone, 1989). Where escalating costs have forced policymakers to reconsider models of social services in general and school-based services in particular, privatization has been proposed more frequently. The private contractor is sometimes perceived as using more sophisticated, cost-saving techniques. Without the obligation to pay fringe benefits or provide supervision and without union contracts specifying working conditions and hours, districts may regard independent contractors as a more flexible and therefore more cost-effective work force.

Because much funding for special education is tied to caseload size, school employees charged with placement decisions have at times been accused of subjectivity in their judgments, as if the sole basis of their employment is their ability to increase or maintain their caseloads. Such a sentiment was expressed by a Minnesota state legislator, who proposed that "outside experts" determine eligibility for special education in the public schools, rather than relying on employees who are "ensuring some of their own jobs" (Smetanka & Hotakainen, 1994, p. 1).

However, the provision of psychological services to public schools through independent contracts can cost more than employing staff school psychologists, particularly when specific services, such as assessments, are the focus of the contract:

1. In the absence of comprehensive services, referral rates can increase, leading to more costly special education services. Research shows that it is more cost-effective to *prevent* academic and behavioral problems than to attempt to *remediate* them (e.g., see Shapiro, 1988; Zins, Conyne, & Ponti, 1988). Where prevention and early intervention services are limited or not available, a "refer-test-place" cycle is typically established, with referral alone the best predictor of special education placement (Ysseldyke & Algozzine, 1983).

1. In addition to the higher costs associated with special education instruction, the district must provide triennial re-evaluations in accordance with federal mandates. In districts where psychologists play primarily gatekeeping roles, this refer-test-place cycle is largely responsible for the spiraling costs of special education and is the impetus for many districts to seek less costly service providers. However, by limiting purchased services to eligibility assessments and reevaluations, these districts will likely see increases in placements and ultimately increased costs. Expanding the roles of providers, rather than purchasing narrowly defined services, is more cost-efficient in the long run (Fagan, 1985; NASP, 1992b).

2. Hiring individuals who are not trained or licensed for school practice and who are not directly supervised by the district could increase the district's vulnerability to costly due process hearings (see example above).

3. If the private contractor makes errors or provides incomplete services, district staff (or additional independent providers) may end up training the contractors or correcting/completing their work, which adds to the cost.

4. Unemployment compensation, severance pay, accrued leave payments, and other related costs may follow if privatization or co-location results in layoffs of district employees.

5. The provision of *comprehensive* services via independent contract is likely to cost more than the provision of the same services by district employees, assuming comparable credentials, particularly if payment is made on a per service or per hour basis. If the independent contractor provides assessments comparable in scope to those conducted by school personnel—including not only sufficient testing but observation of students in their instructional settings, diagnostic teaching and intervention, extensive reviews of educational history, interviews with staff and parents, attending planning conferences, and so on—these assessments would likely be as expensive as those offered by hospital and clinic staffs. If consultation, prevention, counseling, and other psychological services are included in the contract, costs to the district would increase proportionately.

At first glance, per diem or per case/project charges of independent contractors seem inexpensive compared to salary and benefits of employees. However, when comparing the services of a district-employed psychologist with the *same* services of per diem or per project contractors, many districts may find that the employee saves money (Fagan, 1985). For example, a private provider charging $200 per day for evaluation and consultation services will cost a district $36,000 for a 180-day school year; the same district can *employ* a recently certified school psychologist for $28,000 per year. Adding approximately 20% to 25% for employee benefits, the employee costs the district less.*

Independent contracts are rarely written to cover the full extent of services provided by district psychologists, such as participation in eligibility and placement meetings, counseling students, consultation with teachers regarding behavior management, classroom observations, program evaluation, crisis intervention, and staff development and training. A survey of state school psychology associations (Mars & Canter, 1993) identified a number of situations in which employees were replaced by less well trained personnel, providing more limited services. Exceptions to these trends include the provision of comprehensive services (rather than per diem services) to small and rural districts by school psychologists employed by private and other public agencies, including intermediate districts or educational "cooperatives." These arrangements are typically undertaken

---

* Cost figures are based on salary and benefits as specified in the 1994–95 teacher contract for the Minneapolis Public Schools; cost comparison would vary to some degree depending on the conditions of school district contracts and salary scales.

as a practical alternative to hiring (or finding) part-time employees, as the salaries and benefits paid to agency employees may not result in any cost savings to the contracting districts (Allen, 1993: Fagan, 1985).

Accountability

Do independent contractors offer equal or more effective services? It is often argued that private psychologists provide specialized skills that are generally unavailable in the public school setting. Some specific services, such as the evaluation of a low-incidence disability or of a foreign language–speaking student, may require the services of "outside experts," leading to occasional or short-term independent contracts. However, school psychologists possess training, experience, and specialized skills and knowledge typically not found among clinical psychologists in the private sector or in public mental health centers. They have the understanding of the day-to-day operations of the schools and of special education regulations, can provide an array of educationally relevant services, are able to accommodate the special needs of teachers and students, and are more likely to be involved in and understand school reform practices such as site-based management. System-employed school psychologists are more likely to be flexible in scheduling and can be more sensitive to the needs of district students and teachers than can independent providers, who usually are not familiar with either the school system or the student population.

Administrators may argue that independent contractors are more accountable because of the threat of competition and lack of employee tenure and seniority benefits. If the LEA is not happy with the private contractor, it will refuse to renew the contract. Similarly, it is argued that independent contractors are more productive because they are not bound by union rules, and private agencies can easily dismiss unproductive workers.

However, the threat of competition ends when the contract is signed. Although in theory the contract can be canceled or not renewed, the LEA may have few options once it lays off its own psychologists. Furthermore, to save money the LEA most likely hires the providers offering the cheapest services available, who may not be the most-qualified or best supervised professionals. Effective collaboration among school personnel and staff consistency is essential for student success; thus, constant turnover of providers is undesirable. Once a contract is signed, LEAs will be reluctant to change to another provider.

On the other hand, school employees are more likely to be loyal to the school district, enhancing continuity: private providers are more likely to be loyal to their company or to their own practice. They may seek more lucrative contracts and thus increase problems associated with staff turnover.

The LEA gives up some of its ability to hold providers accountable when it is no longer able to supervise services or set standards for either practice or professional growth. This can be only partially controlled by requiring state certification/licensure of providers. The "chain of command" is far more difficult to engage when the service provider is a private contractor rather than an employee. Depending on the contracting agent and conditions of the contract, ineffective independent providers may be no easier to terminate than are ineffective school employees.

School districts have recourse to hiring and retaining unqualified, incompetent, or ineffective employees during their first years on the job, as tenure is generally not granted for 2 or 3 years. Beyond the probationary period, districts wishing to dismiss an employee may need to prove gross insubordination, illegal activity, or gross malpractice due to conditions of union contracts. However, school districts typically conduct employment and criminal background checks and require health examinations, as well as minimum levels of credentialing, to assure a qualified and healthy work force. These front-end efforts help reduce the risk of ineffective or incompetent employees.

Although it may cost the LEA more in the short term to establish an ongoing, system-based work force, studies show that organized workers are more productive and have a lower turnover rate (NEA, 1990). Contractors may cut corners by hiring less credentialed, less experienced, and transient staff at lower wages. For example, staff from several districts in Oregon and Minnesota recently reported proposals to replace credentialed school psychologists with unregulated "psychometrists" at much lower levels of training and salary (Canter & Crandall, 1994a).

Impact of Purchased Services

The short-term and long-term impact of purchased school psychological services versus employee services is not well established empirically. Because each arrangement is different, comparisons cannot be easily made or results generalized. Furthermore, there are very few studies available.

The Georgia Association of School Psychologists conducted a survey of psychologists and special education directors regarding the use of contracted services (Canter & Dryden, 1993). When independent contractors were hired to provide evaluations, this was generally the only service provided. In 78% of the reported cases, the evaluator did not attend placement or eligibility conferences; 54% did not observe the child in the classroom setting. Furthermore, the services were not generally considered adequate—86% of the respondents indicated that there typically were insufficient data to make a placement decision. In many instances, special education directors in Georgia reported that they no longer used independent contractors because of the inadequacies of these services.

Similar surveys in Michigan, where privatization in schools has been a long-standing concern, raised significant questions regarding the quality of contracted evaluations. The evaluations were reportedly of "poor quality, incomplete, and more time-consuming with serious consequences to students and liability to schools" compared to school based services (Russell, 1993, p. 17). One could argue that these districts got exactly what they paid for—narrowly focused evaluations. Too often, school administrators hold the misperception that purchased evaluations are equivalent to the evaluations of school district employees. At least in Georgia and Michigan, some administrators quickly learned that this is not necessarily true.

As illustrated by these two examples, much of the data collected about the impact of purchased school psychological services address assessment services only, as this is the most prevalent contracted service. As one of the following case studies demonstrates, purchased *comprehensive* services, although not necessarily cheaper than district employee services, can overcome most of the shortcomings of independent contracting while sometimes providing a more practical arrangement.

CASE STUDIES: PURCHASED SERVICES FOR SCHOOLS

Four case studies are presented that reflect a wide range of contractual arrangements and their impact on the provision of psychological services in school settings. Two of these cases represent the downside of independent contracting, where services of employees have been supplanted and the quality of services apparently compromised in an effort to save money. The remaining two cases demonstrate approaches to contractual services that reflect current professional standards and that either *supplement* existing services or *establish new service options*.

Replacing Employee Services

In the early 1990s, NASP initiated a task force to address increasing incidents of contracted services replacing some or all of a district's school-based psychological services. In addition to the national surveys of practitioners and state associations noted earlier, the task force provided support and information to district personnel, sometimes successfully. However, situations such as those of Blue Island, Illinois, and Wayzata, Minnesota, discussed below, are becoming more common. Although empirical data have not yet been collected regarding the impact of contracted services in these and other districts, anecdotal information is available and provides some insight about the decision-making process used and the potential outcomes.

Blue Island, Illinois

In the spring of 1993, this blue-collar, suburban Chicago school district faced budget retrenchment with a proposal to eliminate its two school psychologist positions (J. Zilinskas-Arciniegas, personal communication, May 17, 1993). Mandatory services would be purchased via independent contract. A major rationale for this proposal was the assumption that the cost of district psychologists' evaluations was equal to the number of students evaluated in a given year divided by the psychologists' salary for that year. Using this formula, the school board determined that each psychologist's evaluation cost the district approximately $1,000, whereas independent evaluations could be purchased for a mere $250–$375 a piece.

Unfortunately, this calculation was based on the all too common belief that school psychologists *only* test students. Members of the school board did not take other services into account, although a number of other services were indeed provided by the district's two psychologists, including behavioral consultation and participation in multidisciplinary team planning.

The psychologists in Blue Island sought support for preserving school-based services through several resources: they contacted their union, they contacted the Illinois School Psychologists Association, and they contacted NASP. Collective bargaining laws in Illinois did not prevent supplanting union contract employees with independent contractors. Strong letters from both the state and national associations highlighted the cost-effectiveness of comprehensive psychological services and problems associated with privately contracted assessments (Davids, 1993; Durbin, 1993).

Regardless of these efforts, the two positions were eliminated, effective with the 1993–94 school year.

Impact of Privatization. The outcome of contracting in Blue Island has been informally reported (J. Zilinskas-Arciniegas, personal communication, December 1994). The two psychologists found positions in neighboring districts at higher salaries. Blue Island schools purchased assessment services to address mandatory special education eligibility assessments and reevaluations. School staff reported frustration with these new services, as they were no longer receiving consultation about students' academic and behavioral needs, and they reported that the evaluations were not as comprehensive as those provided by district psychologists. Some teachers reported that they were reluctant to refer students because of the lower quality of services. They reported that contractors spent less time with each student and have recommended reclassifying a number of students, leading to more frequent disagreements within building teams and an increase in the number of minority opinions filed. Despite teacher concerns, Blue Island continued the contractual arrangement in 1994–95; neighboring districts have begun consideration of similar arrangements.

Wayzata, Minnesota

In an effort to alleviate budget shortfalls, this suburban district proposed eliminating two of five school psychology positions and contracting for mandatory evaluations in the spring of 1994 (K. Wojkowitz, R. Anderson & P. Struck, personal communication, January 23, 1995). Because of a relatively strong Teacher Tenure Act, Minnesota districts are prohibited from eliminating tenured staff positions and replacing the same services with independent providers; two Wayzata psychologists were relatively new and untenured. Unlike their counterparts in Blue Island, however, the Wayzata psychologists attempted to fight this proposal without any additional support from state or national associations. The outcome was the same—the two positions were eliminated.

Impact of Privatization. Both psychologists who were laid off in Wayzata found employment in other districts. The remaining three district psychologists continued to provide services to their assigned buildings (two to three schools each), and several licensed school psychologists (all with limited or no previous professional experience) were hired to conduct evaluations at the other district schools at a rate of $20 per hour. The district psychologists provide a wide range of consultation and intervention services, as well as eligibility evaluations. These comprehensive services however, are limited to those schools served by a district psychologist. Students and teachers at the other schools have access only to eligibility assessments.

Principals and teachers have expressed frustration with the inequity in the delivery of psychological services across the district. The competence of the providers has not been questioned, but their limited role is regarded as a major drawback despite apparent cost savings. Several other school districts in surrounding communities have implemented or considered similar private contracts.

Purchasing Supplemental Services

Minneapolis

School districts, regardless of size and resources, often need support services that, for various reasons, are not available or sufficient to address a specific need. Such services might include an evaluation of a non-English speaking student or a student with an unusual, low-incidence disability, a consultation from a psychiatrist or neurologist regarding an atypical disorder or medical condition, or services to address a short-term backlog of reevaluations. Where there is a need for services to *supplement* existing services, independent contracts can offer a cost-effective alternative to employing specialized personnel or to risking inadequate services to atypical students.

The Minneapolis Public Schools employ 23 full-time-equivalent school psychologists to serve 44,000 students. Despite a gradual increase in psychology positions, the growing demand for mandated services, particularly special education reevaluations, has created a dilemma in the delivery of quality (and timely) psychological services. Rather than curtail other essential services (such as behavioral consultation and staff training), independent contractors have been hired at peak periods (usually, late fall and late spring) to conduct some of the special education reevaluations.

This model of purchased services has proved effective because it includes appropriately credentialed personnel who (usually) are familiar with the school district, it is task-specific, it limits purchased services to situations requiring little if any follow-up by district employees, it is easily coordinated, and it controls costs.

Personnel. In Minnesota, individuals holding a school psychology license from the state Board of Teaching may be employed by school districts directly or provide services to school districts via independent arrangements, or they may work under supervision at other public and community mental health agencies. The employing school district receives partial salary reimbursement from the state for the school psychologists' services. Clinical psychologists in private practice must hold a license from the Minnesota Board of Psychology and may market their services to school districts through independent contracts. Districts may receive state approval for a lower level of reimbursement for these specific services that address special education needs, such as mental health services.

In Minneapolis, preference is given to licensed *school* psychologists, not only because a greater portion of their cost will be reimbursed but because school psychologists are more familiar with the special education rules and procedures that must be addressed in reevaluations. Furthermore, preference is given to individuals who have previously worked in the Minneapolis schools. Retired staff members and staff members on leave of absence have been recruited and frequently hired to provide reevaluations. Individuals interested in contracting for reevaluations in the Minneapolis schools are screened by the program facilitator and references are sought when needed. Fortunately, during the past few years the district has been able to contract with licensed school psychologists exclusively, most of whom had previous (successful) experience in the district.

Assignments. The program facilitator coordinates assignments for contractors. Staff psychologists screen referrals for reevaluation at their assigned sites. Only formal assessments are assigned to contract personnel. Furthermore, the referral is screened to determine if the student attends school regularly and is likely to establish rapport easily with an unfamiliar adult. Referrals that are likely to involve controversy regarding placement or long-term follow-up are not assigned to nondistrict personnel. Beyond these criteria, referrals are assigned to contract personnel to help address a large workload at specific sites; generally, two or more assessments from the same site are assigned to contract psychologists to increase their efficiency.

The independent contractor is expected to complete the following tasks in a timely manner for each assigned assessment: (1) review relevant records, (2) interview relevant school staff regarding the student's progress and staff concerns, (3) conduct all relevant components of the psychological assessment (which may include interviews with parents), and 4) complete a brief written report that addresses assessment questions. Attendance at team conferences is not required, but relevant information must be provided to the staff psychologist serving the site.

Costs. Several different approaches to paying for contractual services have been attempted. Generally, the district pays independent contractors at an hourly or flat rate per contracted service, such as $500 for a workshop or $5,000 for a set number of days of consultation. In the past, Minneapolis schools paid private psychologists a set amount per day worked or the district's hourly rate of pay for teachers (as set by union contract) for the hours needed to complete an assessment. However, neither of these approaches was satisfactory. Although the amount of money allocated in the department budget for contracted services was fixed, the amount of time needed to complete a given assessment is highly variable and somewhat unpredictable. Professionals also vary considerably in the amount of time needed to write a report. Thus, it was difficult to anticipate how many assessments could be assigned to independent contractors, and the department ran a risk of running over the budget limit.

Using data collected by staff regarding the amount of time spent on assessment activities (Canter, 1991), it was decided to pay independent contractors at the hourly rate of pay for 6 hours of work per assessment, regardless of the actual time spent. At the district's current hourly rate of teacher pay ($18 per hour), this reflects a payment of $108 per assessment. This is far below the charges of community agencies and private practitioners for comparable assessments (which could cost from $300 to $500 or more). However, it has been regarded as a sufficient payment for those contractors using private work as a supplement to retirement or other income. Private contractors have reported that their assessments sometimes take less, sometimes more than 6 hours, but that 6 hours seems to be a fair average for a reevaluation.

Aside from the relatively low cost of these assessments, this method of payment also allows for an entirely accurate prediction of the number of assessments that can be purchased given the year's budget and it allows for concrete recommendations regarding budget needs.

Impact. In any given school year three or four independent contractors may be hired to conduct a total of 30 or more evaluations. During the 1993–94 school year, 75 special education reevaluations were completed by five independent contractors, with another 300 completed by district psychologists. Of the five private practitioners, three were former staff psychologists—one recently retired, one recently resigned to take a part-time position with a local clinic, and one recently resigned to be home with young children. A current part-time staff member was hired through an independent contract to work additional hours, and a recent retiree from a neighboring district was also hired. School personnel frequently reported a high degree of satisfaction with the work of these extra staff members, and no complaints were reported.

The total cost of these purchased services (1993–94) was approximately $8,000 minus state reimbursements (approximately 50%), for a net cost of about $4,000, a little over $50 for a comprehensive psychological reevaluation! Coordination time was limited to approximately 15 minutes per referral. For each assessment a written report was filed promptly, with a minimal amount of follow-up, if any, required by the district psychologist. As a result, staff psychologists began the 1994–95 school year without any backlog of overdue special education reevaluations.

In addition to fulfilling legal obligations regarding due process timelines, these purchased services allowed staff psychologists to spend an estimated 450 additional professional hours serving other district students. Some of these hours were undoubtedly spent complying with other due process activities, such as initial eligibility assessments, but many were allocated to teacher and parent consultation, student counseling, and staff training, services that often get short-changed by assessment demands.

Fortunately, there are many part-time and recently retired school psychologists in the Minneapolis area who seek additional short-term employment. A smaller community would likely have more difficulty finding a similarly credentialed, experienced work force in the private sector.

Rural Tennessee

The provision of comprehensive psychological services to small and rural school districts poses a number of challenges. It can be difficult to attract trained personnel to remote areas or to positions requiring extensive travel; both preservice and in-service training opportunities are often limited in small communities; budgets and enrollment in small districts may not justify hiring full-time support personnel; single professionals find themselves isolated and called on to be experts in all situations. In many states one solution to this dilemma has been the organization of intermediate districts or cooperatives through which individual districts contract for comprehensive services. Established as public agencies to provide special education and other support services, these units employ psychologists, teachers, and others who are allocated to contracting districts to provide whatever services are desired. Rather than hiring a part-time school psychologist to serve a one-school district, the district buys services from the cooperative agency. The agency, in turn, provides the district with appropriate allocations of all contracted services. A psychologist employed by the cooperative, for example, might be assigned to two or more districts and receive all salary and employee benefits directly from the agency.

Intermediate districts and educational cooperatives are public agencies, functioning much like large school districts. Similar arrangements for support services can be made between districts and private agencies, such as community mental health centers. The Cherokee Mental Health Center provides such services in eastern Tennessee (Allen, 1990; 1993). A multiservice agency, Cherokee includes a school psychology division providing contracted services to eight rural school systems and seven Head Start programs. These services do not replace those of district employees but provide services otherwise unavailable or impractical due to the small size of the districts, shortages of credentialed personnel in the area, or need for specialized (early childhood) services.

The Cherokee model succeeds because it offers comprehensive school psychological services; establishes long-term relationships with contracting districts; employs highly qualified, appropriately credentialed school psychologists; provides professional leadership and supervision; offers access to other mental health and medical professionals; and provides "outsider" objectivity while developing "insider" familiarity with systems and staff.

Services. Although specific services vary with each contract, Cherokee's school psychologists provide a wide range of services, including psycho-educational and developmental assessments, classroom observations, teacher and parent consultation, intervention planning and implementation, developmental therapy, counseling, administrative consultation, team-building activities, and mental health consultation to Head Start centers. Because the agency is a comprehensive community center, staff psychologists also have access to the expertise and consultation of clinical psychologists and medical staff, who in turn are available to assist in providing services to the center's contracting districts. In addition, the mental health center has served as an internship site for school psychology trainees. Such a range of services would not likely be feasible for any of the small contracting districts if employing a single individual to address all service needs.

Long-Term Contracts. Cherokee's psychologists are often perceived as insiders despite their external employment due to long-term relationships with schools and districts. Some districts have contracted with Cherokee for many years and have enjoyed the continuity of services delivered by the same individual year after year.

Professional Qualifications and Supervision. Cherokee employs trained, credentialed school psychologists to provide services. All providers hold Tennessee Department of Education school psychology certification, and most hold the credential of the National Certified School Psychologist and Tennessee State Board of Examiners in Psychology as well. In addition, Cherokee's school psychologists are supervised by a doctoral-level school psychologist. Opportunities for ongoing professional training and experience are available through work in other divisions of the mental health center and interaction with the related professionals (clinical psychologists, developmental specialists, medical staff).

Independent Perspective. Although primarily invested in the needs of the children and districts they serve, Cherokee's staff also reflects some of the advantages of outsiders. Cherokee's school psychologists are often perceived by parents, teachers, and administrators as independent, unbiased consultants and mental health experts (Allen, 1993). On the other hand, psychologists employed by school systems may have difficulty gaining credibility because they are regarded as insiders who are subject to the same political and administrative pressures as other district employees.

Exclusive commitment to a school system can interfere with advocacy for children's needs. Independent providers can place children's needs above district priorities, although this may risk renewal of the contract. On at least two occasions, Cherokee has lost contracts because its staff persisted in advocating for children's interests despite pressure from administrators (Allen, 1993).

Impact. The Cherokee Mental Health Center model provides high-quality school psychological services in a manner that is highly efficient, given the parameters of service delivery in rural areas. Part-time and full-time positions in rural districts frequently go unfilled, resulting in piecemeal services that are unlikely to meet accepted professional standards or provide continuity. By organizing multidisciplinary services into one large unit, Cherokee can offer both highly trained staff and a range of specialized services to a number of contracting districts that could not otherwise afford to buy services from a number of individuals. A philosophy of commitment to the districts and communities enables staff from Cherokee to attain the familiarity of insiders without giving up the independence and credibility of outside experts. Furthermore, Cherokee serves the profession of school psychology by maintaining a commitment to professional standards and training of future professionals.

THE FUTURE OF PURCHASED SCHOOL PSYCHOLOGICAL SERVICES

Any attempt to predict the future of purchased psychological services by schools is certainly limited by the unpredictability of reform movements in both health care and education. What is certain is the fiscal crisis facing all levels of government as politicians, professionals, and advocates debate the means to support educational and social services for children and families.

As the responsibility of public schools grew beyond teaching the three R's, so has the clientele of public schools expanded to include infants, toddlers, and young adults; children and families from very diverse cultures and speaking many different languages; and individuals with mild to severe disabilities. Federal legislation that initially funded a wide range of services to the historically underserved has created a clumsy bureaucratic system of spiraling costs and equivocal outcomes. Ironically, mandates that provided the impetus for rapid growth in school-based support services in the 1970s and 1980s also established a seemingly endless loop of reactive gatekeeping practices that thwart proactive services known to produce positive, long-term results. In the 1990s public schools face the dilemma of reducing or eliminating those services that could do the most to enhance "education for all children." Enter into this fray the option of purchased psychological services.

Factors Affecting Trends in Purchased Services

Demone and Gibelman (1989) note that a variety of factors will affect the future of purchased services, including politics, ideology, role delegation, and actual experience. In school psychology, political, ideological, and functional issues are significantly intertwined. Although mental health services have been provided in public schools as far back as the 1920s, many districts had little access to these services until special education mandates created funding in the mid-1970s. The demand for school psychologists increased dramatically, but the roles of these broadly trained professionals consequently narrowed, focusing more on eligibility determination than on the overall instructional and psychological needs of students and systems. The requirements of credentialing bodies and the positions of national organizations clearly suggest that broader roles are desirable. However, the reality of regulations and funding sources continues to limit the roles played by many school psychologists.

As school districts continue to seek short-term solutions to financial problems, limited purchased services (e.g., for mandated assessments) may be appealing alternatives to school-based employees. More comprehensive purchased service options will also appeal to districts in areas with a shortage of credentialed professionals or in those where school-based comprehensive services to individual small districts would be impractical. As such services become more common, state credentialing boards and professional associations will likely work together to establish standards for independent providers that are more consistent with the standards of school-based practice.

However, there already is indication that limited contractual arrangements may have negative, long-term consequences where those services have *replaced* more comprehensive school-based services. Therefore, the actual experience of purchased services may eventually lead to a serious rethinking of funding and service priorities. Changes in standards, such as those proposed by NASP and APA, may lead to a redefinition of "independent contract" and "part-time employee" status.

Changes in legislation, in both education and health care, pose the most significant opportunities and challenges for purchased psychological services in the schools. Proposed changes in federal regulations from the Office of Special Education Programs (OSEP) (NASP-NASDSE-OSEP, 1994; OSEP, 1994) reflect a shift in philosophy—away from categorical models of assessment, instruction, and funding and toward a more preventive and prescriptive role for support personnel, particularly school psychologists. These proposals are perhaps years away from wide-scale implementation but clearly suggest a change in direction that would affect the way school services are funded. If funds were no longer tied to gatekeeping activities, services could readily become more comprehensive and less deliberately fragmented.

Comprehensive Models and Purchased Services

Under more comprehensive service models, what would be the fate of purchased services? As noted above, private or public agencies offering comprehensive services in rural areas might provide practical alternatives to hiring part-time employees. More typical school systems will likely see greater advantages to developing or continuing full-service school-based models. Within those systems, however, there will likely be an increasing need for special consultants and short-term projects offered through independent providers, county agencies, or co-located services. If public schools continue to be responsible for addressing the health and social needs of children and families, they will have to engage in more substantial partnerships with agencies and individuals that can deliver those services—public health care providers, family mental health clinics, and community-based treatment programs.

Changes in the funding of general health care may lead to greater competition among both private and public providers of mental health services, and school districts can expect aggressive solicitation from these providers. Managed health care is limiting client bases for many agencies, hospitals, and independent practitioners; these providers in turn are seeking contracts with school districts for both limited and more extensive services. Some school systems already provide services through collaboration, co-funded grants, and contractual arrangements with managed care systems, which may pay for themselves via third-party reimbursements, including insurance and Medicaid.

The Challenge of Service Integration

The biggest challenge facing both providers and employers will be to establish a system that offers high-quality and appropriate services at reasonable cost. Further, the growing emphasis on service integration challenges school and community professionals to develop more collaborative relationships (Talley, 1995). Given the power of teacher unions and the standards advanced by professional organizations such as NASP, it seems unlikely that comprehensive school psychological services will be readily turned over to independent providers. In addition, there is no evidence that schools and children would benefit from such a change. However, it also seems unlikely that *all* support services for children and families can be adequately managed (or funded) without collaboration across various agencies and providers in the larger community. Although employment of psychologists with training in school organization, educational assessment, and behavioral consultation is essential within public schools, greater access to therapeutic mental health services for children and families is essential within the larger community. Logistically, schools may offer greater access to a greater array of services.

CONCLUSION

Today, purchased services represent a significant threat to comprehensive school-based psychological services in many districts. Under the current climate of retrenchment in public education, the risk of reduction or elimination of school psychology positions and a concomitant increase in privatization of mandated services, particularly assessments, remains high. This risk will likely remain high as long as school psychologists practice within narrow gatekeeping roles—indeed, the profession of school psychology in general would be endangered if its viability was defined by one task (Bardon, 1994). Fortunately, the call to reform education, particularly special education, is increasingly heard beyond the halls of academe and professional associations. Proposals from regulatory and funding agencies suggest that we are moving closer to a restructuring of public schools that will allow children greater access to support services and which will allow professionals greater opportunities to provide comprehensive services.

Within comprehensive service models there should be plenty of room for school-based, co-located, and purchased services working together. Such integrated arrangements would ensure the availability of professionals who understand school systems as well as children's educational and mental health issues, who meet specific standards of training and credentialing, and who effectively collaborate across areas of specialization and organization.

REFERENCES

Allen, W. (1990). Working in a community mental health center provides an entirely different perspective. *Communique, 19,* 16.

Allen, W. (1993). Comprehensive contracted services: Assets to the field of school psychology. *Communique, 22,* 2, 4.

American Psychological Association, Committee on Professional Standards. (1981). *Specialty guidelines for the delivery of services: Clinical, counseling, industrial-organizational, and school psychology.* Washington, DC: Author.

Bardon, J. I. (1994). Will the real school psychologist please stand up: Is the past a prologue for the future of school psychology? The identity of school psychology revisited. *School Psychology Review, 23,* 584–588.

Bergan, J. R., & Kratochwill, T. R. (1990). *Behavioral consultation in applied settings.* New York: Plenum Press.

Canter, A. S. (1991). Effective psychological services for all students: A data-based model of service delivery. In G. Stoner, M. Shinn, & H. Walker (Eds.), *Interventions for achievement and behavioral problems* (pp. 49–78). Silver Spring, MD: National Association of School Psychologists.

Canter, A. S., & Crandall, A. (1994a). Hiring psychometrists: Issues and response guidelines. *Communique, 22,* 2–3.

Canter, A. S., & Crandall, A. (Eds.). (1994b). *Professional advocacy resource manual: Preserving school-based positions* (4th ed.). Silver Spring, MD: National Association of School Psychologists.

Canter, A. S., & Dryden, A. (1993). Contracting out for assessments: The Georgia survey. *Communique, 21,* 9.

Davids, J. (1993, March 3). Letter to the Superintendent, District 130, Blue Island, IL., on behalf of the Illinois School Psychologists Association.

Demone, H. W., & Gibelman, M. (1989). The future of purchase of service. In H. W. Demone & M. Gibelman (Eds.), *Services for sale: Purchasing health and human services* (pp. 399–422). New Brunswick, NJ: Rutgers University Press.

Durbin, K. (1993, March 12). Letter to the Superintendent, District 130, Blue Island, IL., on behalf of the National Association of School Psychologists.

Fagan, T. K. (1985). Cost-effectiveness considerations in the delivery of school psychological services. *Rural Special Education Quarterly, 5,* 8–12.

Fagan, T. K. (1995). Trends in the history of school psychology in the United States. In A. Thomas & J. Grimes (Eds.), *Best practices in school psychology* (Vol. 3, pp. 59–68). Silver Spring, MD: National Association of School Psychologists.

Franklin, M. (1995). Implementing school psychology service delivery programs. In A. Thomas & J. Grimes (Eds.), *Best practices in school psychology* (Vol. 3, pp. 69–80). Silver Spring, MD: National Association of School Psychologists.

Gibelman, M., & Demone, H. W. (1989). The evolving contract state. In

H. W. Demone & M. Gibelman (Eds.), *Services for sale: Purchasing health and human services.* New Brunswick, NJ: Rutgers University Press.

Graden, J. L., Casey, A., & Bonstrom, O. (1985). Implementing a pre-referral intervention system: Part 2. The data. *Exceptional Children, 51,* 487–496.

Harvey, V. S. (1992). Conducting a self-evaluation of school psychological services. *Communique, 21,* 10.

Kelly, C. (1994, May 16). Letter to the Superintendent, Rochester Public Schools, on behalf of the National Association of School Psychologists.

Kruger, L. J., Wandle, C. H., & Watts, R. P. (1992). The recession and downsizing of school psychology in Massachusetts. *Communique, 20,* 23, 26.

McKee, P. W., & Barbe, R. H. (1994). Independent evaluation: Maybe, at the school's expense. *Communique, 23,* 1, 6.

Mars, K., & Canter, A. (1993). State associations address threats to school-based employment. *Communique, 21,* 9–10.

NASP/NASDSE/OSEP. (1994). *Assessment and eligibility in special education: An examination of policy and practice with proposals for change.* Alexandria, VA: National Association of State Directors of Special Education.

National Association of School Psychologists. (1992a). *Guidelines: Contractual services in school psychology.* Silver Spring, MD: Author.

National Association of School Psychologists. (1992b). *Position statement: Advocacy for effective school psychological services.* Silver Spring, MD: Author.

National Association of School Psychologists. (1992c). *Standards for the provision of school psychological services.* Silver Spring, MD: Author.

National Association of School Psychologists. (1993). *Position statement: Employing school psychologists for comprehensive service delivery.* Silver Spring, MD: Author.

National Association of School Psychologists. (1994). *Standards for training and field placement programs in school psychology.* Silver Spring, MD: Author.

National Education Association. (1990). *Contracting out: Strategies for fighting back.* Washington, DC: Author.

Office of Special Education Programs. (1994). *Improving the Individuals with Disabilities Education Act: IDEA reauthorization* (Draft). Washington, DC: Author.

Prus, J., Draper, A., Curtis, M. J., & Hunley, S. (1995). A summary of credentialing requirements for school psychologists in public school settings. In A. Thomas & J. Grimes (Eds.), *Best practices in school psychology* (Vol. 3, pp. 1237–1248). Silver Spring, MD: National Association of

School Psychologists.

Russell, D. (1993). "Contracting" creates concerns for Michigan school psychologists. *Michigan Psych Report, 21*, 1, 17.

Schwartz, J., Mars, K., & Pionek, B. (1995, March). *The influence of contracting on school psychologists.* Poster presentation at the annual convention of the National Association of School Psychologists, Chicago.

Shapiro, E. S. (1988). Preventing academic failure. *School Psychology Review, 17*, 601–613.

Smetanka, M. J. & Hotakainen, R. (1994, December 11). Out of control: The spiraling costs of special education, part 4. *Minneapolis Star Tribune,* pp. 1, 16.

Talley, R. C. (1995). APA policy and advocacy for school psychology practice. In A. Thomas & J. Grimes (Eds.), *Best practices in school psychology* (Vol. 3, pp. 191–203). Silver Spring, MD: National Association of School Psychologists.

Ysseldyke, J. E., & Algozzine, B. (1983). LD or not LD: That's not the question. *Journal of Learning Disabilities, 16*, 29–31.

Zins, J., Conyne, R., & Ponti, C. R. (1988). Primary prevention: Expanding the impact of psychological services in schools. *School Psychology Review, 17*, 542–549.

9

Purchasing Substance Abuse Services: Experience from the Perspective of a Voluntary, Community-Based Agency

Steven Kraft and Margaret Gibelman

This chapter focuses on the development of a public-nonprofit agency partnership to deliver community-based substance abuse services. A case study approach provides insight into how and why agencies enter contractual arrangements, the movement from loosely constructed contracts to more formalized arrangements, and the short- and longer-term impact on the mission and operations of nonprofit agencies. Of particular concern to the social services community is the potential for goal displacement and resource dependence, as evidenced in this case. Finally, the lessons learned from this experience are summarized by looking at the options that might have been pursued by the contracted agency and that might have more directly led to the desired service outcomes and strengthened community delivery capability.

Purchase of services (POS) is now the predominant mechanism for funding social services, substantially overshadowing other revenue sources of nonprofit agencies. The evolution of such arrangements, since the early 1960s, has created opportunities to expand the range of services offered to an enlarged client population. At the same time, these contract relationships, as they have evolved, have resulted in profound changes in the mode of operations and types of services offered by voluntary agencies.

This discussion focuses on the period from 1970 to the present. New York State had received money for substance abuse services from federal block grants to the states. Prior to this period there were far fewer substance abuse services in New York State, and those that did exist were offered largely through public agencies. As a result of the availability of new federal funds, the primary source of funding for community-based substance abuse services in New York in the late 1970s was the Department of Substance Abuse Services, a state agency that, in turn allocated monies to different types of agencies for the purpose of providing related services. Some of the provider agencies were under voluntary auspices; others were public. Not-for-profits took on an expanding and important role in substance abuse prevention, education, and treatment.

This case study of POS in the field of substance abuse focuses on one voluntary agency in a large suburban community outside New York City. One of the authors was a participant-observer in the processes described. This agency is governed by a voluntary board of directors representing the broad community of interests.

TOWARD A COMMUNITY-BASED MODEL

Why did New York State significantly expand its use of contracts as a means to provide substance abuse services? Studies conducted under the auspices of the National Institute for Drug Abuse in the 1960s and early 1970s revealed that participants in outpatient substance abuse programs generally experienced dramatic reductions in drug use, improved employment status, a reduction in criminal behavior, and other positive behavioral outcomes (Tims & Ludford, 1984). Concurrently, federal support for and emphasis on community-based programs grew exponentially in the late 1960s, in part reflecting the movement toward community-based treatment and away from residential care for a variety of social and psychological problems (i.e., mental retardation, mental illness, physical disability).

Substance abuse treatment within a community environment took several forms: short-term residential programs, methadone maintenance combined with rehabilitation counseling, outpatient daytime therapeutic communities, and less structured, nonresidential treatment programs. The multiple services offered by Heaven Place (a fictitious name) stressed drug prevention in its broadest sense, encompassing adolescents and youth at risk for a host of psychosocial problems associated with substance abuse. Hours of business were largely concentrated after-school, evenings, and weekends to accommodate to the needs of younger people.

Support for community substance abuse prevention and treatment programs has waxed and waned with the fluctuating emphasis on treatment versus law enforcement approaches. Congressional funding for the programs of the Alcohol, Drug Abuse, and Mental Health Administration (ADAMHA) of the Department of Health and Human Services has been the main source of support for treatment-focused programs; such support is predicated on the assumed interaction of emotional difficulties, alcoholism, and substance abuse (Karger & Stoesz, 1994).

The Anti-Drug Abuse Act of 1986 (P.L. 99–570) again stimulated community programs, with federal oversight of state plans to expand treatment efforts (Institute of Medicine, 1990). This act established the Office of Substance Abuse Prevention (OSAP) within ADAMHA and emphasized programs and services for youths and families at high risk for substance abuse (Saunders, 1995). The scope of the 1986 Act was expanded in the form of the Anti-Drug Abuse Act of 1988 (P.L. 100–690) and an emergency supplemental appropriation in 1989 for treatment and prevention that increased funding while at the same time requiring states to spend the funds for specific populations (U.S. Bureau of Justice Statistics, 1992).

In 1990 the Office of Treatment Improvement was established, with the charge of distributing basic substance-abuse block grants and planing and implementing new treatment approaches (Saunders, 1995). More recently (1992), Congress consolidated training, demonstration and service programs into a newly created Substance Abuse and Mental Health Services Administration, with separate centers for treatment, prevention, and mental health services within the National Institutes of Health, U.S. Public Health Service.

Treatment for substance abuse has traditionally been offered through a mix of public and private programs, with increasing latitude to the states to design their own delivery systems. The public sector has primarily focused on inpatient programs, although these are often administered through not-for-profit organizations. Clients, excluding those who enter treatment through the criminal justice system, often qualify for treatment on the basis of some form of means test. The focus of the private, non-state-supported sector has been on hospital-based and outpatient programs that tend to serve those with private health insurance, and who represent the middle and upper class (Institute of Medicine, 1990; Saunders, 1995).

The boundaries between the services offered and the characteristics of the clients served by public and private agencies have blurred with the wide-scale use of POS arrangements. In these arrangements, the public

agency purchases substance abuse treatment services for a client population it designates. Thus, private agencies, often the recipient of government contracts, have enlarged the scope of their client population.
Adjustments in service orientation may also be required as part of the contract, as will be discussed below.

It is important to note, however, that outpatient programs, exclusive
of those providing methadone treatment, encompass a large variety of
types. Variations include programs that emphasize one-to-one counseling
focused on emotional, spiritual, or practical issues, programs involving
daily, multiple, or weekly individual or group sessions that may focus on
emotional, spiritual, or practical uses, but including 12-step self-help, medical, or psychiatric components, or a combination thereof (Gerstein et
al., 1994; Smythe, 1995).

THE AGENCY

The agency under discussion, which for these purposes is entitled Heaven
Place, began as a grass-roots community organization in the 1960s. Its primary focus during its early years was on prevention services, and its programs were largely administered and implemented by nonprofessional
community residents. This high level of community involvement is considered the key to success in the delivery of prevention services. The model
also emphasizes the use of community residents in the actual delivery of
services (Saunders, 1995).

Heaven Place prevention efforts initially focused on the provision of
information and education but evolved into a more comprehensive
approach in which substance abuse is viewed as one of many risk factors
for individuals and families. Therefore, the prevention effort considers
the totality of individual circumstances, including risk of family violence,
criminal activity, school problems, suicide, and family breakdown
(Saunders, 1995).

Prior to its involvement in contracting, there was no secure or singular source of funds for this grass-roots agency. Board members initiated
efforts within the community, such as raffles, pancake breakfasts, and
other such events, to raise funds. There was also a membership composed
not of service recipients but of community resident supporters. In addition, the majority of services were provided by nonprofessional volunteers.
These volunteers led confrontation and educational groups and conducted
informal one-to-one counseling.

The Agency Enters a Service Agreement

The state substance abuse agency, seeking to deliver its services through community-based agencies, began its contracting process by identifying those agencies already providing substance abuse services or that had a demonstrated interest in extending their services into that area. Between 30 and 40 community-based agencies in one suburban county were provided contracts. Some of these agencies were approached by the state. The agency under discussion was one of those receiving the earliest contracts from the state. The initiative, in this case, came from the state, which had become aware that this relatively small agency, which encompassed one large school district and several towns and villages, had developed a committee (the precursor of the formal agency), the Committee Against Narcotics. This committee had, on its own, initiated community meetings to bring attention to the issue of substance abuse and to involve the community in building strategies to address the problem. In addition, the committee itself got into the business of direct service by sponsoring confrontation groups, conducted by lay people who had some exposure to this type of service provision.

It was the board of directors that acted to respond to the new stream of contract funds available through the county Drug Commission, which was an independent, not-for-profit intermediary between the state funding agency and community agencies. The Drug Commission actively solicited community groups with which they might contract. Since Heaven Place was already involved in substance abuse services, it was among the agencies approached in the late 1960s. The board responded affirmatively.

The original contract provided sufficient funding to hire one half-time professional (without specification of the person's credentials) and pay some operating expenses. With approximately $30,000 in initial contract funds, a part-time director was thus hired. This was the first paid staff. The agency continued to offer the same types of services it had prior to contracting, only this time with public subsidy.

The original conceptual base on which the agency operated was substance prevention and referral. Thus, the emphasis on community education and client education through education groups and confrontational encounter groups focused on the dangers of substance abuse. Such services, from the start, included a drop-in center, encounter-type groups, and provision of community information and public education.

During its precontract years of operation, the agency was not very favorably received within the community, and there was resistance to its presence. With the expansion of services and greater community outreach available through contract funds, the agency came to be better known— with mixed results. One of the objections to the agency voiced by the professional community was Heaven Place's use of lay volunteers as service providers.

In response to community concerns, the board established two advisory boards. One was a professional advisory board and the other a community advisory board. The latter consisted of leaders in the community, including clergy, the superintendent of schools, local elected officials, and PTA officials. The professional advisory board consisted of psychiatrists, physicians, social workers, psychologists, and nurses. The purpose of these two boards was to advise the board of directors about the creation of agency policy and to establish a vision for its future based on community need and input.

The professional advisory board strongly recommended the hiring and use of professional staff. The agency's board, in response, requested from the Drug Commission additional funds to hire a professional staff person. The money was granted. The professional advisory board was involved in the hiring of the staff. The initial focus of the new full-time director, who held an MSW degree, was to engage in public education and outreach. The result was a huge growth in membership and in community interest and by the second year, a significant increase in contract funds, which allowed for the hiring of two more full-time professional staff.

Thus, until the time that Heaven Place received its first contract, it was a volunteer-run, grass-roots effort. Within a year and with heightened visibility, contract funds were used to professionalize and to legitimize its place within the community.

Toward Greater Public Control

During the first several years of contracting, the provisions of the contract were extremely broad, allowing the highest level of discretion to Heaven Place. The accountability for the delivery of these services was minimal; the agency was asked by the funding source only to keep a count of the number of people who came through the door and to submit a monthly report regarding the nature and extent of the services delivered. Clinical records were not required, nor were there specified expectations about the nature of service, beyond a prevention focus (which could mean almost anything).

There were two developments that emerged to change the service approach of Heaven Place and its relationship to its funding agency: one internal to the agency and one external. The external development concerned a movement from the nonprofit county Drug Commission as the conduit agency for funding to creation of a county department, the Department of Drug and Alcohol Abuse, to provide comprehensive planning and ensure services county-wide on a fiscal and service compliance basis. The creation of this department superseded the functions heretofore performed by the independent county commission; the latter was dissolved.

Initially, the agency reflected some of the key advantages of a contracted provider in that it had tailored its services to the needs of the community, and the level of community commitment and the availability of community resources allowed it to offer services to more than double the capacity required under the terms of its contract. As a result, the agency was able to maintain its commitment to delivering services to large numbers of non-substance abusers. In addition, the agency was able to offer a variety of recreational services to adolescents in the community, which served the dual purposes of reaching out to potential clients, as well as complementing the more clinical services offered.

However, when the new public agency assumed the oversight responsibility, the fundamental nature of the contract was changed from prevention to treatment. The public agency viewed treatment as the main functional purpose of the community agencies, whereas Heaven Place saw its function as that of prevention, including overall health promotion for the community. The agency's concept encouraged a comprehensive approach, in which services were delivered to all families and adolescents needing them and in which any dysfunction was seen as a possible precursor to substance abuse.

Similarly, during the early years of contracting, the agency's client population consisted primarily of adolescents and youth and their parents. Most of the adolescents were substance abusers, but a significant proportion, perhaps as many as 40%, were considered at risk. The funding agency began to exert pressure on Heaven Place to modify its target population, foremost by including adults as primary clients. The county also expected the agency to exclusively treat people with manifest and documented substance abuse problems. The at-risk cohort was to be excluded.

In addition, a unit of service accountability rate was instituted, and only treatment-oriented service were reimbursable. Thus, many of the outreach, street work, recreational, and other prevention efforts of Heaven

Place were no longer considered fundable programs. However, by this time the agency was raising higher levels of independent community funds through donations. The prevention efforts were not discontinued; rather, the funding of these efforts was no longer public.

The agency was now required to document, in clinical records, the course of and progress in treatment of each client served. A more and more rigorous oversight system was gradually introduced, including forms developed by the public agency for completion by the Heaven Place staff. Their bureaucratic processes came to be imposed on the contracted agency.

At the same time, the agency was expanding its community support and adding professionals to its list of board members. The agency saw a need to professionalize its services, the first step toward which was the hiring of an executive director. The expectation was that the executive director would recruit and train a professional staff. The agency's professional advisory board, composed of people in related professions (psychologists, psychiatrists, social workers), expanded its functions to represent the board in regard to holding the executive director accountable for the quality of professional services. These developments were complementary—leading the agency away from a loosely structured volunteer group to a more formalized professional agency. This direction was in line with the wishes of the board and the focus of the county department, which sought increasingly more sophisticated services.

Thus, during the early years of contracting, the funding source changed from a not-for-profit group acting as a conduit of contract funds to county government assumption of the bidding, negotiating, contracting awarding, and oversight responsibility. There were continuous problems with cash flow in both the earlier and later structural arrangements. Each year, the agency submitted a contract renewal proposal to maintain and expand its services, and each year the agency was approved for an increased budget. After approval a formal contract was issued that included a line-item budget, service specifications of increasing detail over the years (what was to be delivered to whom and in what quantity), and the form of monthly financial and service reports. (Quality measures were notably absent; such emphasis on outcomes of service and quality of service were to become a feature of contracts in the 1990s.)

The agency was given an advance of 25% of the entire contract amount, which at its highest point reached $200,000 per year, constituting approximately 50% of total revenues. The procedure for funding was the submission of monthly claim forms by the agency and reimbursement of those claims by the conduit agency. However, there were several crisis points in the process. Each new year's contract signing was generally late so that in the beginning of each fiscal year the agency was operating without its contractual funds. Claims were often not paid on time, and therefore periods of financial crisis were not unusual. However, because of the significant community support for this agency, including direct financial contributions, it was always able to pay its bills. Board members either enhanced their community fund-raising or loaned the agency money to continue operations and were repaid when the county paid its bills. Typically, the public agency was 3 months behind in the payment of its bills. On a few occasions, the payment of bills required that the agency borrow money, often from the personal pockets of members of the board of directors.

The county, in the first several years of the contractual arrangement, paid for about 25% of the total service funds of the agency. The proportion of contracted funds to total revenues continued to increase. Raising other sources of funds for support of agency programs was downplayed; the new "first money" policy was a disincentive to procurement of additional revenues (see discussion below).

The County Calls the Shots

As noted earlier, during the 1970s and after the county took over, it began to define the nature of the services for which it would pay. For example, it defined what constituted eligibility for substance abuse services, what constituted substance abuse itself, what was treatment, and what was prevention. Community needs came to be less an issue—surely to the funding agency and in some respects even within the board—and the wishes of the funding agency became dominant. New regulations also extended, not surprisingly, to fiscal oversight, with both paperwork requirements for Heaven Place and questioning of expenses. Nevertheless, the amount of contract funds continued to rise, augmented by new contracts from federal sources such as the Comprehensive Employment and Training Act of 1973 (P.L. 93–203, 87 State, 839.) (CETA) (the latter only tangentially related to substance abuse).

Thus, contract funds from other sources led to an expansion of the types of services offered by the agency, some completely out of the realm of substance abuse. The board justified taking on new functions, citing its overall concern with the well being of the community.

Growing Restrictions

During the Reagan administration, federal funds for substance abuse services were threatened. New York State acted in response to budget cuts of 25% and offered fewer dollars for contracts, as contracted services were easier to curtail quickly than publicly provided services (Gibelman & Demone, 1989). This approach was neither unusual nor unexpected, given the sociopolitical climate of the era. The block grant approach instituted in 1981 provided states with the flexibility to tailor programs as they saw fit. Cuts in programs in response to diminished federal funding was likewise a state issue.

The county, acting under state guidance, also sought to develop new fiscal contract policies. For example, the county, with the approval of the state, developed a policy known as "first money." This policy created the expectation that all money raised by the contracted agency was to be considered part of its substance abuse budget and to be used first, before contract funds. Thus, the more money the agency raised independently, the less it would receive under the contract. Heaven Place had little recourse, as the contract terms had become largely a unilateral decision.

This new policy was, in fact, formalized in the contract's boilerplate. Heaven Place had to request and receive authorization to "roll over" its surplus funds, with the public agency maintaining that this permission was at its discretion. At the same time, the funding agency was not increasing funds commensurate with the number of units of services being provided. This was rationalized on the basis of the agency's positive bottom line. The agency's executive director urged that the board test the legality of these regulations in court, but the board decided on a more conciliatory course. Basically, the stance of the board was to avoid making waves as long as the county agency actually did not reduce funds.

This conflict reached an important turning point when the conduit agency began communicating its expectation that the agency charge a fee for service. The agency resisted the change for several years, with the county threatening to withhold funds and terminate the contract. The agency finally capitulated.

Following the institution of a fee-for-service policy, the nature of the service and the demographics of the clients served changed dramatically. Services to adolescents gradually diminished and were partially replaced by services to young adults, many of whom were referred from the criminal justice system. Thus, instead of serving voluntary community youth, the agency began serving primarily mandated young adults. Recreational services disappeared, and individual therapy replaced group work as the primary modality.

The agency began to have trouble maintaining its contractual service capacity because the vehicles of outreach by streetworkers and recreation disappeared. Conflict developed on the board of directors as to the desirability of these direction changes. Although the board was aware of the impact of the changes it endorsed, it reluctantly opted in favor of following the flow of dollars and the corresponding restrictions about the use of such funds. Now clients are mandated, focus is on clinical intervention and one-to-one rather than group intervention, few adolescents are served, responsiveness to the community has diminished, and fees for service are required. Fees for service and contract funds are the primary sources of agency funding, with a substantially decreased role for the advisory board, less fund-raising, and less community outreach.

Today the agency is a small outpatient substance abuse clinic providing primarily individual treatment to a mandated population and is consistently performing below its units-of-service capacity. All of the original benefits to the agency from POS arrangements (expansion of services; variety of service offerings; use of trained volunteers, community legitimation) have been lost or diminished, except for location of the services within the geographic community. Now that the agency serves primarily adults, even the geographical benefit is somewhat lost, as many adults are reluctant to access substance abuse services in their own communities for fear of being recognized. The use of local resources in volunteer time and money has been reduced to a small proportion of the agency's budget, compared to its previous level of more than half. The community's power to determine the nature of services needed and the means of implementation have also, not surprisingly, been lost.

LESSONS

Purchase of services should encourage local community involvement rather than negate it. Contracts should be used for capacity building, rather than supplanting what the agency is able to do and has been doing. Self-sufficiency should be a goal, depending, of course, on the demographics of the community and its ability to attain self-sufficiency realistically. Instead, resource dependency is the result.

Growth is enticing. The availability of more money and the possibility of program expansion proved irresistible. And why not? During the initial years the strings attached to the contracts were nonapparent and/or nonobtrusive. However, this seductive relationship soon evolved into one less favorable from the contracted agency's point of view, with both short- and longer-term effects.

The power of the purse has been so great that many nonprofit agencies have begun to resemble quasi-public agencies. For example, in this case study the community agency had to meet increasingly detailed reporting requirements as well as respond to shifts in service priorities. The demographics of the clients served changed dramatically. Services to adolescents gradually diminished and were partially replaced by services to young adults, many of whom were referred from the criminal justice system. The public agency was also able to entice the community agency to institute fee-for-service arrangements, in opposition to long-standing policy to the contrary, and to shift away from a prevention orientation.

The failure of the public agency to pay its bills promptly affected the financial stability of the nonprofit agency, particularly as an increasing proportion of its revenues came from government contracts. And perhaps more important, the community's power to determine the nature of services needed and the means of implementation have also been lost.

This case is not unique. It is important, however, to aggregate information on the impact of such contractual arrangements on the service-rendering capability of nonprofit agencies. In an era in which we anticipate substantial decreases in public social services resources, the potential impact on the contracted voluntary sector will be profound.

REFERENCES

Gerstein, D. R., Johnson, R. A., Harwood, H. H., Fountain, D., Suter, N., & Malloy, K. (1994). *Evaluating recovery services: The California Drug and Alcohol Treatment Assessment: General report.* Chicago: National Opinion Research Center.

Gibelman, M., & Demone, H. W., Jr. (1989). The evolving contract state. In H. W. Demone, Jr., & M. Gibelman (Eds.), *Services for sale: Purchasing health and human services* (pp. 17–57). New Brunswick, NJ: Rutgers University Press.

Institute of Medicine. (1990). *Treating drug problems* (Vol. 1). Washington, DC: National Academy Press.

Karger, H. J., & Stoesz, D. (1994). *American social welfare policy: A pluralistic approach.* New York: Longman.

Saunders, D. N. (1995). Substance abuse: Federal, state, and local policies. In R. L. Edwards (Ed.-in-chief), *Encyclopedia of social work* (19th ed., pp. 2338–2347). Washington, DC: NASW Press.

Smythe, N. J. (1995). Substance abuse: Direct practice. In R. L. Edwards (Ed.-in-chief), *Encyclopedia of social work* (19th ed., pp. 2328–2338). Washington, DC: NASW Press.

Tims, F. M., & Ludford, J. (1984). *Drug abuse treatment evaluation: Strategies, progress, and prospects* (National Institute on Drug Abuse Research Monograph No. 51). Washington, DC: U.S. Government Printing Office.

U.S. Bureau of Justice Statistics. (1992). *Drugs, crime and justice systems: A national report from the Bureau of Justice Statistics*. Washington, DC: Author.

10

Homemaker and Home Health Aide Services in Veteran Affairs: Purchase of Care in a Federal System

Harriet Davidson, Elaine Hickey, Lois Camberg, Margaret B. Davidson, Donald C. Kern, and James R. Kelly

Two converging trends in recent years have led to the development of the Veterans Affairs (VA) Homemaker/Home Health Aide (H/HHA) service and the form it has taken. First is the great expansion of demand for home care services nationally (Ory & Duncker, 1992), and second, the growing popularity of public purchase of care from the private sector (Smith & Lipsky, 1994). This case study examines the implementation of the H/HHA service, a federal program to deliver home care services to eligible veterans by purchasing care through local agencies.

BACKGROUND

Expanding the Demand for Home Care

The increase in demand for services provided in the home has been driven by several factors. Prominent among them is the fact that the elderly

*This chapter is based on research commissioned by the Office of Geriatrics and Extended Care through the Management Decision and Research Center, Veterans Health Administration.

population has been growing steadily, and their health care needs are expanding as well. In 1992, Medicare provided health insurance for more than 34 million elderly at a cost of $120 billion. Because the elderly are large consumers of home care (although younger disabled patients are accounting for a steadily increasing percentage of clients), home care services are expanding to meet the demand that accompanies the aging of the population.

Another factor that has spurred the growth of home care is the continued reduction in average length of hospital stays that has occurred over the past decade. Driven largely by changes in health care financing and reimbursement and by efforts to contain costs, this decrease in days spent in the hospital means that much convalescence occurs in an outpatient setting. For the elderly in particular, who often live alone, this creates a need for services and assistance in the home.

A third factor that has contributed to the expansion of home care is the fact that technological advances have made it easier for more care to be given outside the hospital. For example, new equipment and changes in treatment philosophy have allowed such regimens as chemotherapy and administration of oxygen to be given on an ambulatory basis. Conversely, low-tech home care services are expanding because of the realization that much unskilled or personal care is appropriately given in the home.

It has been estimated that over 7 million older Americans are dependent on others for assistance with activities of daily living, such as feeding, dressing, toileting, and mobility tasks (Pepper Commission, 1990; Scanlon, 1988). Many patients who were previously thought to need institutionalization because of these limitations can be maintained with minimal services in their own homes.

An additional reason for the growing popularity of home care is that it is thought to be a substitute for at least a portion of inpatient long-term care. Although research findings are not conclusive, in-home care is likely to substitute for some acute hospital days (Hughes et al., 1992) and may also substitute for nursing home care for a small subgroup of patients (Kane & Kane, 1987), but the extent to which it is truly a substitute for inpatient services has yet to be determined. Still, it is likely that for many patients, if it is not a direct alternative, in-home care does provide a bridge between an institutional setting and complete independence in the community.

Another related reason for the growth of in-home care is the persistent belief that it is a less expensive alternative to institutionalization. However, there is no empirical basis for this conclusion, and some researchers have demonstrated that it can in fact be more costly than certain types of inpatient care (Kemper, 1988; Weissert, 1988).

Finally, and perhaps most important, the growing demand for home care is fueled by the fact that it is overwhelmingly preferred by patients. Because it is seen as deferring the need for nursing home care and is a less drastic alternative, both patients and their families want home care services.

Purchasing In-Home Care

The second trend that has helped to shape the VA's H/HHA program is the growing popularity of POS in the United States (Demone & Gibelman, 1989; Dorwart, Schlesinger, & Pulice, 1986; Davidson et al., 1989) and the use of purchased long-term care services by the VA in particular (Camberg, Knight, & Grinffin, 1990). Purchase of services has long been considered to have many advantages. It is generally thought to be a cheaper alternative to governmental provision of care, to increase competition and thereby encourage quality, and to allow for flexibility in the provision of services.

The increase in flexibility is particularly important for VA, a national system with mandates to serve veterans in all regions of the country, in both urban and rural areas. Purchasing care, as opposed to providing it from a VA facility, means that the system does not have to develop its own expertise, staff, and administration in different areas. Without building or expanding permanent facilities, POS mechanisms allow VA to use as many services as needed for any period of time, to distribute them geographically to meet local demand, and to cut back easily when the need subsides.

Although the advantages are extremely important, there are potential disadvantages in purchasing care from the private sector. Private agencies, especially those that are widely dispersed, may not be as easily regulated or monitored as a VA service under centralized control. It may be harder to access certain services in the community than at a VA center at any given time, because they are either expensive or take time to establish. Further, in the periods when demand is high in the private sector, it may be difficult for VA to locate a sufficient number of providers. Agencies may not be available when needed.

HISTORY OF CONTRACTING FOR LONG-TERM CARE IN VA

The Department of Veteran Affairs has a 30-year history of contracting for health care services from community providers, particularly for long-term care. The oldest POS program providing long-term care in VA is the community nursing home (CNH) program, which has been operating since 1965. Although VA provides extended care internally through its own 131 nursing home care units, adult day health care programs, inpatient respite programs, and hospital-based home care services, each of the 172 hospitals in the Veterans Health Administration (VHA) system refers eligible patients to community nursing homes that are under contract to VA. Through these contracts the VHA is able to provide unlimited care to veterans who require it for a defined service-connected disability and up to 6 months for eligible veterans who do not have service-connected disability status.

The purchase of nursing home services in VA was initiated because of the realization that patients were being inappropriately cared for in hospital beds at a higher cost than necessary. Veteran Affairs administrators recognized that there may be an increased need for nursing home beds for a relatively short period, depending on many factors, including the future rate of military conflict. Purchasing nursing home care from the community provided the necessary flexibility, allowing the supply to expand and diminish with the demand. Further, the POS mechanism allowed the nursing home placement of elderly veterans in different regions of the country close to their homes and families without new construction, thereby saving substantial capital expenditures.

It is important to note that although the CNH purchase mechanism is generally referred to as a contract it is not a true contract, but rather a purchase agreement. An agreement is negotiated and signed, and the rate is set for the life of the agreement, but no specific amount of purchase is guaranteed. If the facility needs a bed for a patient and the home has a bed available, VA can purchase it under the prearranged terms. This mechanism allows VA to buy the service at the desired rate and allows the nursing home to avoid the constraints of a formal VA contract and the obligation to accept all patients.

As the CNH program enters its fourth decade, it is clear that there has been substantial variation in its size, scope, and success across the country (Weaver, Guihavi, Conrad, Maoheim, & Hughes, 1995). During the 6-year period between 1988 and 1993, the average number of veterans placed under contract in CNH facilities by each medical center decreased from 183 to 129. Much of this decline was due to the fact that budget allocations became discretionary at the local level for 1 year (1989) and the CNH program sustained cuts. As of this writing, the average VA medical center has contracts with 20 different nursing homes, and agreements cover an average of two states.*

In the most recent survey (Weaver et al., 1995), VA hospitals reported that, on average, they were able to place all but 4% of veterans who were appropriately awaiting nursing home placement. A small number of sites, however, could not find beds for up to one-quarter of CNH-eligible veterans, largely patients who were ventilator-dependent, who were combative/assertive, or who had a contagious disease.

HISTORY OF THE HOMEMAKER/HOME HEALTH AIDE PROGRAM IN VA

Although the nursing home program has been serving elderly and disabled veterans for 30 years, until June 1993, H/HHA services were not available to them through VA. The VHA had a long-standing interest in providing home-based services as well as inpatient extended care, but it had neither the authority nor the finances to do so. In 1990, however, Congress passed a law that gave the VHA the authority to conduct a "pilot program to furnish medical, rehabilitative and health-related services in non-institutional settings" to eligible veterans; and in 1993 it gave the VHA authority to use a portion of existing CNH funds to purchase the services to "obviate or forestall nursing home care" (VA Directive 10-95-018). The VHA determined that this pilot program would consist of H/HHA services, such as assisting the client with bathing, toileting, dressing, preparing meals, taking medication, and using medical equipment and that these services would be purchased from vendors in the community and coordinated by facility-level VHA staff.

Although the authority for the pilot program was extended for an additional year and eligibility requirements were relaxed, the authority of Congress formally ended on September 30, 1995. As of this writing, the program is still functioning but on an interim basis and is awaiting renewal.

CONTRACTUAL RELATIONSHIPS IN H/HHA PROGRAM

On March 4, 1993, the directive defining the specific characteristics of the home care program was issued by the VA central office. The directive

---

* Only two facilities currently have no CNH contracts; the maximum number of contracts at any one facility is 73.

offered all interested VA medical centers the opportunity to apply to participate in the program. Applicants agreed to meet specific funding, management, and patient selection requirements and to be part of an evaluation of the pilot, as mandated by Congress.

The program directive specified that medical centers could use up to 15% of their existing CNH budgets to purchase home health services, as long as the per patient cost did not exceed 65% of the average CNH per diem rate. The directive also provided broad guidelines for the structure and management of the program, the selection of community health agencies, and the monitoring of quality. The greatest management restrictions were that the H/HHA program be integrated with existing community care services and that no additional staff be allocated for the management of the program.

More specific criteria were given for the selection of patients to receive services. For a veteran to be eligible for H/HHA services, an interdisciplinary team must make the clinical judgment that the veteran would otherwise require nursing home placement. In addition, the veteran must meet at least two of the following eligibility requirements: residence in a nursing facility; dependence in one or more activity of daily living (ADL) tasks (such as eating, dressing, bathing, toileting); dependence in three or more independent activity of daily living (IADL) tasks (such as shopping, meal preparation, medication management, and transportation); age of 75 years or older; history of high utilization of hospital and outpatient services; clinical depression; living alone status; or significant cognitive impairment (particularly behavioral problems). The original (1990) legislation mandated that eligible veterans have a service-connected disability rated at 50% or higher. Legislation enacted in 1994 changed this requirement to allow participation by all veterans who met the other eligibility requirements.

Overall management of the program, as well as guidance for its implementation, was handled by the VA Central Office of Geriatrics and Extended Care in Washington, DC. However, within the set parameters, individual facilities were permitted a great deal of latitude so that they may implement and manage the program to best meet the needs of their local veteran population.

The flexibility that was allowed at the local level was evident in the wide variety of processes used to purchase H/HHA services from local agencies. Most local staff chose to purchase care on a per case basis and did not have written agreements with agencies prior to ordering services. The absence of a formal contract or agreement between the VA facility and the agency had the advantage of allowing VA to tailor the service to the specific veteran, and the patient could be part of the process.

At the same time, however, the informal nature of the arrangements allowed for potential misunderstandings that might have been avoided had the local guidelines been more clearly articulated. In the instances where VA staff did establish written agreements prior to ordering agency services, problems were less likely to occur. Agreements that included hourly rates, descriptions of the number and types of services to be provided, a time frame for reassessing client need, procedures for increasing or adding to service packages, and some kind of quality control mechanism were seen as helpful in clarifying relationships by the facility staffs that had them.

Identifying agencies in the local service area was always an informal process, as long as the agencies met basic certification, training, and continuing education requirements. The choice was limited by the geographic area in which the veteran lived, and attempts were made to maintain continuity of care if the veteran had previously received services from a specific agency. Other than that, facility staffs reported that they relied mainly on networks of colleagues in the private sector and/or professional reputations to identify area agencies.

A final aspect of the purchase arrangements for this program at the local level was the fact that prices were not negotiated in advance. The overall restriction that the price had to be less than 65% of the per diem rate for community nursing homes set the maximum that could be spent on services, and local staff reported that there was generally little variation in rates for service within specific geographic areas anyway. As a rule, clinical personnel ordered services, and as long as they could be provided by a local agency within the fiscal limits, competitive bidding did not occur.

Description of Clients Served

A majority of VA medical centers took advantage of the opportunity to participate in the pilot program. As of December 1994, 119 VA centers had applied for and received approval to institute H/HHA services (Kern, Hickey, Davidson, & Davidson, 1995). Those that did participate were dispersed throughout the continental United States and Puerto Rico, and facilities varied in size, type, academic affiliation, and presence or absence of an on-site nursing home.

There was wide variation, too, in how rapidly and extensively the facilities implemented the program. Many administrators expressed concern about the ultimate cost, ongoing availability of funding once the pilot phase ended, and demand for services and thus limited the number of veterans they enrolled. From the first enrollment on April 1, 1993, through December 31, 1994, a total of 3,061 veterans received H/HHA services. The average number of veterans enrolled per facility was 10, with as many as 34 at a single VA center. From the beginning, the program served a wide variety of patients. Although the average age of clients was 67, they ranged from 23 to 100 years old. As reflects the growing number of disabled younger persons in home care (Gould & Haslanger, 1993), one-quarter of all enrolled veterans were below the age of 60. Approximately 7% of those receiving services were women, roughly the same as the proportion of women in the general veteran population.

All veterans who received H/HHA services during the pilot program time frame met established eligibility requirements. The most common reason for eligibility was dependence in two or more ADLs, noted in 70% of enrolled veterans.* Many who received H/HHA services also had major disabilities. Fifty-three percent required a wheelchair, one of four used a walker, and an equal number were paralyzed. In addition, a significant number of veterans were cognitively impaired. Only one of three was classified as fully independent in cognitive skills for daily decision making. Further, the population of veterans enrolled in the homemaker program had very limited social supports. Almost a third had no one in their home, and another 10% had someone in the home who was unable to help. On average, veterans received one homemaker visit per week, averaging 4 hours, and two home health aide visits, averaging 7 hours.

Although all of the facilities complied with the mandated eligibility requirements, within these criteria there were significant facility-level differences in the types of veterans who received services. For example, VA facilities with a strong long-term care or geriatric focus most often prioritized patients with debilitating chronic disease, advanced age, or functional deficits. Facilities that focused more on acute care stated that they found the program most useful for veterans recently discharged following an acute illness or surgery, who would otherwise require short-term nursing home placement for recuperation. At least one psychiatric facil-

---

* Assistance with bathing was required by 78% of enrolled veterans. 70% needed help with personal hygiene, and 68% required help in dressing. Housekeeping was the most commonly requested homemaker service (81%), and assistance with bathing was the most common home health aide procedure requested (82%).

ity used the program mostly for veterans with chronic mental illness, patients who are particularly difficult to place in nursing homes but who could remain in the community if they had adequate support. The program was also used to provide hospice care, especially for veterans in the final stages of AIDS. Both administrators and clinicians felt that the flexibility to use the program to meet the specific needs of their patient population was essential to its success.

IMPLEMENTATION AND EFFECTIVENESS

As can be surmised from the above discussion, the H/HHA program addressed what was perceived as a tremendous unmet need in the elderly veteran population and appears to be serving many clients who might not otherwise have received care. But how is it working on a day-to-day basis?

In examining the implementation of the program, two dimensions are particularly important. The first addresses the question of how the H/HHA program is meeting the goals of patient care. How well is the elderly, frail, and disabled veteran being served by the program? The second dimension concerns POS as a mechanism for delivering this service to this population. Does the implementation indicate that purchasing private H/HHA services by VA is an efficient and appropriate method of delivering care?

Measuring Patient Care in an Evaluation

It is generally accepted that there are three important parameters by which to assess effective implementation of a health care program overall and home care services in particular: quality of care provided, access for the identified populations, and costs of the program. Although these parameters are difficult to define and even harder to measure, public agencies have an obligation to set up mechanisms to address them in order to understand the degree to which a program is effective.

When the H/HHA pilot program was established by Congress, a concurrent evaluation was built into it. This evaluation was designed, within the limits of the program*, to address questions of quality of care by exam-

---

* Because of the way the pilot program was structured, it was not possible to obtain a control group of veterans who were not in home care or who

ining patient satisfaction and quality of life, access to care by assessing the scope of services and profiles of patients served, and costs by determining whether the original funding mandates were met. Although an evaluation of this sort cannot give definitive answers, data collected do provide some information about how the program, as implemented, is meeting its goals.

Quality of Life and Patient Satisfaction

As part of the evaluation, a sample of 637 veterans completed a questionnaire at entry into the program and again approximately 6 months later. The questionnaire asked their perception of their physical and mental health status, satisfaction with care, and social support. Analysis of data indicate that, overall, the frail and elderly veterans in the H/HHA program perceived a change for the better during the 6-month period. The proportion who thought their general health was fair, good, or excellent (as opposed to poor) went from 51% at entry to 60% after six months of H/HHA service. The percentage who stated that they left their house or apartment more than once a week rose from 40 at entry to 49 after 6 months in the H/HHA program. At the start of the program, over 62% reported that their health interfered with social activities with friends, relatives, or family; after 6 months this declined to 51%.

The evaluation indicated that there had been an improvement in the clients' self-reported mental health, too. Five questions relating to the extent to which they saw themselves as nervous, downhearted, blue, and the like were asked at the beginning and again at follow-up. According to this measure, 62% of veterans had a positive emotional outlook after 6 months, compared to 55% at entry.

Although these improvements in health status and social activities may seem modest, they were observed in a setting of significant chronic progressive illness, where the general expectation is a perception of decline in health and quality of life. Thus, even a small change in the direction of improved status can be considered an indication of positive program effects.

In addition to the data from the questionnaire and agency records, the evaluation included site visits by the research staff to 13 VA medical centers participating in the H/HHA program. Sites were chosen to represent

---

could otherwise serve as a comparison to the demonstration group. The sample of veterans who participated in the evaluation was nonrandom.

different regions of the country, type of facility, size of the local H/HHA program, and number, if any, of nursing home beds. In some ways, findings from the site visits were more descriptive of the benefits of the program to patients than the other data.*

Several important themes relating to patients' quality of life emerged. The H/HHA services increased patients' feelings of safety by monitoring them in their own homes. Veterans stated that they felt more secure in carrying out routine daily activities and taking prescribed medications. It was clear that home care services increased social interaction, provided emotional support, and alleviated isolation and loneliness for many elderly veterans. The site visits confirmed that the H/HHA program improved veterans' ability to meet their personal needs, lessened some of the anxiety of living alone, and affected the veterans' family relationships in a positive way by providing assistance and respite to caretakers.

The evaluation examined another dimension of care, self-reported patient satisfaction. Two measures of patient satisfaction were included in the questionnaires, and the subject was also addressed in the site visits. Patients were asked to describe the extent to which they agreed with a series of general statements about the program, and they were asked to evaluate how satisfied they were with the help they received with each specific problem.

Overall, 92% of the veterans were somewhat or strongly satisfied with the help they received. Eighty-six percent reported that they were "better cared for now than before," and virtually everyone stated that they would "rather be home than any place else," that the program "made things a lot easier for my family (spouse)," that it would otherwise be "difficult to live at home independently," and that they would recommend the program to another veteran.

Access to Services

The question of whether or not the program afforded access to all eligible veterans who required care cannot be fully answered by the evaluation data. It is clear that it provided H/HHA services to a large and diverse group of veterans, but at the current time no data are available on how many veterans there are in the communities who may have needed ser-

---

* In all, researchers interviewed a total of 98 employees and 28 veterans and family members during the site visits.

vices but were unable to receive them. We do know that there were several clear barriers to access.

For one thing, 50 VA medical centers did not apply to be part of the pilot program. As part of the evaluation, we conducted a mail survey that included 37 of the 50 facilities in order to understand some of their reasons for declining to participate. The most commonly expressed reason was that no special funds were allocated for the program. Nineteen of the centers said that they needed their CNH funds for nursing home placement and were not able to use them for home care services as well. Others cited eligibility restrictions (particularly the initial restriction to veterans with a degree of service-connected disability) and lack of administrative support. Only three VA medical centers stated that they were able to obtain the same services elsewhere or would not have a substantial number of patients who needed the service. Of the 37 facilities in the survey, 6 have since applied to be in the program, and another 14 were planning to implement the program.

Even among participating facilities, however, given the broad definition of needs and inevitable fiscal constraints, it is likely that access has been denied to some eligible veterans. Some facilities used the program liberally, and others, with similar patient populations, used it very little. Budgetary restrictions necessarily require some form of rationing of services, and as has been discussed, each medical center made its own judgments within the central office guidelines. Without a specific articulated rationale, patients were most likely to be enrolled in the program on a first-come, first-served basis until the budget for the fiscal year was depleted. How many other patients could have benefited from the H/HHA program is not known.

Costs of the Program

As has been stated, the original mandate stipulated that the per diem cost of providing H/HHA services could not exceed 65% of the per diem costs of community nursing home care and that participating VA centers could spend up to 15% of their facility's CNH budget on the home care program.

In actuality, both of these goals were met. The average monthly expenditure per patient for H/HHA services was $1,019, substantially below the $3,390 per month spent on nursing home care, and the percentage of the CNH budget obligated was observed.

Although the program thus met its mandated goal, it is difficult to know whether the obligated funds were adequate. At the time of the evaluation the program was just starting up and not fully operational at all sites. In addition, for many months eligibility was restricted to veterans with at least a 50% service-connected disability, which greatly limited the number of patients using the services. Finally, because the obligation was determined as a percentage of the CNH budget, it is possible that a larger proportion of the monies was needed for CNH placements or at least that while the H/HHA program was new and untested, facilities continued to use the CNH option more often.

Unanswered Questions About the Services Provided

Some of the limitations of an evaluation of this type have been described. Quality of care in home care, difficult to measure at best, was only tangentially assessed in this evaluation, and it was not possible to adequately answer questions of access to care. From the information we have, we cannot determine if the per diem costs were low, if they were depressed because use was restricted, if the initial amount allocated was overly generous, or if the programs were indeed very efficient.

Certain problems are endemic to any home care program—lack of continuity of care and aides who are not well trained, are unreliable, or are unable to handle the needs of elderly clients (Ory & Duncker, 1992). For the most part, however, local control over the program appeared to be helpful in minimizing most of these problems. The greatest problem that affected services and was reported most consistently was the lack of continuity of providers.

It is important to remember that the program as evaluated is still new. Facility staff have expressed concerns about long-range quality control and their ability to monitor and affect outcomes of care.

LESSONS LEARNED

As the study shows, purchase of services (POS) can be an appropriate mechanism for providing noninstitutional health-related care to veterans. Community-based services can be delivered efficiently to a large population of patients who live in many parts of the country. Our evaluation demonstrated that the program produced a high degree of satisfaction among patients and families and among VA facility administrators as well.

The fiscal restrictions appear to have worked to keep the costs of the program under control, and the budget cap, for the time being at least, has been maintained.

Because the program is new and has not yet withstood the test of time, these conclusions come with several caveats. As of this writing, there are no permanent mechanisms in place to monitor ongoing quality of patient care or to determine if access exists for all who need services. A wide range of processes is used to purchase care from local agencies, and although the absence of a formal written agreement can enhance flexibility, it also can lead to misunderstandings as well. Although VA administrators and clinicians alike appear to be satisfied with the program, there are concerns that, because no additional personnel are allocated to it, staffing may be inadequate in the future. There is similar concern that the lack of budgetary flexibility will hamper local facilities' ability to respond to changing veteran needs.

PROBLEMS AND ISSUES IN THE POS DELIVERY SYSTEM FOR VA HOME CARE SERVICES

Although it is clear that the use of POS mechanisms for this program has many advantages, problems and constraints still exist. Three issues that have been touched on in this chapter were especially salient in its implementation. They are lack of budgetary flexibility, inadequate staffing, and the possibility that if the program served all eligible veterans who needed services, funds would not be adequate.

Most facility managers and fiscal officers felt that imposing a mandated cap on the CNH budget for the H/HHA program was not the best way to allocate funds. They believed that a lump sum allotment with local discretion in spending would allow VA facilities to respond better to the needs of veterans in their district and expand or decrease services as these needs changed.

The fact that no additional staffing or money for extra staff time was allocated to administer the program was a major issue for facilities. Both administrative and clinical staff were expected to conduct the program with no additional resources. Senior managers felt that they needed more administrative staff to help negotiate the best rates from vendors, coordinate services, and monitor billing. Additional clinical staff were also needed to screen potential recipients, monitor services, and conduct periodic re-evaluations.

The question of budgetary limits raised the concern that the program had been kept within the cap because it had to be. There was a clear perception on the part of local staff and administrators that the program could well grow beyond the facility's ability to pay for it if all eligible veterans were served.

Role of the Political Process

Most VA central office administrators who participated in establishing the H/HHA program from the beginning do not think that political pressures played a role in either encouraging or inhibiting its development. Veterans service organizations often put pressure on Congress at the national level and on facilities at the local level, but neither were at work in the case of this program.

It is, of course, true that all government funding and especially federal funding is vulnerable today. Organized veterans feel an entitlement to services and are concerned that the government may not honor its commitment to them. Privatization and purchase of care from private sources are of particular concern to veterans organizations for the very reason that many policymakers value it: if the service is purchased without a commitment in buildings and dedicated staff, it could be taken away as easily and not necessarily as appropriately as it was given.

Monitoring and Accountability

As noted above, the H/HHA pilot program was established with a built-in requirement for evaluation. Unlike the CNH program, which has established a thorough and continuous monitoring and evaluation process in addition to state and federal inspections, the H/HHA program has no formal structure for ongoing monitoring or evaluation. Nor do most states have a formal certification or monitoring system for home care services.

Although there are inherent problems and difficulties in monitoring a federal program of such diverse services in different regions of the country, in both urban and rural areas, it is important to establish some measure of whether purchased services are received by the client and how adequate they are. It is unclear whether ongoing mechanisms will be established to monitor client complaints and maintain a level of quality. The pilot program showed that, with a commitment of resources, the program can be monitored, even as its local autonomy is preserved.

THE FUTURE

According to our best judgment, the program looks secure for the near future. From all indications, home care services are being delivered reasonably well and are greatly appreciated by elderly veterans. It seems clear at this point that the program fills an important need, extending the continuum of long-term care services offered by VA to the community.

The Department of Veteran Affairs is currently facing the challenge of providing for the health care needs of disabled and elderly veterans for the next several decades. Current projections suggest that the elderly veteran population will continue to grow; an estimated 39% of all veterans will be over 65 by the year 2010. As of 1994, over 77,000 veterans were in nursing homes in the VA system (Department of Veteran Affairs, 1991). Many other veterans, not currently in VA and VA-CNH nursing homes, may be in need of services as well. In the general, nonveteran elderly population, it has been estimated that for every person in an institution, there are another four in the community using some type of long-term home care services (Senate Special Committee on Aging, 1988). The trend toward the use of home-based care is as important as ever.

The POS mechanism also appears to be satisfactory for this federal program. It allows local flexibility in providing services "as required" at the facility level and eliminates the need for VA to get into the business of organizing and staffing its own home care programs. As of this writing, the problems and drawbacks of the program appear to be outweighed by the advantages. The challenges of caring for an aging veteran population are great and complex, but our case study suggests that the POS mechanism may be the ideal response to the problem.

REFERENCES

Camberg, L. C., Knight, J. W., & Griffin, J. (1990). *Contracting for community nursing homes services by the VA: Final report.* West Roxbury, MA: Health Services Research & Development, Northeast Field Program. Brockton & West Roxbury Medical Center.

Davidson, H., Schlesinger, M. Dorwart, R., & Schnell, E. (1991). State purchase of mental health care: Models and motivations for maintaining accountability. *International Journal of Law and Psychiatry, 14,* 387–403.

Demone, H. W., Jr., & Gibelman, M. (Eds.). *Services for sale: Purchasing health and human services.* New Brunswick, NJ: Rutgers University Press.

Department of Veteran Affairs. (1991). *Annual report.* Washington, DC: U.S. Government Printing Office.

Dorwart, R. A., Schlesinger, M., & Pulice, R. (1986). The promise and pitfalls of purchase-of-service contracts. *Hospital and Community Psychiatry, 37,* 875–878.

Gould, D. A., & Haslanger, K. D. (1993). Home care prospects in an era of health care reform. *Journal of Ambulatory Care Management, 16* (4), 9–19.

Hughes, S. L., Cummings, J., Weaver, F. M., Manheim, C., Braun, B., & Conrad, K. (1992). A randomized trail of the cost effectiveness of VA hospital-based home care for the terminally ill. *HSR: Health Services Research, 26,* 800–817.

Kane, R. L., & Kane, R. A. (1987). *Long-term care: Principles, programs and policies.* New York: Springer Publishing Co.

Kemper, P. (1988). The evaluation of the national long-term care demonstration: Overview of the findings. *Health Services Research, 23,* 161–174.

Kern, D. C., Hickey, E. C., Davidson, H., & Davidson, M. B. (1995). *The homemaker/home health aide evaluation project: Final report.* Boston, MA:.Boston Management Decision and Research Center, Health Services Research and Development Service.

Ory, M., & Duncker, A. (Eds.). (1992). *In-home care for older people: Health and supportive services.* Newbury Park, CA: Sage Publications.

Pepper Commission (U.S. Bipartisan Commission on Comprehensive Health Care). (1990). *Access to health care and long-term care for all Americans: Recommendations to the Congress.* Washington, DC: Author.

Scanlon, W. J. (1988). A perspective on long-term care for the elderly. *Health Care Financing Review* (Suppl.), 7–15.

Smith, S. R., & Lipsky, M. (1994). Privatization in health and human services: A critique. *Journal of Health Politics, Policy and Law,* pp. 233–253.

U.S. Senate Special Committee on Aging. (1988). *Aging America: Trends and projections.* Washington, DC: U.S. Government Printing Office.

Veterans Health Administration. (1995). VA Directive 10-95-018. Washington, DC: Department of Veteran Affairs.

Weaver, F. M. Guihavi, M., Conrad, K., Manheim, L., & Hughes, S. (1995). *National survey of VA community nursing home program practices: Final report*. Chicago: Hines VA Hospital, Midwest Center for Health Services and Policy Research.

Weissert, W. G. (1988). The national channeling demonstration: What we knew, know now, and still need to know. *Health Services Research, 2,* 175–187.

11

Privatization and Human Services Contracting: A Legal Review

William J. Curran

As Governor Dukakis points out in chapter 2 of this volume, there is nothing new about government, at any level in the United States, contracting for public services. The use of contracts by government agencies can be traced back for at least a century in many aspects of public responsibility.

The novel feature of contracting in the fields under investigation in this volume is the broad reversal of governmental policy from public operation with government employees and facilities to an almost complete privatization of the various programs still funded with tax dollars.

Make no mistake about it, the subject matter of this volume is privatization, not the everyday operation of contracted services. This point having been accepted, the greater focus of this chapter will be on policy matters as affected by legislation and by contract negotiation, with the lesser emphasis, although still included, on contract drafting, contract provisions, and the legality of specific arrangements in one field or another.

PRIVATIZATION AS GOVERNMENT POLICY

Privatization in the provision of human services by government is by definition a policy decision, not merely an ad hoc effort evidenced over time. To be most effective, this policy should be provided for in legislation. This suggestion is made not merely because the new law provides guidelines for administrative personnel in carrying out the policy, but because it indicates broad support for the program by individual legislators whose support is often needed later. Also, the legislation provides the basis for obtaining further funds or a change in allocation of funds from the same legislative body.

Privatization of human services, including deinstitutionalization of patients and residents in publicly operated hospitals and other facilities, has proved to be quite popular in legislatures at both national and state levels in the United States. The popularity spans the political spectrum. Liberal and moderate lawmakers have favored the proposals because they so often promise to increase quality of services, improve the rights and welfare of formerly institutionalized people, or reach a formerly unserved or underserved population. For conservatives, privatization sounds wonderful because it suggests "a smaller government" with fewer publicly owned facilities and less operation by "government bureaucrats." Sweetest of all for conservatives, the advocates of privatization usually promise substantial reductions in budget costs over time.

Of course, we are not suggesting that all of these promises have been realized in every conversion to privatization. In fact, some of the promises are mutually inconsistent. Nevertheless, at this stage in history, privatization in the human services field continues its popularity with legislators. The only groups providing organized opposition to privatization in this field have been labor unions and perhaps some other organizations in various states representing public employees. These groups have been influential, not so much in stopping privatization as in placing obstacles in the path of the trend. These obstacles have not always been bad policy, however. Dr. Demone, in chapter 5, mentions Massachusetts legislation requiring findings in privatization plans that the new programs provide savings and do not result in broad restrictions or reductions in needed services to patients and clients.

There may also be opposition to contracting for services when consumer groups see some forms of contracting as threats to quality of care or access to care. Such opposition can be found in recent years, as Medicaid and other programs turn to large or even mega-large contracts with managed care organizations known to have a strong interest in cost cutting and limitation of services.

What Should Be Privatized?

The broadest policy question that could be asked is, what types of human services are appropriate for privatization and what are not? From a legal standpoint, there don't seem to be any complete prohibitions. Neither the federal Constitution nor state constitutions reserve any human services areas as solely to be operated in public facilities and by public employees. (The exceptions in constitutional law are probably the judiciary itself, other elected officers, and public officials named explicitly in constitutions.) Questions could be raised about separation of church and state in a statutory program of privatization that authorized operation of human services, under a contractual system, solely by religious organizations. However, even such a plan is not on its face prohibited; the question of constitutional validity would require judicial examination.

We come back to the issue of appropriateness. Are some delegations or complete privatizations inappropriate? Governor Dukakis suggested in chapter 2 that the operation of prisons is a questionable field for private contracting. His emphasis is mainly on public safety problems and control over human freedoms. Certainly, there are some contracting plans in operation across the country, but the prison systems remain largely government-operated. Privatization may become a more serious alternative in this field as the political drive for more prisons and longer and harsher criminal sentences grows in state after state. (The prison budget in California is already larger than its state university expenditures.)

I cannot suggest any other field as large and sensitive as prison operations. However, I would also raise queries about full privatization of regulatory agencies, including those concerned with health and social welfare. The problems that might occur here are related to the independence of the regulators to resist pressure, conflict of interest, and the preparation and enforcement of administrative regulations.

There are currently movements in Congress to place limitations on the federal Food and Drug Administration. Conservative political forces have targeted that agency for severe restrictions in operation and even total abolition of the program. One less-radical proposal involves contracting out review of applications for new drug licenses if the agency does not act to approve or disapprove the application in a specified period of time.

This kind of proposal raises serious dangers for the public. It is difficult to imagine private agencies with the scientific skill, experience, and independence of judgment needed to take on highly stressful, time-constricted tasks like this. The potential for legal liability for the massive public harm that could be done by even one dangerous drug released to the market would be enough to deter most serious scientists from any competitive bidding on such individual contracts for services to review a single questionable (long-delayed) new drug. The pressure to approve the drug would be extreme.

The difficulties of full privatization of the functions of the federal Food and Drug Administration would be a multiplication of the problems just discussed. They are similar for any regulatory agency.

Legislative Provisions and Budget Restrictions

In terms of law, the legislatively supported privatization plans often go significantly beyond setting broad policy, especially at the national level. Because these programs are very largely a budgetary or financial operation—all contracting for services is a financial tool substituting for the operation of public facilities and salary items of public employees—the influence of ways and means committees is quite substantial. Also, there is considerable participation in shaping the programs from budgetary officials on the presidential and gubernatorial sides of the legislative process.

Not all of the requirements are set forth in the substantive legislation itself. The further requirements will often be found in budgetary provisions attached to the departmental or agency budget as a whole. It must always be kept in mind that, although broad-scale public contracting (in large contracts to large private agencies) may be new to the human services field, it is "old hat" to legislators and budget directors. The sophistication about public contracting in these groups is therefore very high. There will be a tendency, however, for such groups to apply the guidelines and restrictions of other, more familiar areas to the new contractual arrangements applicable to human services.

Some of the types of provisions that may be applied to contracts for services in the human services field in comprehensive privatization programs are the following:

1. The policy of open bidding and the encouragement of competitive bidding for all contracts.

2. The requirement of acceptance of the lowest bid, where practicable and where other factors, such as quality of services and adequate experience in this field, can be considered generally equivalent.

3. The policy of discouraging conflicts of interest by government officials who are negotiating and awarding contracts for services. This policy can take several forms, including prohibition of former government officials working for contracting agencies for periods of time after government

employment and restrictions on officials contracting with agencies in which they have a financial interest.

4. Severe penalties, including forfeitures of contract payments and criminal sanctions against contractors for misconduct or fraud in seeking, negotiating, and carrying out contracts.

5. Provisions allowing government agencies to cancel contracts for good cause, usually related to inadequate performance or misconduct by contractors. These provisions usually require some notice of cancellation and opportunity to answer charges except in emergency situations.

6. Provisions allowing government agencies to cancel contracts without indicating cause or reasons, usually with periods of notice before cancellation. These provisions are usually invoked only for budgetary reasons but may be utilized in other situations.

7. More specialized provisions relating to populations to be served and requiring universal access and nondiscrimination.

8. Policies requiring job security for civil service employees (usually after a period of service) whose positions are eliminated by privatization programs. These provisions are not favored by cost savers, of course, but may be accepted in compromise legislation. These provisions are particularly likely to be sought (by labor union groups) in deinstitutionalizing plans in which the employee positions disappear with the institutions when they are closed. The unions gain leverage for job security efforts as a result of the sheer magnitude of the positions lost due to institutional closings, all within a very short time frame.

9. Policies that require that the privatization/contracted services be obtained at lower cost than the previous, government-owned and/or operated system. These policies may be applied to the total or global contracting system, to individual contracts, or to both. Some programs may contain a specific percentage of cost reduction, on an annual basis or contract by contract.

10. Provisions requiring the establishment of a new administrative unit to govern the overall privatization program. Usually, these units are established within the department responsible for the program.

11. Policies requiring evaluation of contract services and performance and/or requiring ongoing monitoring of contract services and performance by the administrative unit or the responsible government official. There is generally no restriction on contracting out these evaluation and monitoring activities.

12. Provisions for oversight of the entire privatization plan, including services contracting, by the legislative body itself or by a delegated

federal or state official, usually the budget officer or state auditor.

13. Provision for a "sunset law" applicable to the privatization legislation as a whole. This type of provision sets a specific termination date for the program. The legislature must take formal action to extend the program beyond this termination—usually by a general law, not a mere budgetary regulation or continuing resolution or appropriation. The sunset laws are usually tied to evaluation and monitoring. The officials responsible for oversight are often required to make reports to the appropriate legislative committee, providing an overall evaluation of the privatization effort and a recommendation either to terminate the program on the applicable date or to continue it under specified conditions. These reports are usually required substantially before the termination date so as to allow for hearings and deliberation by the legislature.

14. Provisions incorporating, by reference, other laws or budget office regulations applicable to public contracting. Many of the types of policies or requirements listed above will be found to be included in this style of omnibus provision. It is a very dangerous style of drafting for all parties interested in these contracts, because it includes unknown pitfalls for all but the most sophisticated and experienced of contract negotiators. Actually, these unknown restrictions can hardly be avoided, as the legislators and budget directors can adopt restrictions applicable to all public contracting or to particular types or classes of contracts. These legislative provisions or regulations are binding on all contracts cited in them, or at least on the government officials negotiating contracts. It may take a court action to decide whether these "outside provisions" are binding on contracts in which they are not mentioned and in which there is no standard provision incorporating by reference all such requirements.

Several of the other chapters in this volume deal with the various contract requirements listed above. Some of these provisions will be reviewed later in this chapter.

Privatization Without Legislation

Although I do favor new legislation for privatization, there can be programs that will be installed administratively without formal legislation. This is possible because most privatization efforts in the human services field depend on financial arrangements, essentially contract mechanisms. Many longtime civil servants like to keep low profiles. They would prefer not to seek completely new legislation if they can possibly work within existing legislative authorizations. Such officials are familiar with legislative budget committees. They are used to haggling over line-item matters such as employee positions or full-time equivalents to positions. A changeover to contract arrangements for large-scale operations may not be easily accomplished.

Privatization without legislation can probably be achieved if the personnel who formerly provided the service can be moved elsewhere. This is apt to be a slow process, achieved only with the ready cooperation of the supplanted government personnel. The very slowness of the process will argue against calling it privatization. It is more likely to be addressed as a move to contract services on a supplemental or experimental basis.

Perhaps the only programs that can be moved quickly into contract services are new services that have never been the responsibility of traditional governmental personnel or conducted in public facilities. Here the decision can be made to operate the new programs under contract arrangements. Such programs may or may not have been established through new legislation. An example of a new program operating completely with contracted services can be found in chapter 10 of this volume. It is a pilot program for homemaker and home health aides under the Department of Veteran Affairs (DVA). The program was expressly authorized by Congress in 1990. The pilot program contained a built-in requirement of evaluation. This type of program can be called privatization even though it does not supplant previously government-operated functions because the general field, health care services, has traditionally (for the Veterans Administration) been government-operated in government facilities.

Policy-Making by Purchase of Services

Contracts are part of the overall concept of lawmaking, as any good philosopher of law will attest. When between private parties, it is called private lawmaking. When the predominant party in a uniform contracting mechanism is a government agency, the lawmaking is more public and closer to legislative-style law-making. In the field under consideration, a public agency is clearly the predominant party in all of the contracts for purchase of services (POS).

As indicated earlier, the legislature itself can dictate the content of the contracts to a greater or lesser extent. These provisions and others required by administrative regulations will constitute the standard provisions (or "boilerplate") of the series of contracts under the particular program. The term *boilerplate* has a tendency to demean or to trivalize the significance of standardized provisions. These portions of the contracts are of great importance, both to the substance of the contract and in performance and financing details. The standard provisions will, of course, vary with the type of privatization plan or services involved.

Kettner and Martin (in the companion volume,) write of macro- and micro-perspectives in contract accountability. They describe macro perspectives as issues of service design and outputs or client outcomes. They assert further that macro-perspectives are focused on the public agency and its responsibility to citizens. In regard to micro-perspectives, the authors point mainly to fiscal responsibility and operation of the contracts by agencies performing within fiscal constraints. The macro-perspectives of authors Kettner and Martin can also be described as policy-making, whereas the micro-perspectives are strictly contractual or fiscal under the individual contracts and for the program budget as a whole.

The contract mechanism should therefore be recognized as clearly a part of policy-making. The substance of the contracts, the services actually rendered to patients and clients, carry out the policy of privatization in the particular field of the program. The contracts must spell out adequately the types of services, quantity of services, qualifications required for professionals and others delivering the services, and the eligibility criteria for patients or clients.

MONITORING AND EVALUATION OF PRIVATIZATION

But what of the monitoring responsibilities of the public agency? Authors Kettner and Martin (1998) see program monitoring as a macro-perspective and fiscal monitoring as a micro-responsibility. Actually, I would see monitoring as neither of these. I would see it as contract management, a concept outside either perspective. It is essentially an enforcement or implementation tool, not substantive in itself. It is also legal for the agency to contract out the monitoring responsibility. Nevertheless, if the enabling legislation placed the monitoring function as a responsibility of the central office of the public agency, the agency will be held to make the final decisions on monitoring, at least in a formalistic fashion. It is, of course, possible for a legislative body to prohibit the public agency from delegating its responsibility for monitoring a privatization (or POS) program, but I have not personally observed such a prohibition.

Evaluation functions are quite close to contract monitoring. In fact, contract monitoring may be contained under an overall public agency duty to evaluate the success or failure of a particular privatization program. Chapter 4, by Fishbein and McCarty, illustrates contracting out evaluation responsibilities imposed by legislation. It is clear in a reading of this chapter that the delegation to the contractors was quite complete, including public release of their evaluations under their own authorships.

It is also common for the public agency responsible for negotiating, awarding, and monitoring (or evaluating) POS contracts to require the contractors themselves to contribute to the monitoring process by collecting and tabulating certain data essential to the monitoring. The most frequent example of this type of requirement is the collection and tabulation of data on patient and client outcomes and satisfaction with the services.

Another form of contracting out monitoring or evaluation responsibilities may occur when the public agency contracts with a single agency for the entire POS effort. This may be the case, for example, when a managed care organization assumes, under a single contract, responsibility for arranging and operating health services for an entire population (as in Medicaid) for an entire state. These contracts may well include a large part of the monitoring and evaluation functions.

NEGOTIATING POS CONTRACTS

In theory, or in a pure economic state, contract negotiation is a process between parties of equal negotiating strength, where the contract is built from scratch with contributions from each party. Is this the case with POS contracts such as those examined in this book? Far from it. In most of these negotiations, the parties are quite unequal. The public agency holds most of the cards. The draft contract itself is provided by the public agency, and most of the provisions—the standard provisions mentioned earlier and a good part of the policy provisions—are presented on a "take it or leave it" basis.

This is not to say that the prospective private contractor does not have strength. That strength depends greatly on how much the public agency needs the particular private agency. The negotiating leverage of the prospective contractor is greatest in the earliest part of the program's exis-

tence, when no large market has been built, when there are few potential
vendors, and when the public agency has had little experience in negotiating and awarding contracts. Chapter 9, by Kraft and Gibelman, highlights this point.

Even when the prospective contractors are needed, when they have a
current, although usually temporary, monopoly on available vendors of
human services in the geographical areas under consideration, the actual
negotiation is still quite one-sided. Most contract provisions remain standard. Negotiation is apt to relate primarily to the financial aspects of the
services to be purchased and to some other open-ended factors such as
timing of performance, geographical area to be covered, and monitoring
and supervision.

The public agency predominance in negotiating continues over time
and builds up significantly. The administrators and lawyers for the public agency gain experience in all aspects of the process with numerous
vendor-contractors. On the other hand, the administrative personnel and
lawyers of the contractors learn only from the one negotiation they enter.
It is often difficult for private agencies to find lawyers who have any practical experience in the field, especially any prior involvement in negotiating this particular type of contract for this service.

Inexperienced lawyers for new private agencies often will not know
which draft provisions are really nonnegotiable and which can be avoided
or reexamined. They often will not be familiar with the significance of
standard provisions (the boilerplate) and administrative regulations applicable to all contracts of this type. Without this knowledge they can fail to
represent their clients adequately.

In the negotiation process it is not always the private vendors alone
who may feel hemmed in by the rigidity of the public contracting system.
The public agencies also may not want to be constrained by the full negotiating and awarding process. An example can be found in chapter 10, by
Davidson et al.: the DVA utilized a truncated method for establishing
agreements with local private nursing homes to care for eligible veterans.
The DVA first designated selected nursing homes and set a rate for care
that would remain stable during the period of the designation. This designation was negotiated and signed by both parties but was not considered a formal government contract. Then, as each resident was assigned
to a particular local nursing home, the DVA would pay regularly the agreed
upon rate charge. Thus, assert the authors, this arrangement allowed the
public agency to avoid "the formal constraints of a VA contract and the
obligation to accept all patients."

SOME SPECIFIC LEGAL PROBLEMS
UNDER CONTRACTS

There can be many examples of legal problems presented over the course of a series of POS contracts utilized to achieve a particular privatization effort. Some of these are suggested by other chapters in this volume; others are strictly my own.

Misconduct and Fraud in Performance

As noted earlier, there generally are specific criminal statutes covering misconduct and fraud in government contracting. The penalties are usually felony charges. Also, standard contract provisions commonly authorize forfeiture or termination of contracts on the same grounds. In chapter 5, Dr. Demone's case study deals directly with charges of misconduct resulting in contract cancellation. The particular case was quite complex and was mishandled by government officials. Precipitate action was taken on the basis of an exposé story in the local tabloid newspaper.

A provision allowing cancellation without cause was utilized to avoid the effort of bringing specific charges against several contractors named in the newspaper stories. The case illustrates very well the pitfalls of moving too quickly in answer to media attacks. None of the charges seemed to be based on immediate danger to patients or clients. Most did not seem to involve misconduct in specific contract obligations or contract procurement.

A clear lesson to be learned by private agencies in this field is not to panic or try to handle the cancellation by quiet negotiation. As the matter has become public, a public response is necessary. The help of capable lawyers is essential. Rallying consumers and other community leaders to the support of the agency can be extremely helpful.

General Dissatisfaction with Performance

Very serious misconduct or fraud, often related to contract procurement, or flagrant misconduct that endangers patients or clients presents fairly easy case scenarios. Of course, it is never comfortable for the public officials that awarded the contracts to move to take action for forfeiture or cancellation or to support criminal action.

In many of the most egregious situations, however, the problems have been pursued and most of the investigation conducted by other public authorities. The public agency responsible for the POS will cooperate in the investigation and will take the necessary action in regard to the contract obligations.

The situation is quite different when the dissatisfaction with the contractor's performance is more general—a matter of inadequate quality or quantity of services, lack of cooperation in record keeping and monitoring, lateness in making reports, and so on. In these cases the public agency is often alone in its dissatisfaction. How is action taken in these circumstances?

The discomfort of the public agency in taking direct action may result in chronic slowness in recognizing inadequacies, even at the time of contract renewals. This can be particularly aggravating for public officials when it is difficult to find other private contractors to take the place of a traditional community organization that just isn't up to snuff under any reasonable standards.

Must conditions be so bad? From a legal standpoint there are remedies that can be applied to combat the inertia of the public agency. During the course of a contract, specific demands for improvement in record keeping, filing of reports, and other clearly objective performance matters can be made with built-in time limitations for compliance. In the case of failure to comply within the time limitations, action can be taken to terminate the contracts with letters of notice under the provisions for cancellation for cause.

In the more subjective areas of quality of care and patient outcomes and satisfaction, the public agency can still demand improvement during the course of a contract, or it can threaten the contractor with a refusal to consider any renewal. There is no right in any POS agreement for an automatic renewal, or even for consideration of a renewal. The fact of having had a contract for services in this field does not provide any legally vested interest in renewal, even to the extent of due process reasons or hearings. (The potential for legal liability of the public agency for personal injury to patients or clients due to poor quality of care by the contractor will be examined later in this chapter.)

The underlying condition making it difficult for the public agency to take action in these situations is, of course, the lack of competition against the inadequate local contractor. Effort should be made to encourage competitors to enter the particular geographic market. Also, an effort can be made to attract existing higher-performance groups to expand their activities by entering the geographic area where improvement is needed. The use of these strategies requires that the public agency (1) recognize the problem for what it is and (2) make public its dissatisfaction with the inadequate or "permanently failing" local organization.

The reluctance of public agencies to take proactive stances in these situations is understandable. I have noted earlier the tendency of long time civil servants to keep low profiles. In the contracting fields this tendency is manifested in a passive attitude toward attracting new or expanding competition. The public official who remains passively waiting for applications for POS appears to be fair and judicial when making awards of contracts. This is not really the way it should be.

There is nothing improper or illegal in public agencies promoting competition in the marketplace. Of course, the encouragement and information exchange must be quite open and available to all parties. No secret information or promises may be made that provide unfair advantages in bidding or negotiation of agreements to one party or another. Within these constraints, public officials can and should encourage newcomers to enter the field and to offer quality human services at reasonable and affordable rates.

Nondiscrimination Clauses

The legal requirement of nondiscrimination or equal access clauses is common to most public contracting for services. They are a part of the standard provisions listed earlier in this chapter.

These clauses are an example of legislatures imposing on a new public contracting field the policies and restrictions applicable to more familiar areas. It has been common for decades for legislatures, national and state, to impose a policy of nondiscrimination in public contracting. The effort was designed to prevent the discrimination of the past based on race and socioeconomic status, with the usual additional prohibitions against discrimination based on religious creed, gender, and age. A shorthand for all of these is the concept of "equal access" for all parts of the population.

There are difficulties in applying these legal requirements to POS agreements designed to serve special populations and in allowing specialized or religious denominational agencies to seek and to be awarded contracts. The first question that may be asked is whether or not human services contracts can be designed for special needs groups in the population. The

answer is clearly in the affirmative. A legislative body can address special
needs and can, to that extent, "discriminate" in favor of special population
groups, such as the aged, children, women, the disabled of different types,
and so on. These decisions override the general requirements of equal
access and reapply the concept *within the special population*. Difficulties can
often be presented in defining the targeted group, but the concept remains
that such a distinction is legally proper under the legislative mandate.

What about discrimination in selecting vendors or contractors? Such
discrimination may seem warranted when the program has been specially
designed for particular populations. That is, the public agency may wish
to seek contractors with experience and dedication to that field. However,
the public agency cannot discriminate against contractors with no such
previous single-mindedness, dedication, or experience if the contractors
are willing and able to offer competitive bids and can meet program
requirements.

The more difficult question is posed by Dr. Levine (1997) regarding
contracting for human services with sectarian community agencies. This
issue is of particular significance in the human services field, especially
for social welfare services, specialized housing, and health services, where
a large part of the field has been served in the past by sectarian agencies
and hospitals. Can these agencies continue to serve selected sectarian
groups? If such agencies do enter into contracts to serve a broader population, can they preserve a special identity and special goals?

The legislation in this field does not adequately address these questions. The policy of equal access to services by all persons in the population group is applied without mention of requirements placed on
individual contractors who may be sectarian in character and purpose. In
most situations the issue is faced by the local agency itself, as suggested
in Dr. Levine's chapter. If the agency wishes to enter this field and receive
the benefits of the financial support for its operation, the agency will be
required to open its program under the contract to the entire community.

Both the sectarian agency and the public officials awarding the contract will be aware of the traditional role of the sectarian agency. Neither
should expect that this contact requiring equal access would be used to
change the basic character or overall goals of the contracting agency.
Nothing in general law or the legislation would foster this effort. Also, the
fact that the sectarian character of the agency may lead some members
of that church to favor entering services operated by the sectarian group
or may lead some eligible nonmembers to try to avoid that agency—or
hospital, or nursing home, or group housing—is a matter for judgment
by the public officials negotiating and awarding contracts. There may be

clear reasons for selecting the sectarian agency that balance out these issues. To exclude sectarian agencies from POS fields in which they have been preeminent in providing quality services over generations should be decided only on a legislative basis.

Does contracting with sectarian agencies invade the separation of church and state required in the federal Constitution or state constitutions? I know of no such interpretations by the courts. Some state constitutions and perhaps some state legislation may be more specific about prohibitions of relationships that "benefit" denominational groups. If so, these issues should be examined.

The only recent lawsuit that I am aware of that raises issues in this area is still in the very early trial stage in a federal court in Minneapolis. Newspaper accounts do not provide a formal reference to the case, but it is said to allege a breach of federal constitutional law in awarding contracts under Medicaid to Christian Science health facilities and practitioners (Associated Press, 1996). Plaintiffs in the case allege improper care to patients, resulting in personal injury and death when the contractors followed Christian Science teaching and did not offer conventional medical care and treatment.

This case will bear close watching by readers interested in issues of church-state relationships for several reasons: (1) The case specifically involves purchase of human services under a joint state-federal program, Medicaid, such as those examined in this volume; and (2) the issues raised concern the delivery of health services in a direct way, not encountered in the discussion above, which deals with more traditional sectarian groups.

The challenge in this case will involve the application of church doctrine to the actual services delivered, here a prayer-oriented practice without use of traditional treatment or therapeutic drugs. The case can indirectly call attention also to other religious beliefs and practices, such as refusal to perform abortions or to give family planning counseling to patients or clients. The latter area has been dealt with by Congress in some legislation exempting institutions and individuals from federal requirements under so-called conscience clauses. No such recognition has been given to Christian Science practices applicable to health care services.

Another, quite separate area where issues of nondiscrimination and equal access to services may be raised is that of public contracting with large managed care organizations. These organizations regularly engage in cost-reduction efforts that relate to access to care. Among these are restrictions on entry to the programs to avoid high-risk, high-utilization groups and incentives to providers to restrict access to hospitals and to medical specialists.

Public agencies awarding contracts in the fields examined in this volume must exercise care in drafting agreements with managed care organizations to avoid prohibited limitations on access to care or to specific services. Of course, there may be situations where the cost-reduction practices of managed care groups are favored by overriding public policy. These should be clear, however, for all parties to the negotiation of individual contracts.

Conflict of Interest Problems

A growing area of sensitivity in privatization plans is the problem of conflict of interest. (Some would say it is an explosive "mine field" planted all around the subject.) Violations of quite vaguely worded conflict of interest prohibitions can carry criminal penalties, civil fines, and revocation of contracted human services programs.

In earlier times conflict of interest was considered purely an ethical problem. As far as law was concerned (or even most ethical codes), there was a personal violation only when the individual acted on the conflict, succumbed to the temptation or pressure, to the detriment of his or her obligations, such as unfairly or improperly awarding a contract to the agency where a financial interest (or a relative working for the agency) existed. The answer, or curative aspect, for a conflict of interest was *full disclosure* of the potential conflict. The other party could then either grant a waiver of applying any sanction or ask the individual to withdraw from the situation or negotiation to which the conflict applied.

Times have changed. The media have found exposure of conflicts of interest on the part of public officials, especially in contracting activities, a favorite area for public exposure. It has made no difference in many news stories that no public harm was done or that action wasn't taken on the conflict; the existence of the potential conflict is enough to raise public concerns.

Now the existence of a potential conflict of interest is itself a problem. It will require either complete withdrawal from the conflict situation or full disclosure to proper authorities. In many situations, full disclosure will not be enough; withdrawal will be required.*

Administrative regulations are now common in this area for public con-

---

* In terms of legal philosophy, the punishment of the mere existence of a conflict of interest is greatly frowned upon. It is called a "status" offense and has little jurisprudential support.

tracting and procurement, as indicated earlier in this chapter. The potential types of conflict of interest are too numerous for inclusion here. They apply to both the awarding officials and the community private parties involved in the human services field.

A recent new application of conflict of interest rules to this field is worth noting, however. In awarding Medicaid contracts, it is now held that it is improper for a private agency (and its staff) to bid on or receive a contract if that agency or staff was engaged in helping or advising the awarding public officials to establish the requirements, specifications, requests for proposals, or other aspects of procurement for that contracting opportunity (42 *Code of Federal Regulations*, Sections 74.40–74.48). The purpose of the regulations is to assure a maximum degree of effective, open, and free competition for contract services.

Liability Issues in Delivery of Services

The last area I address concerns legal liability on the part of public agencies and private contractors and individuals for injuries or other losses to patients and clients.

The lawyers seeking redress for personal injury to patients or clients who were served under a POS agreement such as those examined in this volume would ordinarily bring lawsuits only against the local community agency and the individual providers alleged to have wrongfully caused the injury. Such suits would be governed by ordinary civil liability law in the jurisdiction. Liability awards would not be limited to the contract amount but can be sought against all of the general assets of the contractor. Nonprofit community agencies may have limited liability in total awards according to the law in some states.

The more interesting question for readers of this volume is the extent of legal liability of the government agency that awarded the contract. In most situations the public agency will not be sued, as indicated above. This will be the expected practice where the public agency has used "due diligence" in awarding the contract and has selected a contractor with a reasonably good reputation for delivering quality services.

On the other hand, can there be grounds for legal liability against the public agency if it is alleged to have been negligent in selecting a community agency that has a poor reputation and a clear record of providing poor-quality services? The answer is in the affirmative. Also, the public authority could be legally liable for negligent failure to monitor the local contractor properly when there have been warning signs, such as previous lawsuits, that should have alerted the public authority to take preventive action. There are general requirements and limitations concerning suits against government agencies that vary in different states, but the concept of liability is now well established across the country.

An example of grounds for liability may be found in the chapter by Dr. Regan (1997) concerning "permanently failing organizations." If these chronic failures include poor quality of care that endangers the safety of patients or clients, the public agency is highly vulnerable to personal injury lawsuits. (In these cases, the lawyers for the plaintiffs will usually bring suit against both the local agency and the public authority.) In fact, this vulnerability to lawsuits—and the accompanying bad publicity—should be one of the strongest incentives to motivate public officials to take action to monitor more closely and to cancel contracts when conditions are not significantly improved.

The previously mentioned lawsuit in a federal court in Minneapolis also seems to raise novel questions about public agency liability for patient injury under POS agreements. In this case it is alleged that local Christian Science agencies and practitioners did not utilize regular medical services or therapeutic drugs. Reliance was placed on Christian Science practitioners. The patient was a teenager who was placed in the agency by parents who were Christian Scientists. The parents and at least one public interest group, known as Children's Health Care as a Legal Right, brought the lawsuit. In addition to issues of separation of church and state in the awarding of the contract, the suit raises questions about public agencies of the federal and state governments letting contracts for health services to sectarian organizations that do not offer regular medical or other health services.

Is there an obligation to assure the offering of reasonable health care services under a health services program? Do the parents of the child have the legal standing to raise these issues against the sectarian group or the public authorities when the parents were Christian Scientists and voluntarily chose to place their child in the sectarian facility? It can be expected that the public interest group will want these issues raised, but the court may not see this case as the proper forum for considering this question where the parents are themselves Christian Scientists.

REFERENCES

Associated Press. (1996, January 20). Payments to Christian Scientists challenged. *Boston Globe*, p. 12.

Kettner, P., & Martin, L. (1998). Accountability in purchase of service contracting. In M. Gibelman & H. W. Demone, Jr. (Eds.). *The privatization of human services: Volume 1. Policy and practice issues.* New York: Springer Publishing Company.

Levine, E. M. (1998). Church, state, and social welfare: Purchase of service and the sectarian agency. In M. Gibelman & H. W. Demone Jr. (Eds.), *The privatization of human services: Volume 1. Policy and practice issues.* New York: Springer Publishing Company.

Regan, P. S. (1998). Purchase of service and fostered failure: A Massachusetts case study. In M. Gibelman & H. W. Demone Jr. (Eds.), *The privatization of human services: Volume 1. Policy and practice issues.* New York: Springer Publishing Company.

12

Epilogue

Harold W. Demone, Jr.

Governor Dukakis provides the reader with a view of a rational decision-making process in the determination of how and why he supported the purchase of human services. These were managerial decisions based on what he understood was best for the clients and at what cost.

Johnston reviews his career similarly. He has occupied the top-ranking human services position in Massachusetts and also held a federal appointment as the regional director (New England) of the U.S. Department of Health and Human Services and had an earlier career as a private agency executive who received contracts from the state. His experiences are unusually broad. Thus, he sees the need for alliances and public interest groups advocating for their cause.

Demone (chapter 5) provides a case illustrating the largely negative role played by the press and elected officials and the stable role played by the bureaucracy, especially at the middle management and service delivery levels.

Fishbein and McCarty (chapter 4) reintroduce rationality to the mix. They focus on quality control, accountability, and monitoring. They accept the principle of purchase of service (POS). They seek cost-effective technologies to better determine where the money went and with what results. They are apolitical.

Etta (chapter 6) provides a 100-years-plus history of a child welfare agency that has received contracts from the District of Columbia and Virginia since 1923. This agency even had a prior 40-year history of direct allocations from Congress. It is a story of survival in very turbulent waters. The Roman Catholic sisters responsible for St. Anns had long-standing political skills.

Gibelman (chapter 7) reminds us of the dangers in contracting. Governments may unilaterally abrogate contracts and not pay for expenses legitimately disbursed For the public sector this is one of the several advantages of privatization: they do not have to discharge public employees.

Canter (chapter 8) takes us inside the public school system, some of whose functions are to be contracted. She discusses the way in which school psychologists dealt with this threat to their domain and the quality of the provided services.

Kraft and Gibelman (chapter 9) explores the impact of contracting on a community substance abuse agency from the earliest involvement with the state. The growing bureaucracy around the contract industry is apparent from this case description, as is the tendency for agencies to grow dependent on contract funds. Goal displacement is a likely result.

Davidson and her colleagues, in chapter 10, demonstrate how the Department of Veteran Affairs (VA), when required by Congress, can effectively contract for services of a kind not previously offered. A 1977 report by the National Academy of Sciences, National Research Council, to Congress concluded, essentially after 3 years of study, that VA should merge its activities into community-based programs and essentially contract with local providers, as in the experiment reported here by Davidson 20 years later. It is not surprising that VA and Congress shelved the 1977 report that Congress had commissioned. This was too early in the changing structure of government, and the veterans' lobby was too powerful an advocate. Then and now they oppose all change. Note that the contracted program was new and lacking prior VA investments.

In chapter 11, Professor Curran has admirably extrapolated the essential legal principles from the several cases relevant to the purchase and privatization of human services. It can well serve as the summary and conclusion for this case book.

In this epilogue the goal is to highlight a few of the more significant public and private policies stimulated by the case presentations. Collectively, the major issues are evident. In our companion book we provide a more comprehensive overview of these concerns (Gibelman & Demone, 1998).

THE DEBATE ABOUT PRIVATIZATION

First is the matter of definitions. In the United States privatization is largely exercised by the purchase of goods and services by the public sector from the private sector. Some of the same issues resulting from this interaction are also surfacing as large for-profit corporations begin to "down-source" (read as contracting) some of their activities. Nor are the turf battles exclusive to the United States. In fact, the more significant exchanges are to be found in Eastern Europe, where privatization in its pure form, as government fully relinquishes a function, can still be found.

Some residual efforts can still be found in the United Kingdom and in France, where public employees' unions are particularly aggressive in their opposition. Central and South America, Asia, and some African countries are also sites experimenting with privatization. Few countries are lacking entrées.

For the human services in the United States, pure privatization would mean the total abdication of the public sector from the financing, planning, delivery, and monitoring of the effort. In today's political climate the elimination of financing would be the ultimate test. Examples of major human services functions frequently cited for privatization now are elementary and secondary public education, corrections, public welfare and public social services, Medicare, Medicaid, and social security.

Despite the energetic assertions of the political right libertarians that the marketplace is the proper locus for these activities, the likelihood of any significant long-term devolution is remote. Even the poor have voices and can be mobilized if the cuts are too dramatic. There is also a long-standing and well-established history for all of these current public engagements. All were at one time the exclusive or substantial function of the private sector, but they eventually were found to be beyond the capacity of the private sector to finance despite the best of intentions. Today the most vigorous supporters of the public financing of these fundamental functions of a democratic society are representatives of the same private associations. Even many of the jails were privately managed, and most of the police were largely private until well into the last century.

All statements are conditional. Overlap was and is common. The shifts are never universal and unequivocal. And if you are wealthy, none of the formal systems needs be relevant. Everything is available on the open market to those with adequate personal resources.

More likely, the real debates will be twofold. One contention will focus on limiting the funding and eligibility for services but not on the total abandonment of the service. The second major policy exchange will be about the issue of contracting, that is, privatization. Probably even this controversy will emerge as an effort to convert governmental programs to contracting to the private sector. In some jurisdictions, for some services, the contracting is to other public bodies, generally smaller and presumably closer to the electorate. Of the 1,400 Massachusetts providers contracting with the commonwealth, about 200 (14%) are public agencies and for-profit providers. The remainder are private, not-for-profit organizations.

IMPACT OF PRIVATIZATION

When privatization does occur and government withdraws from an under-taking, there are certain common features. Smith (1989) studied four crime groups: victims of child abuse, rape, spouse abuse, and elder abuse. Limited voluntary efforts occurred until the 1970s and 1980s, when advo-cates for the several interest groups were able to persuade Congress and the administration to provide federal support for some programs. Given the tentative popularity of programs, the open-end nature of demands, and the resulting limited attention span of our elected officials and the press, the financing tends to ebb and flow. Thus, the victim service pro-grams most dependent on federal financing were the least viable. Those with multiple funding sources generally managed better. Other influen-tial variables in some of the successes were being well organized and active (Smith, 1989). Advocacy was essential.

Agencies can be reorganized into lesser roles. Mental health, alco-holism, and drug dependence have all had their day in the federal sun, and all three have recently suffered from the effort to make them more efficient and organizationally consistent with other branches of the U.S. Department of Health and Human Services. Legislatures will eventually tinker with anomalies, even those that work and are uniquely structured. Even the friends of these programmatic efforts did not vigorously oppose reorganization efforts, but the strong likelihood is that they will all suffer in the name of organizational cleanliness.

But these are all encounters at the margins, where most of the strug-gles occur. Once well established, it is not easy to dislodge existing enti-ties. Yet the more fundamental battles for policymakers are whether to fund or not to fund and how best to deliver the service—with public employees or by POS. The first decision has always been a political one. The latter has only recently been politicized. For not-for-profit contract recipients it has led to a certain loss of innocence. It is not merely that they care more and will likely deliver better services at a lower cost but that they have to be prepared to be attacked in the press and by political adversaries. Doing well was its own reward. Now the unholy duo of the politicians and the press largely determines the agenda, given their response to the important interest groups.

This is not to suggest that the recent politicization of privatization is necessarily bad. However, it does change the rules and nature of the game. When political party caucuses examine your special interests, there is a good chance they will be better informed. Whether this automatically leads in the short run to better decisions is uncertain. Elections enter the debate and divert attention. In the long run, as in most facets of life, more information is likely to lead to wiser decisions. Perhaps improved resources are possible.

Front-page headlines also have their own way of sowing seeds. As they are almost always negative, there may be more losses than gains; but given the size of the privatization phenomenon, that may be the price to be paid. Here, too, there may well be some improved understanding of the issues if the particular can be separated from the overall concerns.

Regarding the human services, as best as can be determined, the growth of contracting began as an apolitical process. Some public administrators wanted to improve the quality of their offerings. Having more rather than fewer options is usually a wise management tool. Certainly, short-term ad hoc efforts are not well served by the hiring of full-time civil servants. It is clearly cost-ineffective to hire people in permanent positions and then try to discharge them in a human resource structure replete with standard civil service protections supplemented by personnel procedures negotiated as part of a labor contract with powerful public employees' unions.

During the past 25 years or so the only growth of organized labor in the United States has been in public employment. Thus, there is a strong interest group protecting public positions, their dues-paying members. There is also a group of scholars, declining in numbers, who follow the teachings of Harry Hopkins from the New Deal. If the activity is to be governmentally financed, it should be governmentally operated.

As privatization becomes politicized, it takes on the color of partisan politics. When the Massachusetts Republican governor campaigned as an advocate for privatization, the opposition Democrats found reasons to oppose the proposition. The chapter by Governor Dukakis, also a Democrat and the immediately preceding governor, is clearly written by a pragmatist. He asks what works best. Thus, neither political party is forever committed to a particular position although the rhetoric might lead you to believe otherwise.

Given some successes in decreasing public civil service positions and converting the savings to contracts, there are important opposing forces. One group simply wants to reduce public expenditures. They are more than willing to close or reduce direct governmental operations if substantial savings result from the change. They are not likely to inquire about the effect on the clients served by the system. Their concerns are quite pragmatic.

The opponents also include a growing group of idealogues opposed to a large federal government. Some are opposed to government of any size. There are those who view themselves as libertarians committed to the survival of the fittest and the marketplace. There are also some public administrators who view the options inherent in POS as allowing them more administrative flexibility. They have lost patience with the rigid controls increasingly inherent in public management. There is also a large group of parents, significant others, and other interested parties who run our public interest groups. They know from personal experience that the private programs are usually better than those operated by the public sector. They have had close personal experience with the state schools and state hospitals. They do not want to see their children stagnate in such settings. (In many states there are groups of parents who institutionalized their children early in their lives, often at the recommendation of their pediatricians, and who now fear that those adult children cannot accommodate to alternative community-based settings.) And there are powerful not-for-profit forces involved as volunteers and as professional staff in community-based settings who see their clients benefiting from contracting.

There are also unions who would see potential new members from the shift in operations as they organize in the private sector. As noted in the chapter by Demone, one important union, principally noted for its public employee members, is committed to following the dollar. If programs are transferred to the private sector, they will move their membership operation to that venue.

Thus, these competing forces have had an impact on the decision-making process. At both federal and state levels new programs are increasingly contracted. Reorganizing activities (e.g., the closing of state institutions) is a mixed operation.

We remind our readers that despite the many forces active in this debate, if specific contracting efforts are traced to their origins, as in tuberculosis, child guidance, or alcoholism, the concerns are neutral. The players merely represented the efforts of some public officials, appointed and elected, to try to deliver improved services to the client population with whom they were identified. Where they took on a life of their own, as in alcoholism in Massachusetts and North Carolina (in Massachusetts, contracts were initiated early, and in North Carolina substantial state resources have gone to maintain large public institutions), dislodging either now would require considerable political capital. It is with new programs and with specialized services that are not likely to be a part of the typical civil service system (e.g., thoracic surgeons) that some flexibility exists or when new medications and treatment procedures significantly alter the demand for services that options surface. The windows are limited and narrow. They need to be exploited quickly.

As an aside, it is to be noted that regional variation exists. The southern states are much more resistant to changes. They remain committed to state-operated services.

As noted earlier and throughout the case studies, costs drive many decisions. The general distrust with government at all levels, the increasing cost of the health industry, the aging of the population, the effort to imprison the nation's drug users, and the desire to avoid taxes all combine to create an atmosphere hostile to expansion of human services.

Life is currently satisfactory to many of the electorate, compared to some mythical negative future options. As with much of corporate America, the bottom line is very current. Only immediate threats seem to stimulate rational attention. A parent, spouse, child, or close friend may need help sometime. They may themselves be in jeopardy, and at that time become less self-centered. The stand in opposition may very well be reversed. Converts can become vigorous allies.

Thus, despite the puffing of wares, the real effort is to place limits on the size of the programs and to reduce the population of potential users by setting standards for worthiness. Privatization and POS will play a role in these negotiations, for they have three advantages: they are not government, they are often more cost-effective, and they are consistent with the desires of the users. Client concern may not be a major factor for low income welfare clients, but for most services for most socioeconomic groups, the concern of the clients will play a significant role.

Fishbein and McCarty highlight a major growth area in privatization. With newspaper headlines focusing on misfeasance and malfeasance in both public and private agencies, accountability is a hot subject. The fear is that it will drive the contracts as it has previously driven government. The inefficiencies of government are not an accident. First, efficiency is not its principal purpose. Almost equally important, each time a series of scandals erupts, another layer of controls is added to limit corruption to the point where it is almost impossible to steal from government at a rate greater than the costs of controlling the theft. Thus, any effort that will provide informed data without corrupting the system with unnecessary overhead is to be rewarded.

In general, despite all the complications, those familiar with the American practice of privatization of the human services, also variously known as contracting or POS, see it as working quite well. Such comparisons are always relative. The wise observer asks: "Compared to what?" In this case, the other options are direct public operations, quasi-public authorities, governmentally operated private organizations or do nothing.

The final issue has to do with for-profit versus not-for-profit operations. In general, if there is a chance to make a profit, for-profit organizations will emerge. To a considerable degree the profit potential in many human services, given the payment structure, is limited. Many have tried the for-profit route. Few have continued. These failed entrepreneurs might as well be not-for-profit. With lowered personal expectations they may well practice as such.

REFERENCES

Gibelman, M., & Demone, H. W. Jr. (Eds.). (1998). *The privatization of human services: Volume I, Policy and practice issues.* New York: Springer Publishing Company.

National Academy of Sciences, National Research Council. (1977). *Study of health care for American Veterans* (Publication No. 91-271 O). Washington, DC: U.S. Government Printing Office.

Smith, S. R.(1989). Federal funding, nonprofit agencies, and victim services. In H. W.Demone Jr. & M. Gibelman (Eds.), *Services for sale: Purchasing health and human services* (pp. 215–227). New Brunswick, NJ: Rutgers University Press.

Index

SP *Springer Publishing Company*

Program Evaluation in the Human Services

Michael J. Smith, DSW

"Smith has written an outstanding introductory program evaluation text for students of the human services. He effectively balances presentation of the major technical concepts in evaluation research with good advice about how program evaluation should be done. Particularly effective are the examples drawn from his personal experiences as an evaluation researcher."

SPRINGER SERIES ON SOCIAL WORK

Program Evaluation in the Human Services

Michael J. Smith, D.S.W.

—Francis G. Caro, PhD, *University of Massachusetts*

Contents:

- An Introduction to Program Evaluation
- A Comprehensive Definition of Program Evaluation
- The First Step: Describing the Program
- The Second Step: Defining the Program Goals
- The Third Step: Designing the Study
- The Fourth and Fifth Steps: Implementing the Program Evaluation and Analyzing the Data
- The Sixth Step: Reporting the Results of Program Evaluation
- Appendices

Springer Series on Social Work
1990 168pp 0-8261-6590-7 hardcover

536 Broadway, New York, NY 10012-3955 • (212) 431-4370 • Fax (212) 941-7842